PRAISE FOR RICHARD B. SCHWARTZ

Proof of Purchase

It's like this guy is just channeling Raymond Chandler on every page. . . . The ending . . . would make Mike Hammer proud.
— Jochem Steen, *Sons of Spade*

In this engaging hard-boiled mystery, one of three in Schwartz's Jack Grant series (Frozen Stare; The Last Voice You Hear), the seasoned California PI looks into the disappearance of an ex-girlfriend at the request of the woman's husband. When her mutilated body turns up in the woods, Grant makes it his mission to track down her murderer. With the assistance of Lt. Diana Craig, an attractive fast-riser in the San Bernardino police department, Grant follows leads that point to his client, as well as to a consortium of underworld bosses who are branching out into a mega-real estate project. The pair find time, between car chases and gun battles, to begin a relationship. . . . Fans of Robert Parker will enjoy encountering Grant . . . .
— *Publishers Weekly*

The Last Voice You Hear

It's not often that an author's second book is as good as the first, and even less frequent are the instances when an author . . . top[s] it with an extraordinary second . . . deliver[ing] a walloping good tale as well. Richard B. Schwartz has done just that. In *The Last Voice You Hear*, Mr. Schwartz places himself on par with our finest contemporary murder-mystery writers. This is a book you won't want to miss. . . .
— Alan Paul Curtis in *Who Dunnit*

The author . . . writes vividly, putting the reader right into the scene. Schwartz explores the meaning of right and wrong, crime and justice.
— Mary Helen Becker in *Mystery News*

The story rockets along . . . a fast-moving, well-told story with a surprising conclusion that blurs the line between crime and justice.
— Joseph Scarpato, Jr. in *Mystery Scene*

Jack Grant, the Vietnam vet and Pasadena-based PI who debuted in Frozen Stare (1989), returns in this engrossing sequel by Schwartz, author of several scholarly studies of Samuel Johnson. Schwartz knows his London, but surprisingly he evokes California with equal ease, mainly with vividly etched strokes. An apparently maniacal killer is on the loose in London, someone strong and very practiced at impalement. So far, so nasty. But when a victim is dispatched in similar fashion in Disneyland, of all places, Jack Grant is called in. He discovers the killer's identity, but there's a problem: there's a method to the killer's madness. Moreover, Grant has an ethical problem of his own: he's plagued by his conscience, since he understands and even sympathizes with the murderer's cause. The cinematic climax takes place high above the floor of the California desert, and Schwartz squeezes every last drop of suspense from his setting. . . . The result is a high-tension thriller awash in sanguinary detail. Paper towels, anyone?
— *Publishers Weekly*

Frozen Stare

I welcome Richard Schwartz to the club. It's been a long time since I've seen two more engaging characters entering the series scene.
— Sandra Scoppettone

Grant and White play nicely off each other and the switch-on-a-switch works well.
— *Kirkus Reviews*

This tale, in the California private eye tradition, has a rousing finish and is an enjoyable read.
— *Publishers Weekly*

A new author devoted to the hard-boiled tradition. . . . Schwartz has the hard-boiled formula down pat. . . . Schwartz does not break any rules in Frozen Stare. . . . He writes crisply. The narrative moves at a slam-bang pace as bodies pile up. . . . As a dedicated student of the hard-boiled school of detective fiction [Schwartz] has learned his lessons well.
— *The Washington Post Book World*

Gives a whole new meaning to the phrase 'cold-blooded murder'. . . . This is a quick read with plenty of action. Schwartz's first novel is a winner!
— *Sarasota, FL Herald Tribune*

This is a delightful tale, full of amusing touches, and the relationship between Grant and his good cop friend, black Frank White, is a joy. I hope that Schwartz can keep this standard up for a long time to come.
— *The Armchair Detective*

Nice and Noir: Contemporary American Crime Fiction

Opinionated but always fascinating, shrewd and smart, but always readable. . . .
— *The Thrilling Detective*

BOOKS BY RICHARD B. SCHWARTZ
FICTION

The Jack Grant Novels

Frozen Stare
The Last Voice You Hear
Proof of Purchase

The Tom Deaton Novels

Into the Dark
The Survivor's Song
Nightmare Man
Death Whispers
Poison Touch

The Gwen Harrison Novels

No Exit

CRITICISM

Samuel Johnson and the New Science
Samuel Johnson and the Problem of Evil
Boswell's Johnson: A Preface to the Life
Daily Life in Johnson's London
After the Death of Literature
Nice and Noir: Contemporary American Crime Fiction
The Wounds that Heal: Heroism and Human Development
(with Judith A. Schwartz)
ed. The Plays of Arthur Murphy, 4 vols.
ed. Theory and Tradition in Eighteenth-Century Studies

MEMOIRS

The Biggest City in America: A Fifties Boyhood in Ohio
Accidental Soldier: A Reserve Officer at West Point in the Vietnam Era
Postwar Higher Education in America: Just Yesterday

EBOOK

Is a College Education Still Worth the Price? A Dean's Sobering Perspective

A GWEN HARRISON NOVEL

NO EXIT

RICHARD B. SCHWARTZ

DARK
HARBOR
BOOKS

NO EXIT: A Gwen Harrison Novel

Published by Dark Harbor Books
First Edition 2022

Cover design: Jana Rade

ISBN: 979-8-9855721-5-5 Paperback Edition
         979-8-9855721-6-2 Hardcover Edition
         979-8-9855721-7-9 Digital Edition

Library of Congress Control Number: 2022912791

Author services by Pedernales Publishing, LLC
www.pedernalespublishing.com

10 9 8 7 6 5 4 3 2 1

Printed in the United States of America

v10

For my Father
Wartime Special Agent in the Federal Bureau of Investigation

Wherever Guilt can fly, Revenge can follow.

Samuel Johnson

I

EARLY WINS

ONE

I am in St. Andrews, nursing an impulse which is now bordering upon an obsession. It is late morning and my cousin Will is playing the old course with three Japanese businessmen. When they finish their round they will decompress over expensive whiskies and £12 Cubans in the *Rusacks* club bar. Will will pass on the cigar and space the single malts so that he can remain lucid as he discusses the short-term and projected long-term relationships between the Japanese and U.S. steel industries. I have had a light breakfast and warm shower and am in search of sport of my own.

I walk up North Street, pass the library, and turn left, making my way to St Salvator's College. The wind off the sea intensifies, as does the accompanying spray. Prince William had been sequestered in St Salvator's because of its relative privacy, though he continued to attract photographers from the fanzines and afternoon newspapers. They freely violated the limits placed on them, but their goal was less to penetrate the inner sanctum of the college than to catch the prince emerging from his quarters to visit nearby pubs or public spaces.

Today they are doing a retrospective, photographing young women, with the college as backdrop, their putative purpose being to represent St Salvator's as a haven for attractive undergraduates. They photograph very selectively, catching open coats, exposed legs, and blond hair fluttering in the cold wind.

Although the town is laced with tea shops and boutique restaurants they gravitate toward the pubs. I follow two of them to a place called

The Eagle and Crow, buy a half pint of Tetley's bitter, and find a quiet corner where I can observe them while I appear to be scanning my *Daily Telegraph*. They join a third person who is drinking lager and picking at a plate of rice and curried chicken. Each of the photographers in turn tilts his camera to coincide with the man's line of vision and then cycles through the memory chip's digital images. When the man stops him and pauses over particular pictures the photographer takes notes. The curry eater is a middleman, the photographers freelancers. They work, he eats and drinks and purchases selected images, which are downloaded to his laptop and sent off to editorial offices.

When the photographers complete their transactions and leave I follow the curry eater. He is thick in the waist, chest, and shoulders with dark eyes, tousled hair badly in need of a shampoo, wrinkled slacks, an unzipped leather jacket and an unbuttoned Polo shirt that hangs over his belt. If we were in the states I would expect to see him at a downscale race track. I follow him to Market Street where he buys some groceries and a bottle of plonk champagne. He walks north on the City Road, passes the bus station, and enters a small residential hotel tucked between a hardware store and tobacconist's. A minute or two later I see him on the third floor of the building, parting the curtains and raising the window to catch the fresh air from the sea.

Twenty minutes later a young woman arrives. She has teased hair, a tight sweater and skirt, and 4-inch heels. She enters the building, a few moments elapse, and the curry eater appears at the window, lowers it slightly, and closes the curtains. I hope that he's taken the trouble to brush his teeth and bathe in the intervening minutes.

That evening Will and I have dinner at an Italian restaurant just off Church Street. He asks me what I did that day and I tell him I went for a nice walk. I don't wish to deceive him but neither do I wish to frighten him. He tells me that he shot an 82 and is very pleased. He also tells me that his clients want to meet with him in Honolulu on their next trip. "I don't deserve all this," he says, "but I'll take it."

A year later I am in San Francisco with my former college roommate; my impulse is now in full control of me. Helen has no awareness of what I have been doing. Even though we are traveling together she works constantly and we only see each other for brief periods of time. My own work has suffered because of what I have come to term my *need* and the time away only makes things worse, since I have greater opportunities to indulge myself. In San Francisco something happens which changes my life.

I am at *House of Thai* in the Civic Center, finishing my dinner when I hear the echoes of a conversation between two men at the bar. The discussion is heated. It has to do with money. One of the men has reneged on a promise. The other leaves the restaurant. I put cash on the table and follow him.

He goes to an Italian restaurant on the south side of Washington Square, where he meets another man. They sit at a table near the bar and eat. Their attitude and demeanor are strained but not yet angry or violent. After a single drink I leave. The room is nearly empty and I do not wish to draw attention to myself. I go outside. In the park there are four men playing Bocce in the twilight. Their dress is stereotypical: short-sleeved shirts, brown wool pants with suspenders and wide-brimmed hats. So are their accents—they are all residents of Little Italy.

They are playing closed-court Bocce and they are angry. I am not an expert on the rules of the game, but I determine the nature of their conflict. They are trading aerial call shots. Two balls tie and a dispute arises as to whether the resulting scores should be cancelled or the shots be played a second time. Agreement should have been secured in advance of play, but since it was not, the result is a shouting match.

I purchase a cone of lemon gelato from a street vendor and observe the conflict. A few minutes later the man in the bar emerges, signals a cab from the line outside the restaurant and heads south. I follow him to Union Square, where he meets with a third man. They are standing between the bodies of sleeping, homeless men on the north side of the lawn. Their conversation is animated and intense. The man I have been following walks away from the other in anger and heads south on Stockton. I follow him to 4th Street and then to Mission. He goes into an alley. I pause, give him time to emerge on Minna, and enter the alley. He is nowhere in sight. I am halfway down the alley when he appears from the shadows and confronts me. He is holding an automatic at his side. He extends and cocks it. I pull my purse in front of me as if I were using it as a shield and slip my nail file into my hand from the side pocket.

He shouts at me and aims the gun at my eyes. I demand to know why. He tells me that he knows I am following him. He asks who I am and threatens to shoot me unless I tell him. I raise my voice, hoping that the sound will carry back to the street and that someone will come to my aid. I tell him that he is mistaken and ask him why on earth I would be following him. He tells me that he saw me at the Italian restaurant and says that he will count to three. If I do not answer he will then shoot.

He is shaking with anger and there is perspiration on his forehead and under his lower lip. When he reaches the count of 2, I throw my purse against his right arm and drive the point of my nail file into his left cheek. His eyes explode in pain. He shoots me and runs out of the alley, holding his hand against his face. The gunshot attracts a passerby who finds me and calls an ambulance on his cell phone. The ambulance takes me to the California Pacific Medical Center at Castro and Duboce.

A .22 caliber round is removed from my shoulder. The wound is cleansed, stitched, and bandaged. I am still sedated when the police arrive. I tell them I resisted a mugger. They tell me I was lucky and warn me about walking alone in the evening in that section of the city. I thank them. I think of myself attacking with my nail file and the fact that I have survived. I feel more exhilarated than at any other time in my life.

TWO

Our lives proceed by choices. We become who and what we are by making decisions. When things happen by chance we still must react to them. When opportunities are presented we must elect or decline them. We are standing at the center of a compass surrounded by directional points. An infinite number of futures lie beyond us in the mist. We choose a direction and begin to walk. What could be more important or more interesting?

My friends and I see less and less of one another these days; I have chosen to leave the center of the compass and indulge my obsession, regardless of the eventual result. I want to follow people and investigate them. I want to know the motives that underlie their actions. I want to know the secrets of their hearts. I want to protect the innocent and I want to help prosecute the guilty. I know who does that and I know where to find them: *www.fbi.gov.*

There is a respected nursing program whose diagnostic procedures include an assessment of the health of the patient's aura. The nurse's hand hovers above the patient's body and traces its outline, searching for signs of systemic order or disorder. It makes sense; our bodies are a mass of interlaced electrical activity. At the same time, our beliefs regarding our auras tell an interesting tale of our hopes and delusions. We want to think of ourselves as angels, not as animals, and it is a short step from the belief in our distinctive aura to the belief in our eventual halo. The fact remains that we carry a scent and when we have committed a crime and attempt to escape, the authorities track us with animals—animals with vast nasal passages and the ability to draw the subtlest distinctions concerning odors and aromas. Bloodhounds and Shepherds rub their noses against our clothing and their brains seize on our most intimate smells. I leave the notion of auras and halos to others. It does not ground me the way that the following of a scent does.

Such work, I thought, would bind me more closely to my family's history on the northern plains. Tracking is more difficult there, with the incessant winds, but if one is shrewd and properly positioned, the winds make it easier to surprise unsuspecting prey. Tracking is both survival and sport. My ancestors were its masters and wind-swept, treeless horizons summoned them like lost lovers.

The FBI site tells me exactly what I suspected. The Bureau investigates everything, from health care fraud to money laundering. They seek specialists of various kinds: linguists, computer jocks, crime scene investigators, lab techs, and, still, accountants. And they're seeking women. Forty-three percent of the FBI's employees are women, but only twenty percent of the special agents.

The arguments for shifting those numbers cover several pages of website. *Women possess different analytical skills, approach problems differently, and have different talents and abilities than do men. Rather than considering them divisive, the FBI believes these differences are complementary.* Thank you very much, I appreciate the thought, but don't expect me to be a tech specialist. I want to be in the alley, with the men, not behind a microscope in a windowless, gray room.

The pay is modest, but I could trade my nail file in for something more substantial. I am between the ages of 23 and 37. I am available for assignment anywhere. I am a U.S. citizen or a citizen of the Northern Mariana Islands. I have yet to be convicted of a felony or major misdemeanor. My uncorrected vision is no worse than 20/40 in either eye; I have no significant hearing impairment, possess a valid driver's license, a four-year degree from an accredited college or university, and suffer from no defects which would interfere in firearm use, raids, or defensive tactics.

I scan the list of critical skills they currently seek, striking out on every item. At the bottom is experience with the physical sciences. My minor in chemistry has finally served its purpose. I complete a battery of written tests, meet the physical fitness requirements, receive a personal interview, and clear the background check. I am accepted and prepare for Quantico. In one month I will relocate to Virginia; in the meantime I read and prepare; in twenty-four weeks I will become a special agent in the Federal Bureau of Investigation.

At Quantico I meet Richard. We pair off because of our alphabetically adjoining surnames. He is a West Point graduate who completed the five years of his regular army obligation, took a five-year night law degree at Georgetown while working days for a beltway bandit firm and still slipped under the Bureau's age-requirement wire.

He helps me with government T O & E charts, criminal law, upper body strength and the basic rules for fast-trackers in complex hierarchical organizations. I help him with physical science and behavioral psychology; I teach him how to follow people in urban and rural landscapes. We rent a two-bedroom cottage in Stafford, a bump in the road beside route 95, and spend our scant leisure time in the Irish bars of Old Town Alexandria, where short hair cuts are common. As we talk and nurse frosted mugs of Harp I watch the clientele come and go—the pentagon types and the hangers-on they attract, the power mainliners and aspirants from the Hill, the suburbanites from McLean and Potomac, the yacht crowd who've moored their Hatterases at the bottom of Duke Street and are looking for Friday night action and the wannabes with eighteen-foot Bayliners, sunburns, and stomachs filled with *Sam's Club* beer, happy to be on land, away from the bumps and slaps of the river and the need to dodge the debris that's floated there from West Virginia. I talk to Richard as we prepare for the next phase of our training; I sit tight and listen to him, resisting the urge to follow interesting ne'er-do-wells into the night. It is not easy.

Finally he catches my attention, talking about his days in an Armored Cavalry Squadron in Germany and the Middle East. "It's organized chaos," he says, "different vehicles all going in different directions. Some are on the road; some are making their own roads. Tanks, Bradleys, humvees, mortar carriers, deuce-and-a-halfs…if you can control a group like that you can control anything. Each has a different role in a common mission, but together they don't really feel like a team. It's more like a group of boys gone wild, all following their own lights and all heading in different directions."

"Just like life," I answer.

"What do you mean?"

"They're finding their own way. Making their own choices."

"Yeah, that's the trouble. We're all on the same frequency and I'm trying to control them, but I might as well be talking to myself."

"Just like God."

"I never had those kind of aspirations. I'd've been happy to feel like a drill sergeant every now and then."

"And you couldn't just follow them…see what they were up to, or what they might have discovered…"

"No, they all did their thing and when we were careful and lucky they all showed up at the end. Sometimes I'd be lucky and could locate my 113 on high ground where I could get a look at them and see where they were positioning themselves. Sometimes we just rolled on through the darkness, hoping the path we had chosen would take us to the right place."

"I know exactly what you mean," I answer.

THREE

Most of the women in the academy have difficulty with the physical training. They run the obstacle course worrying about the individual tasks. They run the distance course worrying about the time remaining and the uphill segments. Whenever I run I focus on the individual in front of me, wondering what he's thinking, why he's doing the things that he does, why he does them in that particular way. I concentrate on one other thing—am I gaining on him? I'm in his head, not mine. My feet and legs and hands and arms move effortlessly, negotiating whatever is put in my way. I am the one who follows. I am the one who tracks. No one escapes my gaze. Nothing breaks my concentration.

The pistol course in Hogan's Alley is designed to trick and to surprise. I am not tricked. The cutout targets are alive. I am in their brains. I know when they will appear and I know who they are. I know their intentions. I know if they pose a threat to me. I put bullets through their cardboard hearts and cardboard foreheads.

The course is calculated. I am instinctive. I see, I know, and I shoot. The men approach the course as if it is a standardized test. They try to understand its ways. To me it is real. It is life itself and I am the one who always walks away alive.

I learn the most important lesson at Quantico; it is taught by a senior agent who repeats it to every class. "Here is the task," he says, "you can never stop thinking. Never stop anticipating. Never stop considering the possible moves of your adversary. You will make assumptions that prove to be wrong; you will go down alleys that prove to be blind; you will arrive at perfectly logical explanations which prove to be false. The trick is to realize that you can't be right instantly, every time. No one is right all the time and no one gets to the bottom of complex cases without digging and scratching and then digging and scratching again. The secret—and the *job*—is to never stop thinking, to never stop refining, to never stop weighing and evaluating. You can't always think the way your adversaries think, because much of the time you will end up discovering that they are stupid, drugged, drunk or psychotic, but you can always outlast them. You have physical skills but, first and foremost, you are a thinker, a *tenacious* thinker. You have the best weapons and the best technical support in the world at your disposal, but your most important weapon is your brain. It is the most lethal weapon in the Bureau's arsenal."

The graduation ceremony is brief. There is a forgettable speaker from the Justice Department and a large sheet cake. He wears a brown suit and polished brown shoes. The cake has white icing and red and blue stars. The fruit punch is orange and sugary. I graduate first in the class and people say well-meaning things that I would consider patronizing if I had not already moved beyond old insecurities. As a reward for performance I am offered a choice of assignments. I pick the field office in St. Louis.

Richard told me that the best way to succeed in a bureaucracy is to achieve some early wins in a setting that's large enough to matter but not so large that your actions can be overlooked in the confusion. St. Louis is perfect. Two and a half million plus in the metropolitan area and a riverfront landmark that terrorists—the Bureau's top priority now—dream of bringing down. The crossroads point for Chicago, Memphis, Louisville, Cincinnati, Indianapolis and Kansas City. Route 44: the major drug highway from Texas and the southwest. The crystal meth capital incarnate. A state with extended metropolitan areas at its boundaries, ripe for interstate crime and Bureau action. The home state of Jesse James and Calamity Jane.

The Bureau office is on Market Street, between the central west end and the river, an area of empty factory buildings, dead boulevards bordered with vacant lots, the occasional oasis of an upscale restaurant, and successful attempts at gentrification near Union Station and the Enterprise Center. A bisecting six lane strip of concrete offers escape to west county or the looming prospect of the riverbank and East St. Louis. No man's land.

Richard is 250 miles west in Kansas City. No guarantee that he would get his first choice, but luck was with him. The interstate—route 70—is our link: a four-lane washboard with billboards advertising decrepit 50's museums and adult entertainment venues, stores with 'cheap cigs', and occasional open fields and raw limestone outcroppings of some beauty. There is an active wine industry parallelling the river with related tasting rooms dotting the highway. In the small towns the nineteenth century is never far away and in the urban areas there are all the comforts of home, though in each case a critical mass of the upscale population has moved away from the downtown. In Kansas City the shopping and dining mecca is the Country Club Plaza area, where no country club is in sight. In St. Louis the cognate area is Clayton, the gateway to the west county suburbs.

I rent an apartment in Richmond Heights, just south of Clayton. A collection of large retail operations, townhouses, condos, and aging rental property, the area is becoming encircled by discount houses, groceries, and yuppie emporiums. Minutes from major arteries, it is a neighborhood in which you could live without a car, assuming you could get across South Brentwood Boulevard without being run over.

My apartment is spacious and inexpensive, but the remnants of the past remain—dark hallways with frayed carpeting dense with cooking smells, wall garbage chutes from which I expect to see four- and six-legged creatures emerge, windows with outdated screens and steel catches that range from loose to uncertain, and bathroom fixtures that were last updated several decades before my birth.

My neighbors are poor couples and small families for whom the rent is a stretch. No playboys and few elderly. I am on the third floor with a good view of the courtyard and parking area. Good lines of fire if they're ever needed. It's a place to start.

The special agent in charge is Tom Donaldson. Edgar's ideal. A lawyer with military and police experience, he wears dark suits, white shirts, and Dillard's ties. You have to look twice to see him in a gray room. His brown hair is cut without style. He has no facial hair, no scars, no identifying marks of any kind. He drives a blue Ford sedan, carries a black umbrella, a worn brown briefcase and an old .38 special. He is quiet and by-the-book and there are no personal items on his desk or office walls. In a lineup he'd be identified as a bank examiner or the guy who fills out the financing forms after the car salesmen have clinched their deals. His tie is always tied and his shoes are always shined, but not highly polished.

"Donaldson," he says, extending his hand. "Welcome aboard."

"Harrison," I answer. "It's good to be here."

"Your name is…Gwen," he says, flipping through my chart.

"Yes, sir."

"We generally just use last names here. With me too. No standing on ceremony."

"Good practice," I said.

"Why?" he asked.

"Because if someone's monitoring our transmissions they wouldn't know if we were talking about junior officers or senior, adults or children, women or men. Army practice: never say 'we're moving our tanks or missile launchers.' You say, 'We're moving our *elements*.'"

"But you haven't been in the Army, Harrison," he responded, again looking at my chart.

"I read," I said, "and I've got friends to advise me."

"Good," he said, pausing. "Let me say something personal, Harrison. I won't do it often. I've read your chart. I'm very pleased to have you here."

"Thank you, sir. This was my first choice."

"I noted that," he said. "Are you settled in now?"

"Yes," I said. "I'm ready to go to work."

"Good. I've got an interesting case for you."

FOUR

"His name is Calvin Taylor. He was arrested in 2007 for trafficking in kiddie porn on the internet. He was acquitted after pleading that the material he provided had been unsolicited and then forwarded accidentally. The defense was preposterous, but the jury was not sufficiently computer literate to understand the technicalities of the claim and decided instead to punt.

"For the last several years he has owned and operated an adult bookstore in Sedalia, which he sold for a recorded price of $275,000. Since doing so he has purchased a home in Wildwood for $1.75 Million, though he has no visible means of support. We recently found his name on an internet troll. No evidence of buying or selling, but his name turns up on multiple mailing lists. Most of the heavy sites and businesses are carefully passworded, but if he shows up that often in public we can only wonder what he's doing in private. Here's his mug shot…"

Age: 52. Height: 5'11". Weight: 230. Brown/Blue. He looked more like a barfly than a sleaze merchant, a guy who came to a trailer court party and stayed until the beer, wine, whisky and paint thinner ran out. In a business with that kind of profit margin you don't have to be a math or marketing whiz to carve out a successful niche. His features were M1A1 porcine: puffy eyelids over thin slits, thick lips, untrimmed, wayward brows. Visible nose and ear hair. Meet Mr. Creepo.

"His computer's in the cubicle next to the conference room. It's all yours."

"So he's on his guard now."

"Not necessarily. We've impounded his computers before. He may think this is part of a routine sweep."

"I'll check it out," I said. I didn't say anything about checking *him* out. I wasn't sure if Donaldson wanted me poking around in the field so early, so I kept my other thoughts to myself and started with the computer. I moved the monitor around so that my back was to the side wall of the cubicle. I didn't want anyone embarrassed by what they might see on the screen and I didn't want to attract any comments on my own tastes and interests. Bureau offices are not like police stations, where practical jokes and running comments are commonplace, but it's still better to mute possible problems before they arise. Donaldson saw me and tilted his head quizzically. "I don't want to distract anybody," I said. He just nodded.

I figured going in that this was the longest of long shots. If a perp's computer is regularly confiscated it's a safe bet that he's not going to use it to incriminate himself. When I began my scans I wasn't simply looking for pornographic material or links to pornographic sites. I was looking for evidence that the hard drive had been scrubbed and sanitized, which it clearly had. He might as well have removed it and marinated it in lye.

I looked at the clock; it was 3:00. I used the remaining two hours to check on the location of Taylor's home and familiarize myself with the streets and roads in the area. If he had been actively seeking a source for unreported income and if he was not using his own computer, then his available options were clear. He could use a phone (risky), the mails (less risky) or make contact through a pay-as-you-go copy center computer or a (free) library machine. Once in, he could use a counter-intuitive email address: mathteacher@charter.net or christianwitness@hotmail.com and his communications would be virtually untraceable. We could work back from sites of known suppliers, but that could take eons, particularly if he continually changed machines and addresses. Better to simply track him and see where he goes—to the UPS Store? The Post Office? The local dirty book store? Or?

Donaldson was called on a case at 4:30. I waited until the secretaries left at 5:00. I didn't know who might or might not be reporting on me through back channels. By 5:25 I was in Clayton, following Clayton Road through the western suburbs. It's the slowest way to go, but in rush hour the traffic moves and it's at least a straight shot. I wanted to familiarize myself with my new battlefield and there's no better way to do it than to proceed step by step, mile by mile.

Wildwood is the newest upscale western suburb. When you push beyond it the prices plummet but the commutes are impossible. Wildwood adjoins Chesterfield, but still has open land, which the developers are scraping and sculpting. To the north lies route 40, providing direct access to the city some 25-30 miles and 45-60 minutes east. The exit for Wildwood is just beyond Chesterfield Commons, a vast strip of big-box stores and chain restaurants, stretched across an enormous flood plain and growing like a tapeworm. The locals call it the 'flats' or the 'bottoms'. It's now bracketed by two discount malls.

Taylor's house was a mile and a half south as the crow would fly if he were looking down at *Wal-Mart, Target, Sam's Club, Mimi's Café*, the *Olive Garden, Longhorn Steak House* and *Red Lobster*. I'm not sure it was worth one and three-quarters mil, but it covered a lot of ground and was itself covered in vast swaths of gray stone. Many of the original oaks and maples had been spared and the driveway had been lined with Bradford Pears leading to large beds of variegated hostas and azaleas. The splashes of color contrasted nicely with the dark hardwood mulch and the stone facing of the house.

Now, I thought, how do we catch Mr. Taylor in the act of being himself and separate him from the surrounding doctors and lawyers and business executives who are unaware of the source of their neighbor's rather considerable ill-gotten gains? The subdivision was not yet built out and the model home had a ten-car visitors' lot from which I could see half of Taylor's house and the end of his driveway. Each house was built on the side of the surrounding hills, with curving driveways and various degrees of privacy. The terrain looked like a reclaimed strip mine. The model home's parking lot was thirty yards above the structure itself, so that I could park there and not be visible to the agents working the potential buyers.

I watched for seven hours, saw lights go on and off and drapes and blinds open and close, but no one entered or left the driveway. I returned on the next day—Saturday—and watched for 14 hours. Again, nothing. On Sunday I arrived at 6:30 a.m. and at 6:45 I saw Taylor's white Mercedes pull out of the driveway. I figured he wasn't going to church.

When I follow someone in a car I bring along a selection of hats that serve as mini-disguises. My nondescript sedan attracts less attention than the hats—say, for example, an Aussie outback special or an overdone white straw and ribbon job from a retro millinery shop. I've also got a baseball cap and a big-hair fright wig. When you look into a rear vision mirror the darkened outline catches your eye and fixes your attention. I change headgear when my car passes out of view on turns and dips. If I'm on an interstate I exit or pull into rest stops, change headgear, and quickly return. It's crude, but it works.

I followed Taylor into Chesterfield. He turned onto Clarkson and followed it to Manchester Boulevard, an endless line of shops, car dealerships, chain restaurants and strip malls. After driving east for eight blocks he turned south into a mini-mall and parked in front of an end unit with a large glass window with small black and gold lettering that read *Your Very Own Address*—a mail drop. I had walked into one once on 36th Street, just west of Wisconsin in Georgetown. I had seen selections from a book advertised on the internet, published by Green Shutters Press. The publisher listed a 36th Street address. I walked there, hoping to pick up a copy, and found myself standing with my back to a shutterless, grimy window, on a scuffed linoleum floor in front of a bank of mailboxes rather than in a quaint cottage with a helpful clerk and the scent of spice in clear country air.

I turned my car around and parked, watching Taylor in my mirror. He opened a mailbox, reached in, retrieved something, slipped it into his shirt pocket, and returned to his car. Whatever it was, it was small.

When he drove west on Manchester I followed him at a distance. He retraced his steps, turning north on Clarkson and driving up the boulevard, past the wide lawns and multi-storied estates of the Clarkson Valley. Clarkson eventually becomes Olive, a major east/west St. Louis artery, but before he got there he turned onto 40 and headed toward downtown. Fifteen minutes later as we approached the Galleria on the left I looked to the right and saw my apartment building. I wondered when I'd see it again.

FIVE

We passed Forest Park and the science center, the zoo and the Barnes-Jewish hospital complex, Union Station and the Anheuser-Busch plant and drove into the bright morning sun as the arch came into view between derelict factory buildings and the edge of Busch Stadium. We were heading for Illinois.

We crossed the bridge and I followed Taylor to route 64, which led to the Chicago/Memphis interchange and, eventually, to Louisville. He continued to drive east, passing the 255 interchange, and eventually pulled into a rest stop. Suddenly I had to decide whether or not to risk exposing myself. It was a gamble, since I could have lost him, but I turned to the left and parked with the trucks rather than with the cars, put on my baseball hat and did my best imitation of a saunter as I approached the rest room facilities from the rear.

From the side of the building I saw the white Mercedes. Taylor was headed directly toward me. I slipped into the women's rest room, waited several moments, left by the rear exit, and found a weathered picnic table in a distant grove of trees. The sight lines were good. Taylor emerged from the men's room, adjusted his clothing, and walked to a table some seventy-five yards away, near the dog exercise area. He was facing in my direction, but by then I had taken out my cell phone and put it to my ear, doing a Chatty Cathy imitation, with animated expressions.

He lit a cigarette and seven or eight minutes later another man sat down at the table with him. He was drinking something from a metal can. He nodded at Taylor, like a polite stranger, and then sat looking in the opposite direction, greeting people as they walked their dogs. He looked like a truck driver, with a plaid shirt, jeans, suspenders, and a baseball cap with unrecognizable logo. While Taylor smoked, he pushed back the bill of his cap and wiped his forehead. I kept talking into empty space, waiting for Taylor to tip his hand. Finally, he did.

When the man finished his drink Taylor offered him a cigarette. The man took it, gave him a 'much obliged' nod, lit it, and continued to stare at the dogwalkers. After a few minutes Taylor rose, leaving his cigarette pack on the table, next to the other man's forearm, and walked toward his Mercedes. The man finished his cigarette, slipped the cigarette pack into his shirt pocket and walked toward his black Explorer. He had picked it up without hesitation and made no attempt to call to Taylor and at least go through the motions of attempting to return it.

I hurried back to my car and slalomed between the parked semi's. Taylor exited the rest area first, followed two cars later by the Explorer. I got on the phone and called the agent on duty back in St. Louis. I told him I was in pursuit of a suspect and asked for backup. Just above French Village now, I was too far from either St. Louis or Springfield to bring in agents from our regional offices. This was also too much of a long shot to lay on a helicopter, so the duty agent—a man named Tillotson—contacted the Highway Patrol. As long as they kept their distance I wouldn't be compromised. I simply needed them to be able to close with me and the car I was following within a matter of minutes.

Taylor turned off at the first interchange; his contact continued and I followed, figuring that Taylor's work was done and he was returning home. The Explorer driver turned off at the O'Fallon, Illinois interchange and headed toward the town. By now I was patched through to the Highway Patrol and was talking to an officer named Clements. I gave him my location and he said he'd close with me in four or five minutes.

Suddenly the Explorer turned onto a side road and into a gravel driveway and I continued on, not wanting to tip him with the sound of skidding tires. I gave Clements the location, drove a few tenths of a mile, turned and drove back, parking in the burn a hundred yards east of the driveway. A few minutes later the Highway Patrol black and white passed me, did a Y-turn, and parked behind my vehicle.

Carl Clements was a tall, barrel-chested black man, at least 6'3" and 240, with a large sidearm and businesslike nightstick. He looked particularly comfortable with the latter. He was wearing a mounty's hat with a broad brim that shadowed his eyes. For some reason or other I was tempted to tell him that I had one too, but I didn't. We talked briefly and approached the driveway on foot. There was some dense honeysuckle and scrub that afforded us concealment, but we didn't know what awaited us on the other side of the spray of leaves, branches, and twisted trunks.

From the edge of the foliage I could see a dilapidated house and detached garage. I told him I'd take the garage and he could take the house. If we went in together and picked the wrong building we would risk being shot in the back, since several windows of the house were aligned with the door to the garage. Besides, I noticed some heavy duty wires going into the garage and figured it might be used for some other purpose than as a bedroom for the Explorer.

I walked around the back of the building, communicating with Clements with hand and arm signals. As I approached the door with my weapon out I could hear a clicking sound inside. I leaned down, looked at the lock and saw that the bolt was leaning against the tongue of the strike plate. I pushed in the door, drew down, and said, "Freeze," loud enough for Clements to hear me. Without looking or speaking the man swung around to his left and threw a paperweight at my head. I dodged, but he hit me square in the left shoulder and though it knocked me off balance I did my best not to show any reaction. The object, a piece of scrap metal, thudded to the floor. It sounded as if it had been dropped from three or four stories. He pulled himself out of his chair, preparing to lunge at me, and I shot him twice in rapid succession in the left knee. The second round caught him slightly higher than the first and there was less of a sound than the slap against shattering bone made by the first.

He collapsed, curled up, grabbed at his leg and knee, and squirmed in a circular motion like a dog rooting around in a pile of dirty laundry on a basement floor.

"If you want to try for three, I'm willing," I said.

He called me a *cunt bitch* as Clements came through the door.

"You all right?" he asked.

"I'm fine," I said. Clements told the man to straighten out on his belly. Then he put his full weight against his neck, wedging his mouth, nose and cheek against the floor, and cuffed him snugly.

"Here's what this is all about," I said, pointing to an object on the desk, resting beside a computer keyboard that was smudged with dirty fingerprints.

SIX

I slipped a pair of tweezers out of the side pocket of my purse, picked up the object, examined it, and then dropped it into a plastic evidence bag.

"What is it?" Clements asked. He was standing above the perp, too far away to get a good look.

"A memory card for a digital camera. Two hundred and fifty-six gigs worth; these puppies go for about 70 or 80 bucks. So (I asked the perp), is this a set of pix from Calvin's trip to Disney World?"

He didn't respond. He was probably contemplating a formulaic 'fuck you' but Clements had split open the left side of his lip and the area beneath his eye was beginning to discolor. I hadn't noticed the extra bump that those results would have required. Clements must have been an expert.

"The thumbnails are on his screen," I said. "He's already downloaded the pictures." I moved the mouse with the side of a No. 2 yellow pencil and then clicked it with the end of the eraser. An image came up of an Asian girl being sexually abused by two men. She looked as if she was nine or ten years old.

I looked at the man and said, "How long do you think you're going to last in the general population of a federal prison?"

Clements winked at me and said, "I'll hold him until your backup arrives...let him think about your question." He wrote down a local address on a card and said, "You can interrogate him here." Then he dragged him to his cruiser with one hand and poured him into the back seat. He wasn't being especially careful about it; maybe he had a nine- or ten year-old daughter at home.

I would have expected the man to be demanding medical attention, but he must have been preoccupied with my question. His left foot was limply bouncing off of rocks and ruts as Clements pulled him by the upper arm and all he did was wince and groan. We would need his testimony to convict Taylor, since so far there was no direct evidence linking the two beyond what I was able to observe, but this kind of trafficking could involve a nasty federal bounce and given the nature of the crime and the future prospects he faced among his fellow inmates, the likelihood was high that he would welcome a deal to help us convict Mr. Creepo.

I called Donaldson and he was there in an hour and ten minutes. He had been at his son's soccer game in Webster Groves and had covered a lot of territory in a short period of time. The tech team preceded him by fifteen minutes. They pulled several sets of prints off of the memory card (maybe we wouldn't need the second perp's testimony after all), took additional prints from the keyboard and a sticky beer bottle at the back of the desk, and gave us the go ahead to check out the computer and the rest of the room.

While they finished up their work Donaldson and I surveyed the room. The striking thing was that every open bit of table and shelf space was covered with empty bottles and cans. The perp may have been many things, but he was not a dedicated recycler. There were beer bottles and soda cans, glass and aluminum iced tea containers, 16-ounce malt liquor cans, Black Jack bourbon bottles in multiple sizes—including airline miniatures—some screwcap wine bottles, and two refrigerator-size aluminum beer kegs.

The desk ash tray was filled to overflowing and adjoining it was a coffee can with three or four inches of murky brown fluid in the bottom and butts floating on the top like tiny, beige barrels of toxic waste. He must have used the butt can as an auxiliary. I wondered why he didn't just empty the tray instead. The waste paper can at the side of the desk was filled with food wrappers and cartons. His preferences ran to Pizza Hut, Panda Express and Burger King. The insects exploring the contents of the can must have shared his tastes. Donaldson slid it to the other side of the room, putting some distance between them and us.

The garage was winterized with some shredded gray insulation sandwiched between the outer walls and pieces of scrap plywood and drywall nailed to the studs. These interior walls were covered with notes and scrawls and in some cases obscene drawings, as if the entire work space was a public toilet. There was a single piece of irregular, remnant carpet under the desk chair. The garage was heated by a black Franklin stove; its firebox was covered with clumps of dirt, suggesting that it also served as the perp's footrest. There was a half cord of mildewed oak and pine logs indiscriminately stacked against a far wall. From the number of droppings near it, it must have served as a domicile for at least one extended family of mice.

The 'desk' was a formica-top kitchen table with pitted chrome legs and deep scratches in the aqua surface covered with pink and black blunt-end, interlaced triangles. Welcome to 1955. The work space included an olive drab two-drawer file cabinet with the price "$2" written on the left side in black magic marker, an iMac computer, HP laser printer and HP flatbed scanner. We checked the file cabinet but it only contained personal papers. The important things were stored elsewhere.

It didn't take us long to find them. In the basement of the main house there was an ancient Amana refrigerator. The door and chrome handle were covered with black handprints; there was at least a quarter inch of dust and grit on the top; its motor sounded like a threshing machine in its death throes. In one of the opaque, stained vegetable crispers was a thick stack of $100 bills and a set of diskettes in a thick plastic box—the Amana and crisper were probably the perp's idea of fire insurance. In the plastic box, the mother lode: a backup set of the images that the man had been peddling, a complete client list with passwords and credit card numbers, a data base of suppliers with records of prices paid and a full, unencrypted list of the account numbers in offshore banks (Grand Cayman, the Isle of Man) to which the wired cash had been transferred. A nice payday for the government. *Taylor, Calvin* was a name that repeated with some frequency, but it was not the only name in the file.

The websites themselves were entitled *Babes in Bangkok, Babes in Hollywood,* and *Babes 4 U.* The graphics were all upscale. This was a set of sites for 'discerning connoisseurs'. I thought of the old magazine ads that asked the question, "What sort of man reads *Playboy*?" They were filled with pictures of lean, well-groomed men in Italian-tailored suits surrounded by sports cars, state-of-the-art stereo systems and miscellaneous male bling. That was the spirit invoked here, except for the sleaze dripping from the edges. Donaldson looked around the garage and said, "So this is Hollywood? It looks more like an outhouse on Tobacco Road."

The distributor's name turned out to be Ridgewell Washburn, Ridge for short. "Sounds like a character actor's name," Donaldson said.

"A real piece of work," I answered. "And rich as Midas. His personal accounts total nearly seven million dollars."

"Lives like a pig," Donaldson said.

"True to his nature," I said.

"We've got enough here to keep a dozen federal prosecutors busy for years," he said.

"*Successfully* busy," I added.

"You're damn right," he answered. It was the most profane thing I had yet heard him say. He quickly added, "Sorry…"

"No reason to be sorry, Skip," I said. "I appreciate your letting me do this my way; it may not always work out this well."

"It doesn't have to," he said, "not with a win like this."

SEVEN

Two days later Richard called me, inviting me to dinner in Kansas City. We had to wait for the weekend. I got in on Saturday about 7:30 and we went to a steak house just east of the Plaza. They had carving utensils as big as Bowie knives but steak so tender you didn't really need them. Also perfect asparagus, perfect baked potatoes, perfect martinis, and perfect red wine. "Is this a date?" I asked, knowing it would make him nervous.

"It's a congratulatory dinner," he said. "You deserve it."

"Couldn't it be both?"

"If I weren't too old for you," he answered.

I just smiled. He didn't relax very easily. He wore a blue dress shirt with a button-down collar, gray wool slacks, and a brown tweed jacket. Looking at the shirt I could feel the starch in the back of my neck. He also had a fresh haircut.

I wore designer jeans, a wool jacket and turtleneck. I felt as if we were still in uniform. After two martinis and a glass of red wine we each started to relax. "The Washburn collar is terrific," he said.

For a moment I thought he was talking about the collar on my sweater. "Right," I said. "There was a lot of luck involved, but with the possibility of over seven hundred indictments (and counting) we made a real dent in the problem."

"You should negotiate for 10% of the ill-gotten gains," he said.

"*That* would impress my mother," I said. "She wonders why we do what we do considering the risks and the rewards. She still hasn't gotten over the fact that I'm not a lawyer or accountant. I take that back. She still hasn't gotten over the fact that I spent a year and a half after college doing counter jobs in European hotels. I wanted to see the world, not go to professional school."

"She just worries about her only daughter," he said.

"I know. And she knows that I'd be miserable in some girly form of work. When I got some medals in high school swimming she was afraid that I'd develop East German shoulders and start dating somebody named Greta."

"There was a girl at West Point named Greta," Richard said, "but she didn't have big shoulders."

"No?" I responded.

"She had big SAT scores," he answered, coaxing a smile.

"College was easy for you," I said. "They told you what classes to take, how to dress, when to go where, how often to get your head shaved, who to salute…I had to decide what to study and who to be."

"I missed all that," he answered, "and I'm sorry. I could have been a hippie."

"Right. With a starched tie-dyed shirt and polished sandal straps."

"Is it really that bad?"

"I'm just kidding. Relaxation is a relative notion."

"Right. This is my version."

"I always heard that the West Point boys were so repressed that when they let go they were utterly out of control."

"Not true," he said.

"Oh? I'm disappointed."

"They *never* let go," he said. "Well…maybe every now and then."

I gave him an encouraging smile. "What have you been up to, Bureau-wise?"

"Same old, same old. Internet fraud. Banking fraud. Securities fraud. I'm changing my desk plate to read 'Frauds 'R Us.'"

"You should enjoy that. You had five years to play with mortars and howitzers and grenade launchers and all that other smoke-and-fire stuff. Now you can see how the rest of the world sins."

"Actually it's not so bad, except for the fact that I need to get myself a proper green eyeshade."

"You get a lot of quick lessons in human nature, I bet."

"Every day," he said.

I didn't tell him that for a time I thought about seeking a job as a postal inspector. Sometimes they get to sit behind one-way glass and watch suspicious individuals for days. It sounded good to me, but I decided I'd rather be walking or driving. One of my jobs after college was to shadow potential shoplifters in the *Nordstrom* at the Santa Anita Mall in Arcadia. It was a challenge because there was so much open floor space and so few nooks and crannies in which to be inconspicuous. I sat at television monitors for hours, watching dressing room scams. I had to force myself to leave work.

"Remind me about your dad," Richard said. "What does he do?"

"He's a lawyer. Corporate stuff, but usually not litigation. Contracts…the fine points of complicated deals…that sort of thing. One of their big clients is the local gas utility. Not very romantic work, but it's steady and it pays well. Everybody wants heat and hot water and functioning cooking surfaces. He always told me to do something more exciting. My mother would interject that he wasn't really serious and that I shouldn't listen to him, but actually, he was. His family had barely survived the depression and the result was that my dad and my uncle were always risk-averse. I'm the family adventurer."

"I'm now the family civilian," Richard said. "My father still puts on his class A's every day and drives down the Shirley Highway to the Pentagon. He talks about how soft it is, since he doesn't have to be there until 6:30 most mornings and leaves promptly at 7:00 every night. With a simple 28-mile commute he's home for cocktails while it's still light. When something flairs around the world he's in every day, usually complaining because he can't take time out for his lunchtime 4-mile run along the river. He's an old time soldier and loves it dearly. When I told him I was getting out after five he was relieved to find out that I was hoping to eventually end up at the Bureau. For him, that still counts as man's work."

"I like the Bureau," I said, "but sometimes I wish we were in the glory days, chasing bank robbers across Kansas or searching the northern lakes in Wisconsin. When I was in grammar school we took a trip there. We saw the site of Dillinger's hideout; it was at least a six-hour drive above Chicago. My mother hated it; I loved every minute. She wanted to go to the beach, follow the sun. I wanted to follow the bad guys."

Before Richard could respond my cell phone vibrated in my jacket pocket. "Excuse me," I said. I took the cell phone out and looked at the incoming number. "I have to take this," I said. "Sorry."

I stepped outside of the restaurant, steering away from the pedestrian traffic on the sidewalk. The evening air was cool and there was a wind coming in from the southwest. A few minutes later I returned. Richard had his hands on the table. He wasn't holding his utensils. He looked concerned.

"I have to go back right away," I said, trying to control my voice. "Donaldson's dead."

"How?" he asked.

"Car bomb."

"What?" he said. "In St. Louis?"

"Yes, in St. Louis. Richard…"

"What, Gwen?"

"My car was in the shop on Thursday and Friday. I was driving a pool car."

"And?"

"Donaldson signed it out this evening. It had been rigged. Whoever blew it up was probably trying to kill me."

EIGHT

It was 1:50 in the morning when I arrived at the field office. The acting special agent in charge, Dale Winthrop, was waiting for me outside when I pulled in. He looked as if he was standing guard. "What happened?" I asked.

"At this point we don't know a great deal," he said. "The bomb was not hard wired to detonate with the turn of the ignition key. Tom was just up the street, driving west, when it went off. We figure that someone was waiting at an observation point and detonated the device when the car came into view. There's an abandoned building that would provide a good line of sight to the license plate. That would have been necessary, since the pool cars are all carbon copies of one another, unless, of course, somebody just wanted to blow up a Bureau car randomly. The kind of device used could have been planted easily. All the bomber would need was access to our parking area. He or she could have simply dropped something by accident, stooped down, slipped the bomb out of his or her coat and attached it beneath the driver's seat. One good magnet and it would be ready to go."

"Was anyone else hurt?"

"No. The street was nearly empty at the time."

"What do we know about the device?"

"C-4. Probably about two pounds. Packed with screws and roofing nails."

"Pure anti-personnel and more than enough explosive to do the job. Middle-east style with the built-in shrapnel."

"Yes."

"They were trying to kill me."

"From the assumed observation point there would not have been a good view of the driver, just the license plate. Particularly at night."

"They definitely were trying to kill me."

"We don't know that, Gwen."

"But it's a good assumption."

"Yes, it is."

"Does the mob ever use devices like that?"

"It's not their usual style. If the Kansas City mob came in as a result of your breaking the porn case, they would have directed a street soldier to shoot you behind the ear. That's their signature and they like to leave it."

"If they can get that close."

"Yes."

"And who controls them?"

"*Controls* is not a word they'd use, but they kick back to Brooklyn."

"That's what I thought."

"Let's go inside," he said, "get some coffee."

Dale was a good agent but a little more coarse around the edges than Tom. Normally he'd use words like 'hit' or 'clip' or 'cap', not 'shoot.' He was on his best behavior. His tone was formal, even courtly. He was trying to be gentle with me. He must have been certain that I was the target. Two pounds of C-4 with a cargo of small shrapnel would have shredded Donaldson. I pushed the image out of my mind; I didn't want it to hold me back.

When I entered the conference room it felt like a funeral parlor. The other agents spoke to me as if I was the victim's daughter, even though I had only known him for a few days. They knew I was the intended target and their expressions of condolence masked their concern for me. Suddenly I had to be the strong one. That was fine. Under other circumstances I might have been seen as talking out of line.

"What are our next steps, Dale?" I asked.

"I think you should lay low," he answered. "You might well have been the target and we don't want to lose you too."

"If this is war, I'm not heading for the locker room," I said.

"Think about this, Gwen. You're vulnerable in too many ways," he answered.

"So are they," I said.

"What do you mean? We don't know who they are; we don't know where they are and we don't know how many of them there are. They can find out where you live and they can find out what you drive. They can position a sniper in any one of a hundred locations. We don't have the resources to sweep your apartment and your car on a constant basis and we don't have Secret Service personnel to guard your every move. If you're out there as a target and they take you out (which won't be hard) they win a second time and I'm out a good agent."

"Thanks," I said, "but I don't see it quite that way." The other agents in the room squirmed as I said that, but they held their expressions.

"Not your call, Gwen," he said.

"I understand, but hear me out."

He folded his hands in front of him and stared at me.

"A bomb is a coward's weapon," I said. "I don't want them thinking of themselves in any other way. And I don't want them thinking they've taught us a lesson. They've just added another line to their rap sheet. When they go down the landing is now going to be a little bit harder. Tell me about the likely observation point. How carefully has it been combed?"

"Preliminary check only at this point," he answered.

"Well, why don't we have a look rather than holding hands here and crying? I'll be surrounded by brave men; I'm not worried." After I said it he paused a moment before responding.

"OK," he said. "Let's go."

NINE

The building was on the north side of Market, just below Jefferson, no more than a few seconds from the field office and only about fifty yards from the detonation point. The flash marks were still visible on the pavement and there was some remaining debris along the center of the street and in the gutter. The first floor windows were too close to the ground; the sight lines would have been easily obscured by any intervening objects, particularly in an area with heavy truck traffic servicing the Enterprise Center and Union Station. The second floor was more promising. The windows in the southwest corner would have afforded a good view of Market and were close enough to the ground to enable an observer with binoculars to read a license plate, particularly after the vehicle passed. The bomber could have identified a Bureau sedan with no trouble as it came into his field of vision and then reached for his binoculars to check the license as the vehicle continued toward Jefferson Avenue.

We went inside and made our way through the crud and rubble to the second floor, which consisted principally of open space with an occasional pile of broomed trash and the remains of fast food wrappers and empty bottles. "Check it out," I said, shining my flashlight. "The plywood covering the other windows looks undisturbed. The nail heads are corroded and there are cobwebs at the edges. You can't reinstall cobwebs. The window in the corner has been used recently. There are pry marks around the plywood and no intact cobwebs." I shined my light on the floor. "The dust has been disturbed. This is where he sat and waited."

"This is the sixth floor of the Dallas book depository. We're looking over Dealey Plaza," Dale said.

"Yes," I answered, "except that he's made a little effort to cover up the fact that he was here."

"But not much," Dale answered. "Maybe he wants us to know he was here."

I didn't respond; I figured I had said enough at that point.

"We'll know more when we've dusted and sifted," he said and I nodded in agreement.

There were no fingerprints found, but our techs got a good shoe print and found some residue on the sheet of plywood covering the window. "What was it?" I asked Dale.

"Nasal discharge," he said.

"And we can get DNA from snot," I said.

"They're checking now," he answered. "There could also be some spit."

"Well, I guess this is the sort of time when you're grateful for the Bureau's king-size data banks," I said.

"Size 10 shoe," he answered. "Actually, a boot. Military type. Vietnam-era. Of course, it could have been purchased from Army surplus, but we're running the names in Washburn's files and looking for people (or relatives of people) who have had military training in the use of explosives. If we turn any possibilities we can check their DNA against that on the sheet of plywood. It's a long shot, but..."

"It's an excellent idea," I said.

"Gwen..."

"What, Dale?"

"Thanks for pushing."

"Thanks for caring about me," I said. "Can I ask a favor?"

"What's that?"

"When we find some possibles..."

"Yes?"

"I want to be there."

"*If* we find some?"

"Yes, *if* we find some."

"You got it."

TEN

We did. It took three and a half days. The individual's name was Carl Hendrix. He turned up in Washburn's files as the recipient of $80,000 in payments over the course of the previous fourteen months. There was no description of the nature of the services he provided. Hendrix had been in the Corps of Engineers and had been given an other-than-honorable discharge.

The OTH resulted from his chronic violent behavior, some of which involved women and the bruising of eyes and breaking of wrist bones. I imagined him with a high forehead and Neanderthal slouch. Dale smiled broadly when he clicked off from a cell phone call and announced that one of the incidents had resulted in the taking of a DNA sample. "And guess what?" he said.

"Mr. Snot Nose is our boy," I answered.

"Bingo," he responded.

"Where is he?"

"Down the rat hole, I'm afraid. His last known address was in Memphis, but he hasn't been there in over a year. No recent credit card activity—at least not in his name—and no cell phone records—again, at least not in his name. Also no record of a hasty departure from Lambert Field; that was our first stop, but none of the check-in clerks i.d.'d him and the closest thing to a Carl Hendrix in their computers was a Carol Henderson, arriving from Spokane en route to Philadelphia. Carl's suddenly the invisible man."

"So we've got an all-purpose scumbag, doing dirty work for Washburn."

"And he probably just got a big paycheck."

"Or was promised one."

"Right."

"How about relatives?"

"We've got a possible. A sister."

"Where?"

"Would you believe St. Charles, Missouri?"

"Would you be surprised if I said I wanted to check her out?"

"OK, but only if I can drive."

"Thanks, Dale."

"Let's do it," he said.

St. Charles, one of the local territorial capitols before statehood, is a thirty minute drive from the field office. With a recently dedicated outsized statue of Lewis, Clark, and Lewis' dog Seaman and a main street dense with shoppes, watering holes, micro breweries, and photo op sites, St. Charles is a tourist magnet, with old brick streets, stone sidewalks and quaint gas lights to complete the atmospherics. Also ample parking. Carol Dretchen, née Hendrix, was bartending at a place called the *Riverfront Tavern*.

Her St. Charles address was outdated. She now lived in U-City, a couple of blocks from *Blueberry Hill*, where Chuck Berry used to perform, but her day job took her to St. Charles and that's where we found her.

Instead of bracing and interrogating her we checked her phone records, both land and cell. Nothing obvious from brother Carl. Either she wasn't in contact with him or they were going out of their way to keep their communications off the books. No calls from Memphis and no calls from repeating numbers except for a set of calls from her daughter Cara, a freshman at Truman State. She had been divorced from Lee Dretchen for fifteen years and he was now living in Portland, Oregon. He was out of her life completely. If Carl *was* calling her he was using multiple cell phones. There were only four calls from public phones in the last year and they were all from Kirksville, doubtless from Cara.

"I say we track her and see where she goes," I said.

"That could take awhile," Dale answered.

"Yes, but how often do we have to find someone who's killed our SAC? I can do it," I said.

"One condition..."

"I know. I'll call for backup as soon as Carl enters the picture."

"And no Bureau sedans."

"Right. He knows what they look like."

ELEVEN

Carol Dretchen lived in a two-family flat a few blocks north of the Delmar loop. U-City runs the gamut from dodgy to chic; her corner of the neighborhood was holding on by its fingertips. I wondered how many of the students strolling the loop, lunching at *Fitz's*, taking in art films at the *Tivoli* and shopping among the multi-pierced patrons of *Vintage Vinyl* were aware how close they might be to an encounter with a homicidal felon. Maybe that's what gave the neighborhood its charm. Besides, where else could you display your new tongue piercing or wear that vulgar-saying tee shirt given to you as a sorority prank?

I followed Hendrix's sister for three days. Each morning she left at 10:00, drove directly to St. Charles, kicked back with a cigarette on a bench along the river bank, worked from 11:00 to 9:00, and returned by 9:45. She ate lunch and dinner each day in the tavern—presumably a fringe benefit—and only stopped twice, once to drop off some dry cleaning and once to pick up some groceries. The same pattern followed for the next three days, except that she stopped once at a bank. I tried not to over-interpret that. Not all people use teller machines and she may have been there to cash some checks or make some complicated deposits. When she worked the following three days also I began to wonder if she ever got any time off. She did. On the tenth day things got interesting.

Each morning I began with a full tank of gas, a rich array of wigs and hats and a reliable pair of binoculars. My favorite set had a lower power than some of the distance monsters, but the higher the power the greater the problem with focus. You see at a vast distance but the object you're observing can jump and twitch if you're not rock steady. I prefer breadth of field as a tradeoff, because it's easier to move between the optics and unassisted line of sight. Every morning I had watched Carol Dretchen intently and every day I had seen nothing, at least nothing out of the ordinary. The same was true on the tenth day, but on that particular day she headed out of town on (as it turned out) a serious road trip and she didn't begin by putting an overnight bag in the trunk or back seat. Either she had everything she needed wherever she was going or she planned to return the same day. Her purse was average size, and though it might have contained a toothbrush and change of underwear it couldn't have contained much else. Curious.

She took 270 to 44 and headed west, in the general direction of Rolla, Springfield, Branson, Tulsa, Oklahoma City, Dallas, El Paso, Phoenix, Los Angeles and Honolulu. I called Dale and told him she was on the move; he told me to stay with her. She passed Rolla but didn't go to Springfield or Branson. Instead, she headed northwest toward the Lake of the Ozarks. Since she wasn't dressed or packed for a vacation I considered some of the more interesting possibilities.

Osage Beach is the spiritual, financial, fast food, and tattoo center of the Lake and *beach* is a stretch term. A dammed river, the Lake has over 1,000 miles of coastline—more than the state of California—but it chiefly consists of endless inlets, straits and backwaters. From the air at night it looks like a long crack in a sheet of dark glass, with countless points and edges. The domiciles thereon range from luxury condos to hot-sheet motels, to cliffside estates and rural, dirt-road cottages. At Bagnell Dam, the structure that created the Lake, there are tour boats, jet ski rentals, discount tee shirt stores, bumper car rides, decayed miniature golf courses, a giant plastic statue of *Mad's* Alfred E. Newman, cotton candy stands, adult lingerie stores, and Texas two-step dance parlors.

With the meandering shoreline of the Lake, Osage Beach actually feels as if it's inland from the Dam, though the travel distance between the two is less than five miles and some portion of the Lake is visible during most of the drive. The town itself is little more than a single highway lined with chain restaurants, gas stations, lawn ornament stores, Wal-Mart, weapon and ammo suppliers, realty offices, indoor children's attractions with names like *Miner Mike's*, and—in the heart of it all—an outlet mall with five restaurants, a thriving cineplex and over 100 stores. All of the usual suspects are there, from Ralph Lauren and Liz Claiborne, to Tommy Hilfiger, Harry, David, the Brooks brothers and all of their partners, young and old. The complex is so vast that shoppers drive from one sector to another, passing their day in search of bargains, shade, soda machines, rest rooms, and paths back to the main highway. It was more than a three-hour drive from St. Louis but for reasons yet to be discovered Carol Dretchen had decided to spend her Tuesday there.

Unless the purpose of their trip is purely utilitarian, most women shop with companions. They'll pick up a bottle of milk or a box of cereal by themselves, but when they're looking for shoes or skirts or serious accessories they usually want to be accompanied by a consultant capable of providing a second opinion. With men it's different. If they want something they go buy it. When they walk into a store they do a quick scan and either deal or leave. Women walk and think and remember. They comparison-shop. They ask each other's opinions. They stop for a glass of iced tea or something involving chocolate. For them, shopping is a tour, not an expedition and stores are more like museums than parts-list catalogues. Carol Dretchen wasn't playing by the rules, so I figured she wasn't at the outlet mall to shop. Neither was I.

I called Dale again and told him where we were. He said he'd call the local police and ask them to stand by. Dretchen parked in front of the *Mikasa* store and went inside for a minute and a half. Before she returned to the parking lot I could see her face in the window. She was either looking for someone sympathetic or someone suspicious. Either way it worked for me. She walked back out to her car, reversed direction, and headed for the *Coach* store.

No woman can shop in *Mikasa* for a minute and a half. It's like *Crate and Barrel* or *Bed, Bath, and Beyond*. The minimum tour is ten minutes. She was in *Coach* for two minutes and fifteen seconds. She got in her car, reversed direction again, and drove to *Perfumania*. She came out two minutes later, holding a card, shaking it in the breeze and smelling the scent on it. Now she was using props. Lame. Amateurs always do that and they always give themselves away.

Standing in broad sunshine she looked at her watch. Women don't check their watches fifteen minutes into a day of shopping unless they're planning to meet someone. When they're shopping they're off the clock. That's the whole point of the exercise. When she got in her car, reversed herself again and drove toward the *Jockey* store, which was a stone's throw from *Coach*, she might as well have put a sign on her back. Attention, shoppers. This one's a ringer. She's here for other reasons and other purposes.

She walked into the *Jockey* store and checked her watch again. She was standing in the window on the right side of the store. I could see the signs behind her for men's underwear. Why would she be standing there? When she emerged, her head was down. She turned left and walked toward the end of the building. She paused at a soda machine, window-shopped the selections, and then went into the women's rest room. When she emerged five minutes later a man came out of the adjoining men's room. She passed him an envelope without speaking and checked out the soda machine a second time. He walked toward the parking lot and I speed-dialed Dale.

"Five feet ten or eleven, lean, with ropy arms and a bad dye job. Late fifties. A lot of miles. Tattoo on his left forearm. A K-Mart quality short-sleeved shirt and tie. He looks like the manager of a dirty book store, dressed up for a visit from the regional manager."

"Carl Hendrix," Dale said.

"As he lives and breathes," I answered.

"Stay on him," Dale said. "The Osage Beach police are ready to join you."

"Let's see where he goes," I said. "He might lead us to somebody interesting."

"Don't lose him."

"I won't."

"And don't get too close."

"Don't worry."

"I've given the locals your cell number. I'll call them and they'll call you."

"Sounds good. Tell them to call quickly. He's getting in his car now."

TWELVE

The car was a generic, black Explorer. The windows were dark. He drove past me and headed for the highway. As he turned right my phone rang.

"Harrison," I said.

"Agent Harrison, this is Sergeant Colby Dreyer," the voice said. "I'm with the Osage Beach police. I've got Officer Lou Bowlby with me and we're at your disposal."

"That's good to hear, Sergeant," I said. I'm following a black Explorer, heading north on Osage Beach Parkway. I'm driving a dark blue Camry, license Victor, Tango, Seven, X-ray, Niner, Charlie. The Explorer's license is Hotel, Four, Bravo, Foxtrot, Three, Echo. We've just passed *Miner Mike's*."

"We'll catch you in about four minutes, ma'am; let us know if the Explorer turns onto route 54."

"Will do," I said.

He did. Then he continued to drive north, slowly and sensibly. No need to attract attention and tempt a pullover when you've recently killed an FBI agent. I had my Royals ballcap on and my earpiece and speaker in place. The police and I had a nice chat as we drove.

"He may be heading for Jeff," Sergeant Dreyer said.

"Or toward 70," I answered.

"Columbia…Fulton…Moberly…KC…St. Louis…lots of choices."

"His sister handed him something in an envelope."

"Money, you think?"

"Could be," I said. "She stopped off at the bank a couple days ago. Maybe some cash, maybe a ticket, possibly both."

"We'll find out soon enough," the sergeant said.

Jefferson City comes and goes quickly. You come up and over a hill, see a flash of fast food restaurants, drive down and through a small pass, check out the capitol on your right and suddenly you're on the bridge, crossing the wide Missouri, except that it's not very wide at that point, though the breadth of the flood plain and the location of the distant limestone cliffs give you an idea of how wide it had been in the past. You're in Lewis and Clark country, if only for a minute or two.

"Columbia or Fulton?" Sergeant Dreyer asked. "We've got a bet."

"Columbia, I think."

"Why?"

"Because that's where the airport is and I don't think he wants to be taken down in the kingdom of Callaway."

"You got that right," Dreyer said.

Callaway County had proclaimed a plague on both the northern and southern houses during the civil war and actually declared itself a separate kingdom. The spirit of independence was still strong there and their patience with bad outside elements was notoriously short.

As I heard Dreyer and Bowlby giggle, Hendrix turned right off of 54 and entered the on ramp for 63, heading due north toward Columbia. Seventeen minutes later his brake lights illuminated and he turned right. Following at a distance of a hundred and fifty yards I passed the small sign announcing the turnoff for the Columbia Regional Airport and followed him in.

There are two facilities at the airport, one for private planes and charters, the other for regular commercial flights. Deregulation had nearly killed the latter, but it was now undergoing a rebirth with multiple flights a day to key hubs. The original parking area was a flat, uncovered square with easy ingress and egress, with newly-installed spillover lots to the north and west. Hendrix pulled in and I drove on, parking in the pick-up and drop-off lane at the front of the facility. Dreyer and Bowlby pulled into the lot, parking behind Hendrix so that we had him sandwiched.

The lane where I was parked was elevated above the lot and gave me a good line of sight. Hendrix was futzing in his car and didn't emerge for three and a half minutes. When he did he was wearing a sport coat and hat. He could almost pass for a businessman. He was also clever enough to include a large lapel pin which would draw attention away from his face and a brief case with prominent labels. Check-in clerks and security personnel are in an ongoing war with boredom and anything out of the ordinary can grab and hold their attention. I figured Hendrix was probably smart enough to distract them in other ways. Yawning is good. So is nose blowing—anything to break up the police blotter images in the backs of their minds. People who are good with explosives are also good at remaining calm. The twitchy ones don't make it out of Det. cord 101.

As Hendrix walked to the foot of the three stairs that led to the building proper, Dreyer and Bowlby were ten yards behind him and had fanned out to give me a clear line of fire. I opened the door of my Camry, got out in a leisurely fashion, and then spun to the left, pointing my weapon at the bridge of Hendrix's nose. "Freeze, FBI," I said.

Hendrix stood in place, still holding his brief case. "Put down the brief case and lay down on the ground with your hands extended," I said. He looked at me skeptically. Then the recognition set in; I was his original target.

"There are two police officers behind you and if I don't shoot you, they will," I said. "Do you have a preference?"

He looked over his left shoulder and then his right. Dreyer and Bowlby were raising their eyebrows in an 'it's in your court' stare. Each had their arms extended and their weapons cocked. He put down the brief case, sank to his knees, and extended himself across the ground.

I cuffed his hands and ankles, hogtied him with a connector chain, put a piece of duct tape over his mouth, and asked Dreyer and Bowlby to help me put him in the back seat of my car, stomach down. Then I closed the door and walked a few feet away from the car and thanked them.

"I don't think he's going anywhere but where you want to take him," Dreyer said.

"I want him to be anxious to talk when we get there," I said.

"If he acts up, hit the brake hard," Bowlby said. "See if he enjoys it more on the floor."

"Gotta be stupid," Dreyer said. "The only places you can fly from here now are Dallas, Denver and Chicago and there'd be a lotta people there waiting to greet him."

"Maybe not all that stupid," I said, opening his brief case. "The desk clerks and security guards there are all waiting for him, but flying in from here takes him directly to the gate area and he can change planes without clearing security." There was a printout of an e-ticket to Toronto inside his brief case. I showed it to them. "He'd probably go straight to the gate or to the smoking lounge (if they still have one) and hide in plain sight."

"Those are clear glass, usually," Bowlby said. "Everybody could see him there."

"They could if they looked," I said, "but next time you're near one, check it out. The people inside don't look at one another. They're all just there to get their fix, not to socialize. And watch the people outside. For them it's a major gross-out. Either they hate the habit or they remember when they had it and now they're crusaders. It's like a leper colony. They feel grateful or superior and just keep walking."

"How long you been doing this kind of work?" Dreyer asked.

"Officially—a couple of weeks," I answered.

"Well, it's been a pleasure working with you. Next time you're at the Lake, give us a call. We got *two* Starbucks now. We'll all go out for a four dollar cup of coffee."

"You're on," I said. "Now if you gentlemen will excuse me, I have a delivery to make."

THIRTEEN

I called Dale as soon as I pulled out of the airport and told him to expect me in about two and a half hours. Hendrix was quiet for most of the trip, though he sniffled a little and made a point of wiping his nose on the back seat. I thought about thanking him for the DNA sample, but just kept driving. When I turned off of 40 and onto Market I called Dale again.

"Special Agent Harrison?" he answered.

"Yes, sir. My estimated time of arrival is a little less than one minute."

When I pulled up in front of the field office Dale was standing there with five agents behind him. I parked, walked around the back of the car, and opened up the right rear door. "All your's," I said.

There was no applause in front of Hendrix, just some rough hands reaching for his extremities and a thin-lipped smile from the SAC. The agents carried Hendrix in without removing the leg cuffs or undoing the hogtie.

"He was headed to Toronto," I said. "And then…who knows where?"

"He's not headed there now," Dale said. "By the way, you should take a day or two off. You've earned it."

"Actually," I said. "I was just about to have dessert at this nice place in Kansas City when this all started…"

"Go for it," he said.

Richard and I had different entrées this time, but we shared a second bottle of wine. He told me I had earned a serious dessert. "Here's something…" he said.

It was called *Chocolate Intemperance*. The name sounded vaguely familiar. The waiter admitted that it was a standard cookbook recipe, "but," he added, "our chef has made some modifications. He starts with a charlotte mold and lines it with a large, rectangular chocolate brownie laced with Kahlua. The center is filled with chocolate mousse and the dish is chilled. It's then removed and drizzled with hot fudge, which forms a shell over the brownie, which has already formed a shell over the mousse. It's then cut in wedges, garnished with whipped cream flowers, and sprinkled with powdered sugar. Some people have a shot of Kahlua with it."

Richard looked shocked.

"You can always share one," the waiter said.

"I want my own," I said. "I also want the Kahlua and a double espresso back."

"Sir?" the waiter said.

"I'll just have a cup of coffee."

"Certainly," the waiter said, and disappeared.

"I skipped lunch," I said.

"I'm not questioning," he responded.

"I know."

"Besides, you've earned it."

"That's what the SAC said."

"He's right."

"I don't know. Somehow it seemed easy."

"There's a difference between something being easy and your making it look easy," Richard said.

"Thanks."

"I told you to get some quick wins and you've certainly done that."

"I don't like the price tag attached to the second."

"I know," he said. "You need some time to absorb what's happened. We've got huge data banks, futuristic technology, instant communication systems and pinpoint-accuracy weapons. It's sometimes over so fast that you haven't noticed the fact that you're standing in a pool of blood."

"Yes. It's a far cry from the days of my grandfather."

"When did you say he was in the Bureau?"

"During the war. He had a spinal cyst that disqualified him from military duty. In those days Edgar only hired attorneys and CPA's and he was a newly-minted lawyer.

"He was never involved with any of the household-name criminals. He could take shorthand; he had studied it in order to help himself take notes in night law school. The Bureau sent him to communist cell meetings; he'd sit in the back row and keep the minutes for Edgar. My mother still has some of the telegrams and directives he received. They're long and detailed. Everything you ever heard about Edgar's micromanaging is true."

"Your grandfather would be proud of you now. I know I certainly am."

As he said it he began to reach across the table to take my hand in his, just as the waiter arrived with the dessert and coffee. I met him half way and squeezed his hand in a friendly manner that offered the promise of more.

"I know," I said. "That's very important to me. I wouldn't drive two hundred and fifty miles to have dinner with just anyone."

FOURTEEN

"Here we are with this romantic dinner and I'm suddenly realizing how little I know about you," he said.

"Not much to know," I answered. "I went to a small college in Ohio, ran around Europe for awhile, worked in New York for a year and a half, then joined the Bureau."

"But you're not from Ohio, are you?"

"I grew up in California, but the family was originally from Wyoming."

"I didn't know there were people in Wyoming," Richard said, "just pronghorn antelope and bears."

"And deer. And moose. And elk. And bighorn sheep. And mountain goats. And some buffalo. And all kinds of things. You're from Pennsylvania, right?"

"Lehigh Valley," he answered.

"Right. I remember you saying that. Stone houses and what's it called…scrapple?"

"Never developed a taste for it."

"Ever miss Pennsylvania?"

"Sometimes. I haven't lived there for nearly twenty years, but it's nice to get back. I would think that you would miss Wyoming. It's unique."

"I never really lived there. My grandfather left shortly after the war. When I was growing up we'd sometimes return for vacations. Now my mother and father go to places like Hilton Head. I'm not sure why. Well, actually I am sure why. I like to go back to the mountains when I can."

"We need that; it's in our genetic code," he said. "We hunted and gathered for millions of years. It's our natural habitat. Everything else is artificial."

"I know," I said.

Before I left that evening Richard told me I should give some serious thought to acquiring a personal life. He put it more gently than that—something about taking some time for myself. Pretty thought. Sweet. He was probably right, but I was thinking about other things and other *needs*.

FIFTEEN

The next morning I met Dale Winthrop for breakfast. For us that was black coffee with a plastic-wrapped croissant and wilted strawberry on a cardboard plate. Dale also had a glass of water, which he used to wash down a trio of peppermint Tums. I didn't ask whether he was countering the effects of the coffee or fighting the symptoms of Bureau stomach.

He congratulated me again on collaring Hendrix.

"His sister's going down for this too," I said. "She passed money to him and flight details on his electronic ticket. He was probably using her apartment as his safe deposit box."

"Right."

"There was an address book in his brief case that might prove to be interesting."

"Yes," Dale said. "We're checking it out. He probably worked for a whole set of disreputables. If we can connect him to certain events it's possible that we can connect them as well. This could end up being very big."

"I hope so," I said.

"You're going to get a call from Washington," he added.

"From Washington?"

"Yes."

"Can you tell me what it's about?"

"Just an attagirl, but it's coming from the Director, who is personally very pleased. The fact that we lost an agent but captured his murderer that quickly helps a great deal. It reassures the public that we're standing between them and danger and that when the bad guys strike there's a quick and effective reaction from the Bureau."

"I'll tell him how much support I had."

"Thanks."

"There was also a call from the *Post-Dispatch*."

"I'd rather not talk to the press."

"The publicity would all be positive."

"I know, but I really don't want my picture in the paper."

"Understood."

"What's next?" I asked.

"Some desk work, but not for too long. It's a computer fraud case."

"Dealing with...?"

"False claims about loan refinancing. They ask for your VISA or MasterCard number so they can run a credit check. Then they go shopping."

Dale knew my preference was for field work, but sometimes there simply isn't any, and besides, electronic theft can do as much damage as armed breaking and entering. I decided to create my own excitement, stopping at Forest Park each morning and running. I was also listening and watching. And following.

The park drew twenty million people when the world's fair was held there in 1904 and it still draws more than half that many every year. With five hundred more acres than Central Park, there's plenty of room to run. And plenty of room to get into trouble. With Marlin Perkins' zoo, a 27-hole golf course, the Jewel Box conservatory, World's Fair Pavilion, Historical Society temple, Art Museum, tennis courts, ballfields, boat house, the Muny outdoor theatre, skating rink, and assorted playgrounds, the park is the city's historical, cultural, and recreational center, luring the wealthy of west county, the blue collars of Dogtown and the Hill, the inner city poor, an army of tourists, and the criminal element that preys on all of them. The endless row of mansions that borders the park on the north provides a comforting sense of security and, for the most part, the park is relatively safe. That doesn't mean that I leave my weapon in the car when I go there.

As I run I tune out the sound of my shoes on the pavement and grass for a moment and focus on my thoughts. How safe *are* we? A high-profile criminal case sets the internet and cable news networks afire. Coverage is constant and omnipresent. When I walk into a bookstore, however, I see shelf after shelf of novels and true crime books, all detailing interesting and exciting cases, any one of which would be sufficient to dominate the airwaves and cyberspace, but how many such cases are there really? The courts are clogged with endless lines of petty criminals and violence flares and blood flows every Saturday night, but how many actual plots are there to kill world leaders and take over the universe? How many world-class serial killers are there, really? One or two a year?

On the other hand, the list of unsolved crimes grows daily. How many monsters have been allowed to run free? How many crimes have continued to escape our notice? The intelligence flow with regard to terrorism is constant. The number of threats mounts daily. Movies and novels provide a rich set of images that are generally much larger than life, but we are still surrounded and we continue to blind ourselves to the realities. The most germ-laden receptacle in the home is the kitchen sink, not the toilet, and the cleanest mouth belongs to the family dog. There are creatures living at the roots of our eyebrows and dust mites beneath our beds that would frighten Godzilla if he saw them through a microscope. For people like me the everyday reality—with all its dangers—is exciting. We're the bacteriologists and entomologists, hunting for creepy things and then cleaning house.

As I turned these thoughts and images over in my mind I saw a jogger following two women. He slowed his own pace to stay behind them. Their clothing was sweaty and tight, outlining their bodies; he was enjoying the view and probably thinking thoughts that he wouldn't want his mother to know. Watching can be a prelude to acting. The women were talking in an animated fashion, apparently unaware of his presence. I increased my pace and as I approached him I slipped the bottom of my jacket up and over the handle of my Sig P320. I stepped it up again and pulled beside him, leaving enough room for him to see the weapon but keeping a sufficient distance to quell any temptation on his part to reach for it. He ran beside me for another hundred yards, began to breathe a little heavier, and then slowed to a walk, left the path, and rested on a park bench. The women never noticed a thing. They were safe in their garden, or at least they thought they were.

When I got to the office there was a note on my desk from Dale. It was short and to the point:

See me immediately.
DW

SIXTEEN

"I just got off the phone with the Director," he said.

"I talked to him two days ago. What's the problem?"

"He wants you to do the full story with the *Post-Dispatch*…let them run your picture."

"I thought we had agreed that I wouldn't have to do that. I told him it would compromise my ability to do my job."

"Things have changed," Dale said.

"What do you mean?"

"The Director believes that the positive press would outweigh any negative impact on your future effectiveness."

"And in English that means…?"

"It means that the Bureau can always use some good headlines and your story would provide them. I want you to see something…"

He reached into the lower drawer of his desk and dug out an old *National Geographic* from 1961. The edge was frayed and some of the pages were loose. There was a picture on the cover of an Englishman in a gray suit, holding his daughter on a kiddie leash. They were watching a member of the Grenadier Guards pacing his post at the Tower of London, resplendent in his bearskin cap and scarlet tunic.

"I understand," I said. "This used to be their battle dress. The redcoats stood out on the battlefield, but if you hit them it was harder to see that they were bleeding."

"It's not about that," he said. "Here…"

He turned to the back of the magazine, where there was a beautiful piece of propaganda, no doubt placed (or at least highly encouraged) by Edgar himself. Entitled "The FBI: Public Friend Number One," it opened with a picture of a line of agents holding revolvers and firing tracers at night on the Academy range. Each man was holding a flashlight in his left hand, which was extended to the left "to misdirect return fire." This was followed by a two-page image of the senior Bureau staff being briefed by Edgar while Clyde Tolson looked on. They were standing in front of a map of the country painted on clear glass. Edgar had his finger on New Mexico; everyone was watching him attentively. The picture was obviously highly posed, the glass used so that the camera lens (which was positioned behind the map) would not be obstructed. There was nothing on the map at all except for a bare outline of the states and national borders.

This was followed by a sequence of pictures dealing with the Academy, an image of a roadblock on a mountain pass in Arizona, the night aglow with headlights and red flares, a picture of the Los Angeles field office with agents studying a blackboard map and corresponding aerial photograph, a picture of the Justice Department headquarters of the Bureau prior to the construction of the Hoover building, a room filled with eager, efficient, and noticeably female secretaries, a discussion of forensic techniques, more night firing of tracers (this time with Tommy guns), and a montage of location shots—surveillance in San Juan, complete with Minox cameras, collaborations with Mounties on the Canadian border, an agent rowing through a Louisiana bayou, a mounted agent in Arizona checking cattle brands for evidence of interstate rustling, and three end pieces.

The first was a goofy story of a tracer (again) hitting the blade of an axe, splitting in two and shattering two adjoining, suspended clay pigeons—a stop motion sequence illustrating the pistol skills inculcated by the Bureau. The last was entitled "Rendezvous! A True-life Spy Drama from FBI Files" that illustrated an encounter between a Soviet intelligence officer and an undercover agent in New York: "The drama [went] unnoticed by shoppers and mothers airing babies."

In between was the capper—a picture of an agent behind the wheel of a sedan with a bright aqua dash and dials, surrounded by smiling "Navajo youngsters" in color-coordinated aqua garb and lipstick "war paint." Their smiles "brighten[ed] the rounds of an investigator from Phoenix," whose own highly-posed smile was a mixture of self-satisfaction and condescension. One of the putative "Navajo youngsters" was a deadringer for Mickey Dolenz of the Monkees.

"We can't get publicity like this anymore," Dale said, "so we take whatever we can get."

"Times have changed," I said, "maybe for the better in this case."

"They *have* changed, but some things are still important. The Director checked your personnel jacket."

"And?"

"There was some information that you had failed to include, so he checked some more. He found out about your ancestor."

"And he wants me to appear in an aqua outfit?"

"Gwen, your great-great-grandfather was an Oglala warrior. He fought with Crazy Horse."

"Not to put too fine a point on it, but a more accurate translation of *Tashunca-uitco* would be *Enchanted* Horse."

"OK. Better still. They're carving a mountain to commemorate him. I've seen it; it's staggering. The face alone is nine stories high. They're sculpting the mountain with Det. cord rather than dynamite, because it's more precise. Think of this as *news*, Gwen, positive news. Your connection is inspirational—the kind of thing that could turn up in grammar school newsletters and Rose Garden photo ops."

"I've seen the mountain too," I said, "and I understand how big the story could be, but I don't want that kind of publicity. I want to be judged on what I do, not by the fact that my great-great-grandfather was famous. I don't want any special considerations and I don't want any special burdens."

"Both come with the territory," he answered.

"They don't have to," I said.

"You'll have to talk to the Director about that; I can't make decisions for him," he said.

"I understand," I answered. "How did he find out?"

"He checked with the Salt Lake field office; they work with the Mormons. Genealogy is very big with the Church. They study immigration records, obituaries, you name it. The Bureau uses their databases all the time."

"I don't want any talk about this around the office, Dale. Please."

"OK, if you don't want to be famous . . ."

"I just want to be effective," I answered.

SEVENTEEN

I managed to dodge the Director for two weeks, working a kidnapping case and a set of related, internet fraud cases. The kidnapping case was closed and the victim recovered; the fraud case was being challenged by an array of gel-haired Chicago lawyers, but the chances for multiple indictments were good. I tried to take some personal leave to further evade the Director's call, but he was persistent and I was finally forced to talk to him and confront the issues.

His attitude was a mixture of anger and incomprehension. "I don't understand this at all," he said. "You're the descendant of someone famous; you're someone who could serve as a role model. Do you have any idea how few *Native American women* we have in the Bureau? Your grandfather was only the third Native American special agent in the Bureau's history."

"With all due respect, sir, I don't want to be the occasion for a headline and I don't want to be stereotyped, even if the stereotype has some positive elements."

"This is a tremendous opportunity," he said, "not just for you, but for the Bureau. The competition for appropriations is bloody beyond belief. Every bit of good news helps. Having a person like you is huge, especially with your track record. The possible benefit is incalculable."

"I'll do whatever I can for the Bureau," I said, "but I don't want to be a poster girl. Just let me do my job. So far things have worked out, haven't they?"

"Yes, of course they have. That's the whole point. Now it's time to smile while we pin on the medals and take the pictures. There's nothing wrong with positive recognition."

"Anonymity has its advantages also, sir," I said.

"Agent Harrison . . . Gwen . . . there are little girls all across the country who dream about accomplishing what you've accomplished. Why won't you let them see you and hear your story?"

"My story's just starting," I said. "I don't want it to end prematurely when I'm seen as some kind of freak or media creation."

"OK, but I can't guarantee that others won't seek out the details. The *Post-Dispatch* is already asking questions."

"Transfer me, sir."

"Transfer you?"

"Yes. To a bigger office in a bigger city, some place where I won't be noticed as easily."

"Are you sure that's what you want?"

"I'm sure."

He paused for a minute and told me he would call me back. Thirty minutes later my phone rang. He was short and to the point. "All right," he said. "Pack up. You're going to Federal Plaza."

"New York?"

"New York."

The itinerant agent's life was not all that foreign to me. My grandmother had long told me stories about my grandfather's Bureau postings. He lived in his car while she lived on trains, traveling across the west with my dad, an infant in her arms. They spent the bulk of their time in Salt Lake, Omaha, Kansas City and, principally, Denver. I saw the pictures many times. The towns were all simpler then and the mountains seemed closer. Evergreens dotted the snow-covered peaks in the stark, black and white, 3x5 photographs. There was a picture of a sign by the side of a mountain creek, warning drivers not to throw trash into what would be their actual drinking water. The cars were thick and clunky and heavy with chrome. The observation cars on the trains were like domed greenhouses with sunlight reflecting from the glass; the men all smoked and—like the women—wore suits and hats. Food was expensive; the waiters were all black and all called George.

My grandmother and grandfather are so young in the pictures that I can barely recognize them. They rode horses in the Rockies and my grandmother even wore western gear. My father floated in the great salt lake long before he could swim and my grandfather and grandmother still tell 'this is the place' Mormon stories.

Now it was my turn to move and since I had lived in New York before I didn't have to think of myself as an itinerant or pioneer. The one thing that saddened me was the distance from Richard. We decided not to have a farewell dinner, but talked instead for an hour and a half, promising to visit one another as soon as time permitted. He told me to be careful. I told him that they'd already tried to blow me up in St. Louis, so New York should be easy.

He laughed politely but didn't sound convinced. Those who haven't lived there are always threatened by the city—two million people in a single borough on a small island, with clogged streets, broken pavement, rusting bridges and aging tunnels. It's a place where it's easy to feel trapped, frozen in place by dark forces—the perfect setting for an apocalyptic film.

II

HUIS-CLOS

EIGHTEEN

Eight days later I was in New York, sleeping on an air mattress in a studio apartment with a faux fireplace and an indirect view of two trees. My furniture was scheduled to arrive, optimistically, in six days. Rents had doubled since my last time in the city, but the sun was shining through my as-yet drapeless window and the familiar horns and street hum below were somehow reassuring. Breakfast was a bagel and coffee from a nearby deli with a Jewish name—*Nate's*—and a Greek staff. The deli occupied two floors; the street level consisted of a bank of refrigerators, a buffet of fruits and salads, and a fifteen-foot sandwich counter. The second level included a carefully-hidden unisex rest room and a set of crowded, slightly-mismatched tables and chairs that would be in constant use within a few hours. A small set of regulars would be leaning their chairs against corner walls as they read through their morning papers. Their ongoing advice: stay away from the salads after 3:00 p.m.

I dressed up for the first meeting with my new boss but when I reported (early) the Assistant Director was out of the city, on a case. His secretary assured me that he was anxious to meet with me, but was, unfortunately, otherwise occupied. She showed me to a desk in a partitionless bullpen, indicated the file cabinet which was assigned to me, and assured me that my computer would be set up by the early afternoon. I asked her if the AD had assigned any cases yet, so that I could begin studying the files.

"You'll have to talk to him about that," she said. "I'm sure he has things for you, but he didn't leave anything with me. Your phone is working and your desk was cleaned this morning."

I could smell the faint scent of Windex that had been used on the gray laminate. The beige phone didn't match the gray desk, but there was a strong dial tone and multiple lines with accompanying buttons. The inside of the desk had been cleaned as well as the outer surfaces. There was not a single paper clip, rubber band, post-it note or loose staple that had escaped attention. I collected various items from the supply closet and began to set up shop. A few minutes later the AD's secretary returned with a handful of materials. "You might find these helpful," she said. They included an organizational table for the office and a month's worth of relevant stories from a local clipping service. The tech support staffer appeared two hours earlier than expected and set up my computer. "I checked with my counterpart in St. Louis," he said. "This is as close to your previous machine as we could get."

It was close enough. I thanked him and as he turned to walk away I googled the AD. His name was Sam Salva. I wondered if Salva had been Salvatore before the family arrived at Ellis Island. The Italians didn't change their names as frequently as the East Europeans, but this was my first *Salva*. The AD was a native New Yorker; there were pictures of him hip by jowl with Giuliani at a Holy Name parade and Italian/American day rally. It was hard to imagine something like that occurring in St. Louis, where the SAC's profile was noticeably lower than in ethnic New York.

A graduate of City College and Fordham law school, Sam Salva was the son of Tony Salva, a former deputy police commissioner, the husband of Julia and the father of Sam, Jr. and Mary Elizabeth Salva. The family Scottie was named Sophie. He was 52 now, six years older than the picture on the screen, but probably still as fit. As I surfed the web stories his press was consistently positive, the high arc of his career resulting from a single case which had propelled both him and the key members of his team into the organizational and media stratosphere.

After 9/11 when Mohamed Atta's 1996 will was found, a team of criminalists from the New York field office found evidence on the document that linked him to a cell that Salva located and summarily closed. The constituent members were then speedily tried and promptly relocated to a federal prison. The Bureau was noticeably quiet about the evidence adhering to the document (which was originally published by *Der Spiegel* and translated by ABC News for general consumption), but the best bet was that a fingerprint of one of the cell members had been found there. In rereading the story I began to remember some of the details of the will, particularly one salient item:

5. I don't want a pregnant woman or a person who is not clean to come and say good bye to me because I don't approve it.

The cell was not linked directly with 9/11, but computer records disclosed that they had plans of their own, all of which involved violence on a grand scale. Salva made all of his charges stick, a significant feat, given the fact that there was minimal evidence linking Atta to the cell. Moreover, he was able to clear the air when motions were filed concerning the chain of evidence and equally capable of fending off a battalion of 'pro bono' attorneys and a brigade of media types demanding the disclosure of information that the Bureau was anxious to keep confidential in hopes that it could lead to further arrests. Salva successfully negotiated the legal and media gauntlet at the same time that he was doing first-rate investigative work. The fact that the cell had plans to detonate devices near the Montefiore Medical Center in the Bronx and the Hillel Center on a branch campus of the City University resulted in a tidal wave of public support, particularly after Salva persuaded the Director to release some of this information to independent examiners, who confirmed its authenticity.

Giuliani had been generous in sharing his own spotlight with Salva and the fact that neither of them was then running for public office multiplied the plaudits that they received and the respect that they enjoyed. Since that event, Salva had sought less attention and more time for new investigative initiatives, the result being that rumors flew concerning the cases which he was likely to be working, since his track record suggested that his activities might be a more reliable barometer of terrorist activity than the public reports and warnings issued by the Department of Homeland Security. The media had even gone so far as to attempt to shadow him 24/7 with the intention of reporting in detail on each of his comings and goings. This necessitated some counter measures and also helped explain the relative reticence of his secretary when I asked her about his plans for me.

As I surfed the Atta stories I wondered if I should add a small pillow to my hat collection, so that I might slip it under a skirt or dress and disguise myself as an unclean, pregnant woman. I'd have to practice arching my back and changing my gait, but the idea was worth considering. A second skirt over the first could be quickly removed along with the pillow, particularly if it was a wraparound. A little Velcro here and there would not be beyond my limited capabilities as a seamstress.

From time to time agents drifted in and out of the office. I introduced myself and exchanged small talk. Several referred to common aspects of my background, so I figured that Salva had briefed them or sent around a memo. At 5:15 his secretary informed me that he would not make it back to the office that evening and that we could meet in the morning at 8:00. I thanked her, shut down my computer, and suddenly remembered that I had forgotten to eat lunch.

I stopped in at *Nate's Deli* on the way to my apartment. The guy who gave me my coffee and bagel that morning—Gus—was still behind the counter, but he either did not recognize me or chose not to give any hint of acknowledgment of my earlier visit.

"Yes?" he said firmly. It was more like an order than a question.

"Turkey, lettuce, tomato, and mayo on whole wheat," I said.

"Anything else?"

I put the Diet Pepsi I'd gotten from the refrigerator on the counter and pulled a bag of chips from the point-of-purchase rack. "Do you have any pound cake?"

He pointed to the candy rack below the counter. "Plain and marbled," he said.

I picked up a piece of plain pound cake, pleased that he had gone to the trouble to mention the fact that they had two kinds. Maybe he *had* recognized me. I gave him some bills and the exact change and he nodded approvingly but didn't speak again.

My brown bag cradled under my arm, I walked out onto 3rd Avenue, surveying the line of restaurants and shops that stretched before me. A man hurried through my line of sight. He was carrying a beige raincoat over his left arm. The weather was warm and sunny and the forecast had predicted as much. I wondered if the coat was concealing something, but resisted the impulse to follow him. I walked down East 50th toward my apartment. As I approached 2nd Avenue I saw a man smoking a cigarette across the street from my apartment. He was standing in the shadows on the north side of the street. If he was hoping to catch a cab he would have walked up to 3rd or at least stood by the curb. If he was waiting for a friend to pick him up he would have positioned himself so that the friend could see him clearly as he drove past the parked cars there.

I thought about Calvin Taylor and his sleazoid friends. Perhaps they had learned of my transfer and were waiting to welcome me in some decidedly unpleasant way. If I ignored him and let myself into my building he could simply shoot me in the back as I turned away from him. I decided instead to slip out a foldup hat from my bag, pull it down far enough to shadow my face, and keep on walking. I walked north on 2nd Avenue, made myself scarce for fifteen minutes, removed my hat, tousled my hair, and returned from a different direction. By the time I got to my apartment he was gone.

NINETEEN

The inflatable mattress was suddenly less comfortable than it had been, probably because I kept rolling off of it so that I could crawl toward the window and check the street below. Instead of an old friend surrounding me with warmth and comfort it had become a launching platform for possible counterattacks.

When I looked out at 2:00 a.m. the man had still not returned. I checked the parked cars along the block for cigarette glow, but each of them within view was dark. I checked again at 3:00 and at 3:30. Still all clear. I slipped my sidearm into its holster, put it next to the right edge of the mattress, fluffed my towel/pillow, and pulled up the cotton throw I was using for a blanket.

The next morning I was at the field office at 7:15, nursing a tall black coffee and nibbling at a rye bagel, re-checking computer files and preparing for my meeting with the AD. I was wearing a gray suit with a black turtleneck, walking shoes that could pass for business loafers, and simple black earrings.

"I've got some bagels in my office if you'd like a second," a voice said. I turned and saw the AD.

"Assistant Director Salva, Gwen Harrison," I said.

"Good morning, Gwen. Since we're both already here why don't you come into my office now."

The room was Bureau minimalist: a simple desk, credenza, file cabinet, and bookshelf. A small gray laptop sat at the right side of the AD's desk. The wi-fi router was sitting on the bottom shelf of the credenza, a plain black Linksys. There was a 5x7 picture of his wife and children on the left side of his desk and a small grouping of photographs on the opposite wall—the AD with Giuliani, the AD with Bloomberg, the AD with the Governor, and the AD with the President.

"We're delighted to have you on board," he said.

"It's good to be here, sir. I've lived in New York before and I was pleased to know that I was being assigned here."

"You did a good job in St. Louis," he said.

"Thank you, sir," I answered.

"You might have noticed that there was someone outside your apartment last evening."

That took me aback. "Around 5'11", maybe 175, mid 40ish, gray at the temples, a smoker?" I said.

"Special Agent Bill Bonner," the AD replied. "Maybe he should have put a sign around his neck."

"I didn't figure him for an agent," I said.

"But you knew he was surveilling something or someone."

I paused for a second, not wanting to get the man in trouble with the AD. "Ever since they blew up the car in St. Louis I've been keeping an eye out. Making his presence known would make sense—if someone *was* thinking about making a run at me, it would be a good idea for us to have someone on the street to let him or them know that our side is watching too."

"Good answer," he said, smiling.

"I appreciate your looking out for me," I said.

"Are you ready to go to work?"

"I *am*," I said.

"How's your memory?"

"Pretty good," I said.

"I don't like to write things down," he said. "Security is a very high priority here."

"Understood."

"I want you to work directly with me on a case. Counterterrorism. Sound interesting?"

"Absolutely."

He opened his desk drawer and took out a manila folder. He didn't open it at first, but instead continued talking. "Increasingly Al Quaeda is using scouts to scope out targets. Reduces our ability to profile and extends the size of the net we have to cast to keep tabs on them. We've been watching a man named David Willets. We believe that he is linked with a local cell. He's not in the city; he lives upstate in Cornwall, New York."

"Just up the Hudson," I said, "above West Point."

"Yes. He lives in a townhouse complex, right on 9W."

"West Point would be a nice target."

"Yes," the AD said, "if they could get in. The academy has been locked down for some time now. You have to have a verifiable appointment to enter the grounds and even then they check you out fairly thoroughly. Mirrors under the car…the whole bit."

"But if they've been doing this for a long time it's become routine. Whenever there's a routine there's a way that it can be beaten."

"Indeed. And life goes on. There's a steady stream of delivery trucks and an ongoing set of construction projects that require supplies that could otherwise be seen as suspicious. Security is tight enough to scare away any amateurs, but a hardened pro could get through."

"Is Willets a pro?"

"We're not sure. We know he's been in contact with one of their key people, but we don't know what role they intend for him to play. He could simply be an observer or go-between. There's no hard evidence that he could actually handle demolitions or fixed-wing or rotary-wing piloting. There may even be no connection at all. These guys like to turn rabbits loose in multiple directions, trying to distract us. The key is the central network, so they give us a lot of misdirection on who's in and who's out, who they might or might not know and who they might or might not know who actually matters. Either way, we always have to check out possible leads."

"You want me to follow him?"

"Yes, but at a distance. We don't want our surveillance compromised and we don't want *you* compromised."

"Understood."

"There's another wrinkle. He comes into the city on a regular basis."

"Working?"

"He appears to be."

"How does he get in? The train from Poughkeepsie is on the other side of the river."

"He drives."

"That's a hard 120 miles a day. Expensive too."

"With E-ZPass around 12-14 dollars to cross the George Washington Bridge and at least forty-to-fifty to park. He could drive part way and pick up a bus—much easier and much cheaper—but he always drives the full distance."

"The Palisades is a nice drive, but that's only half the trip. The closer you get to the city the more complicated your life gets."

"Especially at rush hour."

"You said he lives in a townhouse?"

"Yes, but it's not as upscale as it might sound. The complex was built in the 60's and has gone through several iterations since then. Usually these things end up as public housing, but this one is still viable, even if it's a little ragged around the edges. It's called *Cornwall Park Townhouses.*"

"Fancy name."

"Especially for something that just sits by the side of the highway. It's not even in the village proper, which is between 9W and the river, a mile, mile and a half away."

"Low profile. Easy ingress and egress," I said. "Where does he work in the city?"

"We're not sure."

TWENTY

"No fixed office?"

"No. Each time he comes in he makes rounds. Some of the people he visits have possible links to Al Quaeda, but the vast majority don't. He makes about five or six stops a day, sometimes as few as two or three."

"So these are real meetings, not just walkabouts."

"Yes, but so far we haven't been able to find a pattern. That's where you come in."

"I'll begin today. Do you have a file that I can start with?"

He picked up the folder from his desk and handed it to me. Then he pointed to the left of his desk. "That door in the corner leads to a former closet. There's a desk in there. I prefer that you study the file there and then return it. I also want you to work directly with me on this. I'll be your backup if you need any help. Clear any routine requests with my secretary, Janice."

"Yes, sir," I said, considering the implications of what he had just said. The case was big and I could be at or near the center of it. I was also alone. The signs all said that he trusted me, even though we had just met, which meant that he had done his homework and knew what I was best equipped to do. Either that...or I was being sidelined until he had the opportunity to fully evaluate my work. Or perhaps I was just being sent off on the road to nowhere, where I wouldn't get in anybody's way.

The walk-in closet was a fully-equipped mini-office. The interior space had been extended. There was a toilet inside and a miniature sink as well as an end table with a coffee maker. A ceiling vent had been installed to provide air conditioning and a floorboard electric heater encircled the work space. There was also a Churchill reading lamp, single-line phone and a small yellow pad with freshly-sharpened pencils.

I put my jacket on one of the two white-plastic hangers on the back of the toilet door, sat down at the desk, and opened the file:

Willets, David
dob: 3/10/68, Philadelphia
s of George Philip W and Estelle Sterritt W
B. A., Sociology, Temple U, 1990
J. D., Fordham U, 1993
current addr:
23 Brewster Road, Cornwall, NY 12518
business addr:
unknown
marital status:
single

Subject is believed to be connected with Abbas Al-Madi cell; has been seen in company of two cell members on three separate occasions. (For details see AD.) Reported average income for previous three-year period: $360,275. Position: "attorney/ consultant". No outstanding warrants, no previous indictments or convictions. Two motor vehicle violations (outdated state inspection decal, 1999; exceeding speed limit, 2012). All self-employment documentation and IRS payments in order. Vehicle registration: 2019 Toyota Avalon, NY license TW9 V4H.

Foreign travel: United Kingdom (each year since 1998), Italy (2009), Belgium (1999, 2005), Greece (2017), Ecuador (2018). None in Middle East.

Memberships: ABA, University Club (NY)

Mr. Squeaky Clean, living beneath his means, steering clear of the law, paying his taxes, limiting his personal and professional contacts, hiding in plain sight 60 miles from Manhattan. I called the rental agent at *Cornwall Park Townhouses*. His rent there for 1300 square feet would buy him a single room in Manhattan and he could touch all four walls while standing still in the center and extending his arms only slightly.

There was also a grainy picture, doubtless taken with a telephoto lens. Again, Mr. Unremarkable. Nothing about him attracted attention. Judging by his relation to an adjoining exterior doorway, I figured him for somewhere between 5'10" and 6'. Probably 160-170. White shirt, lightly striped tie, dark suit. His hair was thick and high (a feature he could change very easily) and his face was clean-shaven. The hair was dark with the slightest flecks of gray; his eye color was too faint to read, probably blue or gray. I wondered why those details weren't included in the brief description in his file. Hadn't anyone gotten close enough to check?

I returned to the AD's office, opening the door slowly in case I was interrupting a phone call or meeting. He was sitting quietly at his desk, working at his laptop. I asked him for the names of the cell members and other suspicious persons who had been seen in Willets' company and he wrote them down on a single slip of paper. "Memorize, please," he said.

I studied them carefully and then returned the slip to him. The fact that there was a sprinkling of 'Mohameds' made things both easier and more difficult. I held the names in short-term memory, left the office, and promptly wrote them down on a second piece of paper. Then I checked with Janice about a travel budget and she told me I shouldn't worry. The AD had told her that my project was top priority and that I should be given whatever I needed, within Bureau regs. Then I went to my computer.

I figured that if I rented a townhouse in *Cornwall Park Townhouses* I could be made too easily, so I checked on local motels. There was an AAA 2-star between Cornwall and Newburgh called the *Colonial Inn*.

Ninety-seven dollars a night; simple but hopefully clean. There were car rental agencies in both Newburgh and New Windsor, the latter the location of Stewart International Airport, a converted air force base. I would need to change cars with some regularity in order to maintain anonymity. The migration route to New York, like the final destination, were both predictable and straightforward, so once in the traffic flow no one would be surprised to see a car accompanying them for the duration.

Once into the city things would be straightforward as well. Basically you take the GW Bridge, get on the west side highway, drive a few miles and take West 56th through Hell's Kitchen to midtown. The flash point would be his common destination—the Sheraton parking ramp. If I didn't stay with him there I'd never find him in the city. On the other hand, I couldn't pull in behind him every time we came into town. I'd have to count on the fact that he would park there, then pass him en route, drop the car and be waiting to follow him once he dropped his. Parking on the street wasn't an option. Even assuming I'd be lucky enough to find a space I wouldn't have the opportunity to feed the meter and I'd end up picking up my car at a towaway lot on the river with $100+ tickets, fees, and miscellaneous indignities.

The good news was that I'd brought my hats and hair pieces with me when I drove to New York and I wouldn't have to either resupply them or wait for the movers to come. Since my stuff only took up a small portion of their van and everything was either sealed or boxed I figured I could put off the delivery for a few hours if they arrived earlier than planned. At this point they were shooting for a weekend delivery time, so I could scoot back into the city in lighter traffic if I needed to. Thank God for cell phones.

I put together my notes and freshly-printed maps and went home to collect my things. I'd always wanted to have a closer look at Richard's alma mater, but I didn't expect to be put in the position of protecting it from a possible terrorist attack.

TWENTY-ONE

On the way to my apartment I stopped at *Nate's*. I wanted to buy one of the *Nate's Deli* tee shirts on display in the glass case below the checkout register but I didn't want Gus thinking of me as a first-time-in-New York tourist. I was happy to see that he wasn't behind the counter, since I didn't want anything to spoil our developing relationship. At this point we were at the stage in which he would give me good service and in return I would make no overt efforts to imply that I knew him. The next stage would be the exchange of half smiles and other forms of recognition that would go unnoticed by other customers. Eventually we would reach the point at which we would greet each other, perhaps even by name. It was a long process and I didn't want any unnecessary setbacks.

The shirts came in only two sizes, Medium and Large. They were white with orange lettering and included a line drawing of Nate. The figure looked like Abe Saperstein, the original guy behind the Harlem Globetrotters, but Nate was wearing a cook's apron and reaching toward you with a plate containing a corned beef sandwich and a huge kosher dill. Below the picture was the caption, "The best corned beef in New York." I had plans for the shirt but I couldn't share them with the counter staff.

By 2:30 I had loaded my car and pulled away from the curb. An hour and twenty minutes later I was above West Point, driving toward Storm King Mountain. The sky was dotted with finely-etched clouds against a curtain of blue sky and green mountain peaks whose towering verticals abutted the highway. Brief glimpses of the academy appeared below me to the east. I thought of the Revolutionary War stories that Richard was fond of telling—of the huge chain stretched across the Hudson to protect the river from British naval vessels (pieces still existed and were on display in the Academy Museum) and of the strategic importance of the site.

Kosciuszko himself had designed the defenses. This part of the Hudson Valley was a place of deep history, a history whose changes were once punctuated by a haunting graveyard of mothballed WWII ships down river. Richard had shown me old postcard pictures.

I thought of Washington Irving's home on the river and of the lore and legends of the Valley, the painters who came here to capture the American sublime, of distant views of the Catskills from Storm King Mountain (80 miles on clear days) and the eagles there, described by Melville. I remembered the stories told by Richard's P's (academese for professors) of Lieutenant Arthur Ashe playing tennis on the academy courts and of Pete Dawkins' days there as a P in the Social Science Department, when the cadets spoke of him walking across the waters of Lusk Reservoir every morning on his way to work. What would happen now if the waters of the reservoir were suddenly laced with poison?

Richard talked about Thayer Hall and the adjoining statue of Georgie Patton next to the library. Georgie with his binoculars, "looking for the library," everyone quipped. What if all three were destroyed in a single blast? The supt's quarters—a huge frame affair with a vast wraparound porch—faced the parade ground, across which the Corps marched, resplendent beneath the mountains and above the river. What sight could be more moving or more beautiful to him? What if the Corps was before him in full dress uniform, brass reflecting in the sun and drumbeats filling the air and all were suddenly struck by rockets or strafed by miniguns from a helicopter gunship?

The academy was filled with soldiers, but it had not been poised for attack or counterattack since the Revolutionary War, when Benedict Arnold was ready to sell the property to the British for £20,000. "Whom can we trust now?" George Washington asked. Military maneuvers there are constrained by the youth and inexperience of the cadets and by the sheer narrowness of the post. The latter is always a problem; we have weapons that shoot beyond the boundaries of even the largest military posts; the nagging question is, how do we train the troops to use them without blowing up the surrounding communities? At West Point the mortars have to be aimed at high angles, lest their rounds land on the citizens of Garrison or Highland Falls. Stories are still told about a cadet error in the 1960's that nearly resulted in the destruction of the Bear Mountain Bridge. Too few cranks on an 81mm mortar. Fortunately the wayward round just missed the bridge and plopped into the river below.

West Point's symbolic value was enormous and a successful strike against it would be devastating in both human and political terms. For all of its history and psychological weight it was virtually powerless to prevent a significant incident. It had no greater air defenses than Vassar, just up the road, and while it had a full array of guards at the gate it remained vulnerable to an attack planned at length by experienced professionals prepared to die in the process.

Was that why David Willets had moved to Brewster Road? Did he represent the eyes of an operation that would be executed by shadowy figures invisible among the millions in the streets and subways and alleys of Manhattan? It was all so beautiful here. So attractive…as a place… and as a target—irresistible really, especially in light of the fact that so many of our people were concentrated in Manhattan and focused upon *its* protection. The academy was a plum ripe for picking.

TWENTY-TWO

Cornwall was little more than a village, a collocation of aging wooden houses at the base of the mountain, with a single bisecting highway. The 'downtown' was a group of midscale shops. The once notable *Cornwall Deli* had given up fresh donuts and bagels for stacks of *Entenmann's* boxes and other generic offerings that pulled it down to the level of a *7/Eleven*. A step up from Newburgh, whose slide began decades earlier, the village was now showing tattered edges and the results of a dying economy that was unlikely to ever be fully resuscitated. Ducks still paddled across the Hudson Street pond but the tourist traffic had dwindled to a trickle and the handful of surviving bed-and-breakfasts seldom hung their *no vacancy* signs.

The lot at the *Colonial Inn* was sparsely populated but the building looked as if it had received a recent coat of white paint. Whitewash stain was still visible along the concrete slab beneath the main structure. While some rooms probably still rented by the hour it provided an alternative to the offerings in Newburgh. My room was simple and clean. The dated earth-tone carpeting had been vacuumed within recent memory and the sink and tub had been freshly scoured. The water stain below the cold water faucet had not been completely erased, but the defective washer had been replaced and the faucet no longer dripped. The small plastic vial next to the shrink-wrapped plastic glasses simply indicated *shampoo*, but the two packages of *Ivory* carried their "soap that floats" motto. They rested atop a wash cloth that was so threadbare I could read through it, but that also suggested that it had been washed in bleach-laden, scalding water—for me a more important consideration.

The orange bedspread covered two thin pillows and a thermal blanket with an insulating sheet. Ever since the documentary specials on hotel cleanliness I imagined what such rooms would look like under a CSI's light, but I comforted myself with the thought that my ancestors had counted themselves lucky when they found a quiet spot beneath the sky on the open plains, even though they were surrounded by the local fauna and the waste left in their wake.

The hum of traffic along 9W eventually dissipated and I fell asleep some time after 11:30. I was up at 5:00, preparing to track Willets. I had some rolls that I had purchased at the *Cornwall Deli* and got a large cup of black coffee from the lobby carafe.

The desk clerk greeted me, saying, "Gettin' your plasma, huh?"

"Right," I answered. "Nature's most nearly perfect food, except for Fritos."

I was reassured by the fact that he was wearing a freshly-pressed white shirt, dark tie and jacket, with a small, gold nametag. He pointed to a stack of complimentary local newspapers, inviting me to take one. I picked up a copy and smiled.

"Have a nice day," he said.

"Thanks. You too," I said, and went back to my room to collect my hats and wigs. I was on the road in fifteen minutes. Even though I was taking a risk, I drove through *Cornwall Park Townhouses*, looking for Willets' Avalon. It was only 5:45 in the morning and still in what Richard would have called morning nautical twilight. Fortunately, it didn't take long to find the vehicle. His townhouse was in the first building on the right as I entered the development—the third unit from the left end. The rental office was at the right end of the same building. Except for a single light in an upstairs room in the office unit the building was still dark. Willets' car was maroon; he had ordered the upscale model with the chic tires. The color and the ornamentation would make it slightly easier to follow him. If I had been working with an amateur I would have planned to attach a tracking device to the car, but a *bona fide* terrorist or terrorist associate would have his vehicle swept on a regular basis and I didn't want Willets to have any inkling that he was under observation.

His building had a small grassy area in the back; the lot line was defined by a row of dense honeysuckle that shielded the sensibilities of the occupants from the trash lining an adjoining asphalt road that had existed long before the townhouses were built. I parked on the side of the road, behind the foliage, and positioned myself so that I could see the back of Willets' car when he backed out of his parking space and prepared to leave for whatever work awaited him in the city.

I sat there for nearly three hours. When he left he was in an obvious hurry. I would have preferred to fall into a line of traffic, but it was just his car and mine for the first three miles and I was forced to keep my distance. When we finally came into midtown I rolled the dice a second time, taking an alternate route to the Sheraton garage. When Willets pulled in behind me I slipped on a small black beret, turned the car over to the attendant, took my ticket and walked past him without making any eye contact. He was wearing a gray suit, white shirt, and dark red tie. His brief case was black leather—an outfit as generic as any FBI agent's. His hair was cut shorter than it had been in the pictures I had seen earlier. Following him was not going to be easy.

TWENTY-THREE

In the distance I could see Willets wending his way through the pedestrian traffic. He crossed the Avenue of the Americas at West 51st and proceeded to a small office building on the south side of the street. I passed the entrance and waited outside until he entered the elevator, then rolled the dice again and quickly entered the lobby, checking the light above the door. The elevator had stopped on the third floor. The building was small and the last thing I wanted to do was find myself at the entrance to a tiny office suite with Willets standing there staring at me. I looked at the building index on the wall facing the elevator doors and saw that there were three units on the third floor: *Thomas Henderson, Attorney-at-Law*, *National Capital Inc.*, and *Citizens for a New Consensus*. Then I hurried out to the street.

I found a vendor's cart at the corner of West 50th, bought a large coffee and bagel in a brown paper sack and walked back to the building Willets had entered. I took the elevator to the second floor. The restroom required a key, but there was a recessed service closet at the end of the hallway that afforded me sufficient privacy. I unbuttoned my blouse, removed it, and tied it around my waist, exposing the *Nate's Deli* tee shirt below. I slipped on some sunglasses and a baseball cap from my purse and went back to the elevator.

When the door opened on the third floor I was pleased to see that the office suite doors were made of clear glass. *Citizens for a New Consensus* consisted of cheap laminate desks, each with a large, multibuttoned phone, a stack of bent cardboard placards leaning against the far wall, a single unwashed window and three intense women. They were engaged in a heated discussion. Two were twisting the ends of their hair in knots and curls while the third gestured and pointed at some invisible foe.

National Capital, Inc. was a single room with a single, harried telemarketer pushing buttons and bouncing calls. For a second she looked as if she had three hands. The law offices of *Thomas Henderson, Esq.* (a rare affectation in New York) did not list any other partners or associates on the front door. When I entered there was no receptionist at the front desk, so I made a quick tour of the office, delivery bag in hand. Lawyer Henderson was extremely obliging in choosing an office with a front window, through which I could see David Willets in the client chair. As I attempted to leave I was intercepted by a young woman—presumably the receptionist or receptionist/secretary—who had just come back from the restroom and was still carrying a small key attached to a much larger, plastic one.

"May I help you?" she asked.

"I was looking for Mr. Hendrickson," I said, "but I think I'm in the wrong office."

"This is Mr. *Henderson's* office," she said. "There isn't a Hendrickson in this building."

"Shit," I said. "Sorry, excuse me a sec." I took out my cell phone, punched in the number for the time and temperature, and walked away from the front desk to an adjoining wall. "Carlo," I said, "it's Bet. What was the address on the Hendrickson delivery?" I paused, waiting for a response. "Oh…OK. Next time this happens would you do me a big favor and call me?"

I returned to the front desk. "Sorry," I said. "The guy gave us the wrong address. He called back and somebody else covered the delivery. Must have promised to make it worth our while. Want a bagel and coffee? Best bagels in Manhattan. It's a poppy," I said, looking into the bag.

"Sure," she said. "Thanks."

"It's high test coffee, not decaf. I put in three half and halfs on the side. No sugar. Just that no-cal stuff that's made out of sugar."

"That's fine," she said. "Thanks. Now I don't have to go out for lunch."

"No problem," I said. "Sorry I bothered you."

"Hey, you can deliver free coffee and bagels any time," she answered.

I got on the elevator, slipped my blouse back on and just finished buttoning it as the door opened. I slipped the glasses and ball cap back into my purse, found a quiet doorway on the north side of the street, and waited for David Willets to emerge. Forty minutes later he and Henderson came through the door and walked west. I followed them to *Arnold's*, a bar/restaurant a few minutes from Henderson's office.

The bar was on the first level, the restaurant on the second. I waited for Willets and Henderson to settle in upstairs, then entered the bar, got a ginger ale and some nuts, used their rest room, and went back out on the street. The restaurant is on a square, set back from West 51st, so I stayed in the shadows, making myself inconspicuous. The two men emerged an hour and twenty minutes later, shook hands, and separated.

I followed Willets to Rockefeller Center, where I expected him to meet someone for an appointment, but instead he crossed the street, walked into Saks, bought a silk scarf and a pair of gloves, used the men's room, left, and went into St. Patrick's, where he lit a candle in front of a statue of Mary, knelt, and appeared to pray. Perhaps he was a good Fordham boy after all. Or was he a shameless poseur? Perhaps he was someone who knew he was being followed.

TWENTY-FOUR

Willets prayed for about forty seconds. I took that as an indication that he was either legitimately pious or adept at imitating someone who was legitimately pious, since Catholics are trained from their youth to say prescribed prayers and they learn to do so with dispatch. For a few minutes I expected him to meet someone in the cathedral, having told his contact earlier that he would be positioned on a particular kneeler at a particular time.

He didn't. Instead he checked his watch, left the church, and crossed the street, walking west on 51st. Within the Rockefeller Center complex, on the south side of West 51st, is an Italian espresso bar in the basement of a shop called *Forever Tuscany*. At the street level there is a shop that sells miscellaneous goods—terracotta decorative pieces, olive oils, balsamic vinegars, throw pillows with European images, pictures set in antique-gold frames—and a conventional bar. Next to the bar is a spiral staircase that leads to the espresso bar below, where there are biscotti, a salad buffet, and trays of tiramisu and tubs of gelato set in shaved ice.

Willets entered the store and immediately went downstairs. From the bar above I could see him greet another man and join him at a distant table next to a support pillar which helped afford them privacy. I concluded that Willets was just killing time in Saks and St. Pat's, waiting for his second appointment.

The man with whom he was meeting bore a striking resemblance to Thomas Henderson. Both were in their late forties or early fifties; both were gray at the temples; both wore polished wingtips and dark gray chalk-striped suits. One wore a red tie, the other a black, but aside from their approach to accessories they looked like carbon copies of one another. Perhaps the new man was a lawyer as well and each was simply in the proper New York uniform. West coast lawyers attempt to distinguish themselves from the long gray line by wearing shirts that are clearly custom-made. Stripes on the collar are a particular affectation, but flamboyance is not a priority in New York, where a particular premium is placed on seriousness and gravitas.

When Willets finished his second double espresso and headed for the men's room I walked downstairs, circled around the blind side of the support pillar, and took his coffee mate's picture with my smart phone. Returning to the upstairs bar I sent the image to the AD with a simple request: "Please identify."

Before I could order a second ginger ale I received his response: "Unrecognized. Will check further and notify you."

When Willets returned from the men's room he sat down, conversed with Mr. Chalk Stripes for a minute or two, rose, shook his hand, and departed. I picked up the by-the-glass wine list and read it as he walked behind me. I didn't want him to have a look at my full face in the bar mirror.

He checked his watch as he walked past *Radio City* and continued on to the Sheraton lot. He appeared to be finished for the day—120 miles for two meetings, one only twenty minutes in duration. I gave him five minutes' lead time, figuring it would be gobbled up by crosstown traffic, then passed him on the Palisades. After putting some distance between us I slipped on my baseball cap and sunglasses and took a large paper cup from the holder, nursing the straw as he passed me a few miles down the road.

I was done for the day, but had two contacts for him, one still anonymous. I checked my email on my phone and downloaded a single, brief message: "File online." The AD had posted the information on a secure site. My curiosity aroused, I wanted to hit the accelerator, but

I hung back lest I come up too fast on Willett's bumper and draw his attention.

As soon as I got back to the motel I took out my laptop and went online, leaping through passworded barriers on a site that appeared to be innocuous enough: an online retail hardware store specializing in valves. Strictly for plumbers. Like G. Gordon Liddy.

TWENTY-FIVE

The file was short and contained a recent picture:

Carlton, Robert
dob: 8/24/60
s of Phillip L. C and Annette Radil C
B. S., Economics, Massachusetts Institute of Technology, 1982
MBA, Emory, 1988
current addr:
48 Willow Trace, Armonk, NY 10504
business addr:
Crescent Bank, Rockefeller Center, NY
marital status:
m. Janet Dillon, 1984, 2 children—Scott Alan (b. 1994), Elizabeth Ann (b. 1996)

Subject is Executive Vice President of the New York branch of a London bank (assets: $9B+) serving members of the Saudi community in the Manhattan metropolitan area. His principal responsibility is to invest its assets. Reported average income for previous three-year period: $528,000. Position: "bank executive." No outstanding warrants, no previous indictments or convictions. No motor vehicle moving violations. All IRS payments in order. Vehicle registration: 2019 Lexus RX 350, NY license DR7 L4B.

Foreign travel: Mediterranean (Royal Caribbean cruise 2009, 2012, 2017), Scandinavia (Celebrity cruise 2018), Saudi Arabia (each year since 1998), United Kingdom (each year since 1997). Kauai (2014). St. Kitts (2010). Baja California (2009). Cozumel (2007).

Memberships: MIT AA (Board of Governors, 2001-4), Emory AA, Annabel's Club (London), Westchester Trails CC.

Very interesting, particularly if the Crescent Bank is a money laundry. Even at a half million dollar salary a year, Armonk is an expensive habit, with tear-downs going for as much as three times that amount. Private schools and college for two kids; a $50,000 SUV; monthly country club payments of at least $500; and $10,000 a year for cruises. The *Annabel's* membership particularly surprised me, since it's a Berkeley Square dining club for film stars and media types, complete with liveried greeters and mini tiki torches—definitely not for the buttoned-down. If he *was* a money launderer he'd avoid the spotlight entirely and dine quietly in Pall Mall with the woolly establishment rather than the Gucci-silked glitterati. At least he would if he wished to keep a low profile and avoid unnecessary risk. This could be a possible point of vulnerability which could be exploited.

I called the AD to raise the point, but his cell line was busy. I suddenly realized that I hadn't eaten anything substantial since last night, remembered that there was nothing in the room but two or three ounces of bottled water, and decided to drive into the village. One of the B&B's operated a tea room that was also open for dinner. It sat on one of the principal streets and I asked to be seated in a quiet corner, away from the candle-lit windows that produced a glow designed to help advertise its ambiance.

The menu was simple and unpretentious and so was the waitress, a middle-aged woman named Jane. I ordered cream of broccoli soup, grilled sole, and a glass of Sancerre. When the waitress brought the wine

I was working on some notes—nothing specific, just random jottings on possible scenarios. She asked me if this was my first time at the *Highland Inn*.

"Yes," I said.

"I hope you enjoy it," she answered.

"I'm sure I will," I said. "It's in a lovely setting."

She nodded politely and returned to the kitchen. The wine was good and I ordered a second glass when she returned with my soup. An elderly couple entered the restaurant and requested a table near the window. He made a point of searching out something special on the wine list while she smiled at him and sweetly touched his free hand with her fingertips.

I envied them, not just for their love and companionship but for their apparent innocence. Surrounded by potential terrorists intent on creating mayhem and unleashing rivers of blood, they were enjoying a quiet, anniversary dinner for which they were slightly overdressed, given the restaurant's circumstances. I considered my own position—twelve hundred miles away from a person I cared for, standing between the innocent and the violent, a small bulwark against as-yet unidentified forces with as-yet unspecified intentions. Perhaps I was overdramatizing. I hoped so.

In the twilight I could see the shape of Storm King Mountain in the distance and followed the dense treetops down to the open green spaces at the edge of the village. It was still too early to see any lights dotting the slopes and I thought about the fact that this vast presence had looked like this for thousands of years despite the daily changes surrounding it.

As soon as I returned to the motel I called Richard. It was an hour earlier in Kansas City and he had just returned to his apartment. Very few couples (were we a couple?) enjoy the privacy of a secure phone line, so I decided to take advantage of it.

"How are you?" he asked. (No first name, no familiar term of affection.)

"I'm fine, Richard. How are you?"

"I'm glad to hear your voice. I miss you."

"Really?"

"Of course. What have you been up to?"

"Counterterrorism stuff, initial stages. No clear indications of hostile intentions yet."

"Following leads?"

"Following a person."

"And being careful, I hope."

"Always," I said. "What are you doing?"

"Bank fraud, security fraud, the usual."

"*I* followed a banker today," I said. "Actually I observed him. He wasn't moving."

"Be careful; they're shifty."

"I know. This one works for a Saudi bank."

"A Saudi national?"

"No. One of ours."

"A money launderer?"

"Possibly. His putative job is to handle investments."

"And move money around."

"Right."

"And you're going to call me if I can give you any help?"

"I'm going to call you anyway," I said.

"That's good. That's what I wanted to hear."

"What else would you like to hear?"

"How about that you'll join me in Washington later in the month?"

"Are you just visiting or being TDY'd there?"

"Temporary duty," he answered. "Nothing exciting. I'll be at the Treasury Department, going through some records."

"What are we talking about when you say *join*?"

"Whatever you want it to mean. Office chit-chat in a coffee shop. Dinner in Old Town looking out over the river. Or..."

"Or what?"

"Something more *intime*."

"*Intime*? That sounds interesting. Is that, like, Emmanuel Macron talk for a night to remember?"

"Whatever you want."

"How about a bottle of wine and a foot rub?"

"I could do a foot rub."

"I'm going to hold you to that," I said.

"I hope you will," Richard answered. "When I said I missed you I wasn't just making small talk."

"I like the direction this is taking," I said.

"Good," he answered.

Before I could say anything else each of our phones clicked. "I've got a call coming in," he said. "Here, just a second…sorry, I've got to take it."

"Damn, I do too," I said. "Email me the dates you'll be in D.C."

His phone clicked off before he could answer. I took my incoming call.

"This is Salva," the voice said. "I need to see you right away."

"I can be in in about an hour and twenty minutes, depending on traffic," I said.

"Let's make it first thing in the morning. I have to check some things tonight. I'll know more when we meet. Let's say 6:30; that way you can beat the traffic."

"Movement on our case?"

"Yes. Significant."

TWENTY-SIX

He looked as if he had just returned from a vacation. Rested, alert, no bags under his eyes. A starched white collar that was tidy but not constricting—his slacks freshly pressed, his shoes polished; ready for his close up. I made a mental note to try to find out how he did it. It was 6:20 in the morning, with leaden skies and a light rain over the city. People on the street were shuffling around under umbrellas, searching for awnings and doorways, their eyes fixed on the sidewalk in front of them and the spreading puddles at intersection curbs.

He greeted me, shook my hand, and offered me fresh black coffee, for which I was grateful. I sat down, sipped the coffee, and waited for him to speak.

"We've intercepted something," he said. "Email on a passworded site. Two references now."

I took another sip and waited for him to continue.

"There is an operation and it has a name. *Huis-clos.*"

"L'enfer, c'est les autres."

"What do you mean?" he asked.

"'Hell is other people', a line from the play."

"*Huis-clos* means 'no exit'."

"Right. It's the title of a play by Sartre. It's set in hell."

"That's interesting," he said.

"Somebody's going to lock a door and create hell?"

"So it would seem."

He was being surprisingly cryptic, so I pressed. "What else do you have, sir?" I asked.

"A death. Most likely a murder."

His eyes were wandering. He was probably thinking about the play title and the further information that it could add to what he already knew. I tried to prompt him. "Any one I might know?"

"Charles Pierson."

I shook my head, no.

"A very nice man. Native New Yorker. City College grad. Never left the city, though he had lots of opportunities. Big money offers: corporate…other city and state governments…universities. His dad was a policeman. Charley made enough in the private sector to enable him to buy a brownstone on the upper west side…close to the park…worth millions now. His wife's name is Sherry. Three kids, two still small. We used to play softball in the park on weekends until 9/11. Since then he's been too busy. Sometimes we'd get together for lunch. Lately it's just been carry-out, a few minutes on a park bench…

"They found him in his basement yesterday morning. He was lying across his treadmill. It had one of those devices that you put around your wrist or clip to your clothing. If you slip or faint the string pulls the plug on the machine and the motor shuts off. The symptoms suggested a heart attack, but we checked with his doctor today. He had just been in for his annual physical. Everything was fine—ekg, stress test, the whole deal. All of his numbers were on the sunny side of normal ranges."

"Congenital defect?" I asked.

"None that could be determined. At least not yet. He's been on the table for four and a half hours."

"What makes you suspicious? Couldn't it just be a coincidence?"

"Not likely," the AD answered. "His name was in one of the email messages; it was linked with the operation. The language is convoluted but the bottom line is that the email refers to him as an obstacle that had to be removed."

Salva took a drink of his coffee and stared into space. "He was a dear friend," he finally said. "I have a lot of people with whom I work well, but not a lot of friends like Charley."

"What did he do?" I asked, feeling as if I was somehow intruding.

"A lot," he answered, pausing for a moment. I waited until he was ready to start in again.

"Charley was the Commissioner of the city's Department of Information Technology and Telecommunications."

I guess I should have known that, but I didn't say so. I waited for him to continue.

"The DoITT sounds innocuous enough. The city has telephones and television, databases and networks—the full array of communication systems that need to be managed and maintained. That requires a bureaucracy and the bureaucracy's table of organization is common knowledge, available on the internet to anyone who wants to see it. They have something else, however…"

Again, he paused and again I waited.

"DoITT's original administrative offices were located within two blocks of the World Trade Center. When the towers were hit the offices were immediately evacuated. The city's Office of Emergency Management's Emergency Operations Center was destroyed, along with its computer infrastructure.

"The city's GIS staff were housed in DoITT's administrative offices. Without the Geographic Information System it would have been impossible to manage the rescue, response, and recovery operations after the attack. The whole thing was actually handled beautifully. The GIS staff quickly relocated to the Police Academy; they integrated their operation with the new Emergency Operations Center, and restored their system immediately. They had some significant help from the geographers at Hunter College, by the way, who have been part of the GIS project for a long time. By September 14 a new Command Center was built on a pier in the Hudson River. It was staffed 24/7 and had over 20 GIS workstations with six plotters.

"The central piece of the GIS system is the so-called 'nice map'—technically the NYCMap. The nice map is the base map for all GIS data on the city. Immediately after the attack the state government oversaw daily flights over Ground Zero. The aircraft took photographs, captured the data, and transmitted it to city and other emergency response agencies. The City Fire Department arranged for police helicopters to take digital photos and videos of the site to enhance the information flow and the Mapping Support Unit of FEMA's Urban Search and Rescue Team utilized handheld GPS-linked equipment and other data-gathering technologies to allow the workers at the site to continuously upload data to the nice map.

"This was really important. The flyovers monitored minute changes in the elevation of the site to determine structural weaknesses and shifts in the underground infrastructure, providing constant information on potential collapses that would have endangered the people working there. Thermal imaging detected smoldering fires that could have spread to fuel oil and Freon tanks in the area.

"The GIS maps enabled the city to communicate with the public in a timely fashion—notifying them of utility outage zones, the condition of surrounding buildings, and any emerging ingress/egress problems in lower Manhattan. Most important, the nice map gave the NYPD and the Army critical data on other potential terrorist targets. At the time, of course, many expected additional attacks and the city's bridges, tunnels, and reservoirs were all considered to be at risk."

"And," I said, "the GIS data would include full information on key subsurface features—sewers, water and gas mains, and telephone lines."

"Exactly."

"And there would be key flash points. If you take out the Garden you take out Penn Station beneath it—you kill thousands and stop a significant amount of rail service. In the process you could take out communication systems and throw in some gas main explosions for good measure."

"That's it," he said.

"And Charles Pierson's real job was…?"

"Managing the nice map."

"But he wouldn't be irreplaceable?"

"Ultimately, no. No one is. But if he dies what purports to be an accidental death and no one mentally links that event with a possible terrorist attack we could be caught off guard."

"And there would be a narrow window of opportunity," I said, "the days or hours between the moment of his death and the terrorist strike."

"Right."

"And an attack on the city's tunnels and bridges, with the city enveloped in flames from gas main and fuel oil fires would create a hell without any available exits."

He nodded at me with a look of grim realization. "That's why I thought we should meet," he said.

TWENTY-SEVEN

"So Charles Pierson would have been the go-to guy during any first response phase."

"Yes," the AD said. "There's no one who understands the system better than he did."

"And that's being remedied now."

"As we speak. The nice map crash course is moving full tilt."

"What can I do?"

He reached in his desk drawer and pulled out a list of the individuals with whom David Willets was known to be in contact. "Two of the names on this list are known members of the Al-Madi cell. They were also recipients of the email concerning Operation *Huis-clos*. Special Agent Jim Tenley will follow the first; I want you to follow the second. Abbas Al-Madi himself is heavily insulated. He operates out of a mosque on the upper east side and he is scrupulously distanced from anyone directly involved in terrorist activities. Everything is done through a succession of intermediaries."

"Like a mafia don."

"Yes, only more so."

"But you know that he's involved."

"Yes, but I can't tell you how we know that."

"Understood," I said.

"Al-Madi is very old school. Rigorous in his practice of his faith and very skeptical of modern ways. He keeps his nose clean and never leaves tracks. He's like a monk in a tower cell."

"But he's quite willing to use modern weapons."

"Yes, unfortunately, he is. The person I'd like you to follow is named Malawi," the AD said. "He's already under full electronic surveillance. In the meantime I'm going to put Special Agent Jeff Tillotson on Willets. Have you met him yet?"

"Briefly. The tall man…blond."

"Yes. He'll pick up Willets at the Sheraton parking garage, assuming that Willets comes into the city. If he sees anything you need to hear about, he'll call you on your cell phone. I don't like pulling you off of that assignment, but all of this is related and I need someone on Malawi who hasn't been around long enough to arouse suspicions. The man being followed by Special Agent Tenley is named Attari—two t's, not like the computer games. I want each of you to report on everything you see, *everything*. Where Malawi goes, who he sees, what he's wearing. Any detail could be relevant. The DoITT people are preparing for anything and everything. Sewers and tunnels and gas lines are being checked, bridges are under observation, flash points are being monitored around the clock. The surveillance at Penn Station, Grand Central, and the Port Authority has been tripled. The harbor police are checking everything that floats and the NYPD are checking everything nearby. The three airports have ratcheted up security and the whole eastern seaboard transportation infrastructure is on high alert. Every explosive-sniffing dog is on a leash and hard at work."

"That won't have escaped the terrorists' notice."

"No, but prevention is a fully-acceptable outcome. Apprehension would be ideal, but it may not be possible. I'm hoping that we put them on edge just enough to make them tip their hand. That's where you come in. Every city and federal agency will be watching for foot soldiers and suicide bombers; your job is to watch the ones at the top."

"Where do I pick up Malawi?"

"At the University Club. He lives at Central Park West, but he goes to the Club every morning for breakfast. He then works in the library there. It's one of the top private libraries in America. It's also usually deserted, so if he's meeting someone there it's very difficult to get close enough to him without calling attention to your presence. I've got a new listening device for you to use."

"I was in there once, back when I first lived in the city. Where does he live on Central Park West?"

"South. In the same building as Madonna."

"Wouldn't Madonna be something like the purest possible incarnation of Satan to a Muslim extremist?"

"Yes, but it's a nice building and he likes his creature comforts. Here's his file…"

I took the manila folder from the AD and went into the adjoining mini-office to study it. Karras al-Malawi was a Saudi national, whose family had made a fortune building highways across the desert. He was 47 years old. His official job description was "international financial consultant." He was unmarried, did not own a motor vehicle, and had never been arrested. He had studied in Switzerland and Paris before moving to the states. He had a master's degree from Georgetown—just like Al Haig, but I doubted that they had ever been close. He had lived in New York for the last decade. Like David Willets he was often seen in other people's company, but his work was a shadowy matter at best. I was determined to learn more. Besides, I had all the time in the world—one or two days.

TWENTY-EIGHT

Perhaps it was time to reconsider my prejudice against 'professional' men who lacked offices. The University Club library was nicer than any office I'd ever seen or occupied. I got the quick and dirty tour from the membership secretary, a woman named Elaine Griggs. Miss Griggs (her preferred title) was seventyish and wiry, with tight gray hair and rimless bifocals. She wore a powder blue suit with dark blue scarf and a pin with a prominent pearl.

They say that African griots don't start at the point in question in a historical narrative; they always begin at the beginning. So did Miss Griggs. She began by describing the Renaissance Revival architecture of the building itself, one of McKim, Mead, and White's masterpieces as well as a city- and Fifth Avenue landmark.

"The plan was centered around an enclosed cortille which began as a full colonnade on the first floor, became a three-sided colonnade on the second and shrank to four piers on the third. Since this is a club of educated people the centerpiece of the design is the library. Le Corbusier visited in 1935 and wrote, approvingly, 'In New York, then, I learn to appreciate the Italian Renaissance.'"

I wondered how many times she had repeated that quote. The library itself housed one quarter of their 100,000-volume collection—the remaining 75,000 were shelved in locked stacks—and it featured, Miss Griggs noted, 25-foot murals painted by H. Siddons Mowbray in the early 1900's. The vaulted ceilings were heavily decorated and ornamented; the overall effect was that of a vast private library in a sprawling renaissance mansion. Side tables and armchairs were positioned in dark corners and cubby holes. I felt as if someone in a morning suit named Harris or Taylor was about to descend on me with a glass of sherry on a small silver platter. He would lift it with white-gloved fingers, place it on an embossed napkin, call me *madame* and ask me if that would be all. In the midst of all of this finery I felt somewhat awkward wearing my sensor-amp, a miniature device that looks like a specially-fitted hearing aid and is designed to pick up the slightest sound and amplify it. Effective at fifty yards, it is one of the newest eavesdropping devices in the Bureau inventory.

Miss Griggs informed me that Mr. Malawi was at the Club, and that he was having his breakfast. She also told me that he preferred a particular leather wingchair in the library, one overlooking Fifth Avenue. I found a table and chair some thirty or forty feet away, which would not afford him a line of sight view of me or my activities. I then selected several books from the shelves, all dealing with the history of Manhattan. I stacked them on the table along with some 3x5 cards and a pair of No. 2 pencils. My sensor-amp was concealed by my hair and I added some tinted glasses with thick, broad frames. It wasn't a perfect disguise but it was as close to a mask as I could get.

When he arrived some twenty minutes later I continued reading and did not look up until he had passed me on the way to his favorite chair. When I checked I saw that he was wearing a dark suit with thin gray stripes and heavy leather wingtips. The edge of a starched white collar rose above the top of his suit jacket. After he sat down I gave him a few minutes to settle in before leaning forward to look again. He was wearing a muted, burgundy tie with a matching pocket square. Except for the hundred-dollar haircut and meticulously-groomed moustache he could have passed for an effete individual from the British Home Office. He *would* have been comfortable with a Harris or Taylor presenting him with a chilled sherry, except for the fact that a faithful practitioner of his religion should stick to something less fortified. Then again, there was that need for creature comforts which the AD had mentioned...

After finishing his paper he pulled out his cell phone and punched his speed dial. I could hear half of the conversation perfectly, once I adjusted the sensor-amp.

"It's me... Today?... The usual place?... Where, then?... What time?... Yes, I will."

Not the most helpful bit of information. He was calling someone familiar, someone who would recognize his voice. They were meeting today, but not at their usual location. Willets, perhaps?

When he clicked off he checked his watch. Just then a waiter walked past me and approached him with a demitasse of coffee, which he politely refused. "I must leave," he said.

When he followed the waiter out I was rooting around in the seat cushion of my chair, doing an absentminded professor routine, my face turned away from him. As he exited the club on West 54th I kept my distance, exchanging my reading glasses for small, dark sunglasses. He flagged a cab on Fifth Avenue and I was fortunately able to find one as well. I followed him to Penn Station. I was safe for the moment, since it was unlikely that the station or Garden above would be bombed at a time when he was there. He took the escalator down to the station proper. The tile floors and low ceiling were creating a din in my sensor-amp that resembled an explosion of sound in a steel tunnel. I lowered the volume as I followed him to a ticket window, attempting to position myself in such a way as to enhance my chances of being able to hear his voice among the many around him.

All I heard were loud, disjunct syllables from several dozen voices. After he purchased his ticket he walked to the club lounge behind the stairs and escalators leading to the tracks below. Perhaps he was in search of the coffee he was unable to enjoy at the University Club. I took advantage of the opportunity and slipped into a travel accessory store, buying scarves that would modify my jacket and skirt ensemble and also a wool tam that would draw attention away from my eyes.

He emerged at 9:42, walked directly to a set of steps on the west side of the station, and passed through the control gate. There was no indication of the train on the Track 8 board at the top of the stairway, but I checked the video monitors and the trains currently boarding were all on other tracks. The club lounge must have announced the track of his train prior to the public announcement on the monitors—all part of the club car service. This spared him and other club car passengers from participating in the mad dash that occurred every time the monitor changed, since the area below the monitors, adjoining the stairs, is basically a staging area for nervous passengers anxious to beat each other to the best available seats below.

I followed him down to the track area, sporting my new scarf and hat, watched him board, and approached a conductor on the platform. I rolled the dice. "This is the Metroliner, correct?"

"Yes," he said, "the express."

It wasn't really an express, since it stopped in Newark, Philly, Wilmington, Baltimore City and BWI, but we would be spared Trenton, New Carrollton and enough other stops to bring us into Washington in just under three hours, assuming that Washington was his destination. At least there were fewer stops for me to check along the way. The last thing I wanted was some Alphonse and Gaston routine with one or the other of us jumping on and off the train in an attempt to trick the other.

Malawi seated himself in the club car and I sat in the third row of the adjoining coach. When we pulled out of Newark the club car passengers were served a late breakfast or early lunch (I couldn't see which) with optional wine. I went to the rest room at the end of our car and caught a glimpse of him through the double doors; he was enjoying a glass of the white. When the conductor came through I handed him a government voucher, which he pocketed without questioning me. Malawi stayed in his seat at Philly, Wilmington, and Baltimore City. He was going to Washington.

Each time I was able to catch a glimpse of him he was talking on his cell phone. He was also jotting notes in a small pocket folder. My next flash point would be Union Station. If I got too close to him I risked being made; if he got too far away from me I would lose him. I decided to follow my Sheraton parking ramp plan and get to a taxi before he did.

I worked my way through the cars to the front of the train, hit the platform the moment we arrived, and hurried through the waiting areas, ticket area and restaurant and shop arcade to the taxi line at the front of the station. Fortunately the line was short. At times, when the lines are long, starters force the passengers to share cabs. I had a $20 bill ready to persuade the starter otherwise, but didn't need it. The cab I was assigned was in reasonable condition and the driver spoke English. I handed him the $20 and asked him to drive forward and pull over to the curb. Then I badged him. Sometimes the $20 would be enough; sometimes the badge would be. I wasn't taking any chances.

"I'm following someone," I said.

"No problem. I'll keep my distance. The traffic's heavy as usual; he won't notice me behind him."

Malawi emerged from the station a few minutes later and flashed a two-finger *V* sign to a *Red Top* driver in the middle parking lane. He had called ahead for a Virginia cab. That meant two things. First, we were going to Virginia and second, he was taking no chances on riding in a rattletrap District cab with a driver whose English was shaky. He *did* like his creature comforts.

We followed him along Constitution Avenue. His driver took the Roosevelt Bridge ramp past the Kennedy Center, crossed the river and headed west on the GW parkway. He then got off at Spout Run, heading through North Arlington and into McLean. When he got to McLean, however, he headed south on Dolly Madison Boulevard, driving toward Tysons Corner. I would have thought he would have caught 66 out of

Rosslyn—a straighter shot to the western suburbs. It was probably a traffic issue. There are three rush hours in Washington now and we were still in the second, lunchtime rush. Perhaps Malawi had time to spare or perhaps time was of the essence and while the McLean route was a little circuitous there was less chance of a monster tie-up, since the beltway crosses Route 7 between Route 66 and Tysons and the entire area can gridlock at the slightest flutter of a problem.

This was no place for the uninitiated, since Dolley Madison Boulevard, which is always route 123, becomes Maple Avenue in Vienna and is Chain Bridge Road in parts of North Arlington, McLean, and Fairfax. Within McLean proper, Chain Bridge Road is on the right side of 123 when you pass the old Kennedy house, Hickory Hill, and on the left side of 123 when you enter the village. An address without further directions is virtually worthless.

Tysons Corner isn't much better. The central point of a two-lane rural road in the 1950's, it is now a vast crazy quilt of mega-malls, parking ramps, strip malls, hotels, condos, townhouse developments, restaurants, car dealerships and yuppie watering holes. Private dining clubs and *Ritz-Carlton* suites overlook discount mattress stores, *Tiffany's*, *Gucci*, the offices of innumerable beltway bandit firms, *Red Lobster* and the *Olive Garden*. It's where you go to have a custom car stereo system installed, to buy a Cadillac, to attend a gun show at a mid-market hotel or get a *State Farm* evaluation of the results of your most recent collision. Regardless of the quality of the operation you're visiting, the land on which it sits runs well into seven figures per acre.

All of this haphazard growth has been accompanied by after-the-fact adjustments to the traffic infrastructure. The result is a twisted cobweb of frontage roads, side streets, boulevards that suddenly expand or shrink and short cuts understood only by those who use them constantly. It is the perfect place to lose someone who is attempting to follow you.

Malawi's driver turned left into the principal mall from 123. That was good news. Tysons I (or simply, Tysons) is on the left of 123; Tysons

II (or, the Galleria) is on the right. However, Tysons I is accessible from the Tysons II industrial park; a narrow, two-lane overpass runs across 123 to enable Tysons I and Tysons II shoppers to continue their activities without negotiating the lights and the interminable lines of traffic on 123. If I was Malawi's driver and if I believed I was being followed I would drive into Tysons II, then take the overpass to Tysons I, where the traffic is light and the lines of sight are clear, a place where the following car would either have to commit and expose itself or permit the lead car to fade into the endless lots, ramps, and traffic lanes of Tysons I. Since he didn't do that, I could assume that he did not suspect that he was being followed.

The bad news was that the worse place to follow someone on foot is through a shopping mall. There are dense crowds in which the person can be lost. There are empty corners in which the follower risks being exposed. There are stairs, escalators, and elevators offering escape options and constant opportunities for movements that are both herky-jerky and plausible. The person followed can stop unexpectedly and buy a coffee or ice cream. He can pause in front of a shop window and then look in multiple directions. He can suddenly sit down on a bench and catch you unawares or he can take you on a death march from one end of the facility to the other.

A person crossing an open field cannot stop and look around without tipping his hand that he suspects he is being followed. In a mall he can look anywhere, walk anywhere, sit down anywhere, or simply outwalk you. He can go into a dressing room or toilet and wait for ten minutes to re-emerge, then observe carefully the faces that await him. He can go into large, open areas where his sight lines are clear and you cannot easily follow him: mattress departments, oriental rug departments, single-sex shoe departments. He can go into mazes: book stores, toy stores, costume jewelry departments, perfume and makeup departments, sporting goods.

Malawi's driver headed east around what used to be the landmark Woodward and Lothrop store—now out of business—and headed toward Route 7.

"Watch him," I said to my driver. "He may swing to the left and head toward Fairfax Square" (the upscale mini-mall with cineplex on the other side of the highway).

"I got him, don't worry," the driver said. "You know this area, huh?"

"I've spent some time here before."

"So have I, but it still ain't easy," he answered. "Twenty years ago there were half as many people as there are now."

"And they all have their own way of driving."

"That's for sure," he said. "That's putting it politely. Some of 'em have never seen snow until they get here. When it happens, they freak. Some of 'em ain't even used to dealing with heavy rain. They'll close the schools here when there's a heavy rain; didja know that?"

"I did. Not like Wisconsin or Minnesota, huh?"

"It sure as hell isn't," he said. "Whoops…there he goes."

The *Red Top* driver passed the old Woodie's lot and turned into the adjoining ramp. "He's going to *Nordstrom*," my driver said.

"Sure looks that way," I said.

"There are also some restaurants down in the corner there—*California Pizza Kitchen*, stuff like that."

Malawi wasn't dressed for the *California Pizza Kitchen* and he had already eaten on the Metroliner, but I didn't comment on the fact.

"You want me to wait for you?" the driver asked.

"Yes. Have you got a cell phone?"

"Sure do."

"Give me the number," I said. "If he leaves from a different point I'll call you and you can pick me up."

"Sure thing . . . 703 291-2291," he said.

"Got it," I said, as I entered it into my directory.

"He's stopping," my driver said.

I looked at his registration card on the passenger seat visor. "Thanks, Arnold," I said. "I'll see you soon."

"I'll be here," he said. "Just another afternoon working for the government."

Hopefully not one of our last, I thought, as I hurried after Malawi.

TWENTY-NINE

The Tysons *Nordstrom* store has three levels—the bargain basement, the upper level designer salon and the middle level where the money is made and the foot traffic is heavy. The latter includes cosmetics, purses, jewelry, men's and women's shoes, and the men's department—suits to your right, sportswear to your left, and everything else in between.

Entering from the parking ramp Malawi turned right and window-shopped through the accessories and suit sections of the men's department. He looked at *Robert Talbott* striped ties (now at a tidy $155 each), *Nordstrom* socks, sport coats in 48L (he was probably a 40R), and wool slack separates. From time to time he checked his watch. Then he moved to men's sportswear, checked out the *Façonnable* sweaters, *Nordstrom* cotton slacks, *Polo* shirts and lambskin blouson jackets. He checked his watch again and then walked directly into the men's room behind the cashmere sweater case.

Nordstrom is known not only for its service, but for the fact that their restrooms are clearly marked and readily accessible, not hidden behind a secret panel at the end of a hallway in the farthest corner of the most distant floor. This one had the benefit of proximity to the parking ramp exit. No one followed him in, so he was either in real need of the facilities or meeting someone who was already there. I checked the time of his entry and opened my cell phone/camera so that I would be ready to photograph anyone who exited at approximately the same time as he did.

Since the sales clerks were plentiful and attentive they would notice anyone going in and out; a *Nordstrom* men's room was not the place to hold an extended meeting if you wanted to avoid suspicious eyes. Malawi emerged 10 minutes later. He walked directly toward the shoe department, away from the parking ramp exit. I had a decision to make. Should I risk losing him and wait for any confederate to emerge or should I stay with him? I rolled the dice and waited, figuring that if he had needed the facilities and was also worrying about a scheduled meeting he'd have gone into the toilet sooner rather than dallied and window-shopped.

A few seconds later a man emerged from the men's room who I hadn't seen previously. Tall and thin, he was sixtyish and slightly stoop-shouldered, a caucasian with shoulder-length hair and trimmed beard, both dishwater blond in color, all carefully groomed. Stripped of his clothing he would have looked like a homeless addict who had recently been cleaned up, detoxed and rehabilitated. He was wearing a brown tweed jacket, yellow tattersall shirt, red knit tie, beige slacks, and polished cordovan loafers. A superannuated Amherst English professor home for a shopping trip. I took his picture and waited another five minutes. No one else emerged, except for one of the clerks who had gone in after Malawi had already left.

I walked around the escalator and through the women's cosmetics and purse section, where I would have a good view of the shoe department. Malawi was gone. I walked out into the mall and scanned the *Nordstrom* wing for stores that might plausibly attract his attention. Then I instinctively walked to the railing and looked down to the floor below, the site of *Nordstrom's* coffee bar. There he was.

The coffee bar sells pastries and packaged sandwiches as well as coffee, juice and bottled water. Malawi was sipping something hot from a cardboard cup and talking on his cell phone. On a paper napkin next to the cup he had two shell-shaped madeleines. I wondered if they were stirring memories in him, and if so, of what—pleasure or pain?

I returned to the center of *Nordstrom's*, took the escalator to the lower level, and did my best impression of an engaged shopper. Along the way I picked up a shopping bag and slipped my purse in to bulk out the paper sides. I also slipped on one of my newly-acquired scarves. From the teenage sportswear section—replete with rock videos and high-volume sound—I could see him nibbling on the second of his madeleines. When he finished he walked toward me. I put my hand over my mouth and cheeks as if I was agonizing over a purchasing decision as he passed by, en route to the escalator. From there he went to the parking ramp, got back in his taxi, and left.

The taxi was waiting for him in one of the 15-minute spaces next to the exit. I called Arnold on my cell phone and he picked me up a few seconds later.

"I need to get to Union Station," I said, "before he does."

"No problem," Arnold said.

He slipped out of the ramp, took the circular road which crosses Route 7, hung a quick right, got onto 7 and headed for Falls Church, exiting onto 66 and heading for Rosslyn, the Roosevelt Bridge, and Constitution Avenue. Running against the outbound District traffic, and still too early for the dinner rush into town, he drove at a steady 70 on 66. There was no sign of Malawi's taxi.

When I got to the station I tipped Arnold an extra $20 on the voucher, and hurried inside, where I traded my *Nordstrom* bag for a plastic one, in which I put my scarf and jacket. I unbuttoned my blouse, tarted up my makeup, and put on my sunglasses.

Malawi arrived a few minutes later, just in time for the 4:00 Metroliner. I sat in the adjoining car again and sipped ginger ale while I snacked on a warm sandwich with a piece of wilted green garnish trapped against the cellophane. At 7:00 he walked out of Penn Station and cabbed to the Palace, where he ordered a dry, Bombay Sapphire martini in the Gold Room and, again, earnestly checked his watch.

THIRTY

At 8:00 he walked out to the plaza area. As he checked his smart phone, David Willets walked out of the shadows and took his hand. I looked around for Special Agent Tillotson, wondering if he had been able to stay on Willets. When I didn't see him I called him on my cell phone.

"Jeff...Gwen. I'm at your subject's watering hole. Are you in the area?"

"Hi. I've just been to church." (He had followed Willets to St. Pat's, just across the street.)

"And you're still in contact."

"Yes, and you?"

"Yes, just got here."

He didn't volunteer to share notes with me. Like me, he was reporting directly to the AD. I was pleased to hear that he had been able to stay on Willets and I was curious to know who Willets had been seeing during Malawi's road trip to northern Virginia.

Malawi and Willets came out of the Gold Room an hour and a half later. Hard duty digesting multiple small plates of food, plus wine. Willets walked west, toward the Sheraton; I didn't see Tillotson follow him and I didn't expect to. Malawi took a taxi to his condo on the southwest corner of the park and settled in for the night. I gave him a half hour to come back out on the street but he stayed put.

I had bounced the picture of Mr. Longhair from the *Nordstrom* men's room to the AD. I called downtown to see if he was in the office and available for a meet. He was. He asked if I had eaten. I said, "No, not really," and he said he'd order in some sandwiches.

"Preference?" he asked.

"Whatever they have that's fresh," I said.

"Ham and cheese?"

"Sure."

He also ordered some chips and Goldfish. "I'm a junk food junkie," he said.

He also had a collection of craft beers. "I figure you've earned some, running up and down the eastern seaboard," he said.

I opened up a Founders All Day IPA and took a deep drink. "That's good," I said, "very good."

"The longhaired guy is Leon Donovan," he said. "Malawi usually meets with him in New York. He has no known criminal or terrorist ties. He inherited some money a few years back and knocks around at charity events."

"Why would Malawi meet with him in Virginia?" I asked. "In a department store men's room."

"Probably because the relationship is closer than we thought and involves some information they didn't want anybody with eavesdropping equipment to hear. I've asked the people in Washington to check further on Donovan and see what he's doing down there. He lives out on the island."

"Hamptons?"

"Southold, actually. North fork."

"Maybe Donovan's a sucker and Malawi's using him in some way. Money laundering?"

"Possibly."

"What did he do before he got rich?"

"He was a photographer. Still does some of it from time to time."

"Interesting. Maybe he's doing some private work for Malawi. What did he do—portrait…fashion?"

"Industrial. He did photo spreads for company magazines, that kind of thing."

"So he may know some people."

"Yes, and some industrial sites."

"Maybe Malawi's shopping for targets."

"Could be. Let me turn up the heat a little bit."

"What's up with Willets? He and Malawi had dinner together this evening at the fancy bar at the *Palace*."

"He had a long day," the AD said. "He came into town early, met with a lawyer named Greenlief and an investment counselor named Hastings. Neither has any known terrorist connections. He had lunch alone and then went to the University Club. He spent the afternoon there, presumably waiting for his dinner with Malawi."

"They could have eaten there."

"Better food at the *Gold Room*," the AD said. "Money's never an object with these guys, so why not grab for the gusto?"

"A little more public though," I said.

"Yes, but maybe their plan is to hide in plain sight."

"Do we know anything more about Operation *Huis-clos*?"

"Yes. As a matter of fact, we do."

THIRTY-ONE

"There is no question that Charles Pierson was murdered. I won't go into the chemical details, but suffice to say that he ingested something that resulted in an instant, massive heart attack. Very, very high tech delivery system. The chemical was affixed to the hand grips of his treadmill. It was heat-and-moisture-activated, so that the faster he walked and the more he sweated the more he took in. When he fell over, releasing his grip on the handles, the remainder of the substance dissipated. If we hadn't checked his palms and fingers carefully we wouldn't have been able to detect it. There was still enough warmth left in them to allow the substance to pool at the entry sites.

"We've been checking the DoITT computers and there's been an increase in viral activity. We have plenty of filters to screen for the viruses so the system is not at serious risk, but we count all attempted incursions. Someone is ratcheting up the number of their attempts. It's like field and naval artillery softening up our defensive positions before the actual invasion begins.

"We're also seeing an escalation in electronic traffic within the Al-Madi cell. It's heavily coded and passworded, but there's no question that the volume has increased in the last forty-eight hours. Al-Madi himself has hunkered down, presumably to insulate himself from any possible charges or possible reprisals."

"Tell me some more about the Pierson family, sir," I said. "Wouldn't it be risky to put something toxic on family exercise equipment? The number of children and young women who have heart attacks is very small; if one of them had died our suspicions would have been aroused."

"Usually I'd agree," the AD answered. "If we were talking about the placing of lethal materials on a steering wheel or a doorknob the statistical probabilities would be far more difficult to predict. Exercise equipment is different. People follow routines; it's one of the rules of good practice. Charley was a morning person. Sherry didn't use the equipment until the kids were off to school. The kids didn't use it at all, except for the boy, and then only when he had friends over and they used the treadmill as a toy. Charley watched television while he exercised, the news usually; Sherry watched fitness tapes. All the killers would have needed to do was set up a parabolic microphone near the house or put a miniature mic in one of the basement window wells. Then they could listen to the background sound and heavy breathing, notice the patterns that emerged, make an occasional wrong-number phone call and learn who answered and who didn't at what particular times. All very simple, especially when the pattern followed is so regular and so predictable."

"And they could gain access easily enough?"

"Yes. The basement has an exposed exterior wall with a door. Unfortunately, it's not a sliding door with a 2x4 wedged in the track. It's a standard, outside, panel door with four windows and a generic Yale lock that could have been easily picked. While there was disruption of the dirt that had washed over the cement just outside the door there were no identifiable footprints. Whoever entered the house had slipped on new Totes galoshes in an unusually large size."

"And worn gloves, presumably."

"Yes. There were no fingerprints and no other physical evidence. We checked for sneeze residue and hair and fiber evidence, but the basement was clean. This was a professional job, with a great deal of prior planning."

"Has there been any evidence of attempted tampering with the city's infrastructure?"

"As a matter of fact, there has. How about another beer?"

I wondered if he thought I needed it. I said thanks, took it from him, and popped off the tab as he continued.

"Two city sewer workers surprised an unauthorized individual who escaped before he could be apprehended. He left behind a piece of Det. cord and a roll of electrical tape."

"Where?"

"Third Avenue between 59th and 60th."

"Bloomingdale's and the 59th Street Bridge."

"Right. A significant blast would create a crater that would gridlock traffic and create panic among a large number of pedestrians. A directional blast at the bridge would also take out the Roosevelt Island tram and everyone riding on it at the time. If an incendiary device was used a little farther south it could set the entire store on fire and trap everyone inside. That could kill thousands of people, not hundreds."

"Were any fingerprints or other evidence found?"

"No, not yet."

"And when did this happen?"

"It happened this morning," the AD said. "The sewer crew was doing a spot check of the system; they weren't looking for terrorists or weapons. We were lucky."

"How did the perp escape?"

"He had a confederate who pulled the manhole cover. They were using walkie-talkies. One of the sewer guys saw the device."

"Any noticeable accent?"

"He wasn't close enough to hear anything specific, just close enough to see the perp hold the device up to his ear."

"If they're ready to install Det. cord we don't have much time left."

"Possibly minutes or hours. If we're lucky, days," the AD said.

THIRTY-TWO

My mind was rushing to various possibilities. Should we tighten the noose on the terrorist cell? Start rousting anyone who had given us reason to be suspicious? Suggest to Homeland Security that they raise the terrorist alert code? While I was nursing my beer and thinking over the possibilities, the AD's phone rang.

"Salva," he said. Then he listened for at least two full minutes. "Thanks," he said, "hold on, I'll get back to you in a second." He held his hand over the mouthpiece, turned to me, and composed himself.

"It's started," he said. "We've found a limpet mine attached to a ship with flammable cargo, confirmed C-4 devices in the Lincoln, Holland, and Queens-Midtown tunnels, and suspicious objects on key supports of the Throgs Neck, Triborough, and Verrazano Narrows bridges."

"What can I do?" I asked.

"Interrogate David Willets. Don't hurt him, but don't let him off the ropes either. I don't want you to do it in the city; it could tip off his confederates that we're onto them. I'll ask a local police officer to accompany you. Can you do that?"

"Yes," I said, "but I prefer to do it alone."

"He could be very dangerous," the AD said.

"I'll be careful," I answered.

"Be *very* careful," he said.

"Yes, sir," I answered, put down what was left of my beer, poured myself a cup of thick coffee from the table adjoining his desk, took a sip, and got up to leave. "I'll let you know the minute I learn anything."

"Keep in mind," the AD said, "that we don't need another Abu Ghraib."

"Understood."

"At least don't take any pictures or leave any marks."

"Yes, sir," I said. He had forced a slight smile, a scant hedge against what could prove to be an impending succession of nightmares. "I trust the city will still be here when I get back."

"That's our hope," he said. "We're detaching the explosives from the signaling devices but it's unlikely that we'll be able to trace them."

"They'll use unregistered cell phones with pre-purchased minutes."

"Yes, but we'll find out when the calls come in and at least get some indication of their intentions."

"I'll stay in touch," I said, and headed to the parking garage.

The best time for an interrogation is the middle of the night. Rather than pound on Willets' door and give him a chance to plan some sort of countermove I stayed in the parking lot and phoned him; I told him that I was a Cornwall detective on patrol and that I had seen someone who appeared to be attempting to break into his car. "He left when I pulled up," I said. "I called in your plate and got this number. Sorry to wake you up, but I thought you might have some idea who the person might be."

He mumbled something incoherent.

"The suspect was using a slim jim, so I considered it unlikely that he was a friend or relative. Could you meet me in the lot? It won't take but a minute or two and I want to go over his description with you and verify that no vandalism has occurred."

"Let me find something to put on," he said.

A few seconds later a light came on in an upstairs bedroom, followed by the hallway light, which illuminated the glass frame at the top of the front door. When it opened and Willets stepped out onto his cement mini-porch he was tying a knot in the belt of a red, cotton robe. "FBI," I said, putting the end of my weapon against the center of his spine. "Put your hands behind your back."

As I slipped on the cuffs he said, "What's this about? I thought you said someone was trying to break into my car."

"Should we talk inside?" I asked. "It would attract a lot less attention."

"Of course," he said.

I directed him to walk down the hall toward his living room. The furniture was Danish modern and the three-cushioned sofa on the right wall had an arm with an exposed wood and steel frame. I attached his right wrist to the sofa and sat down in the opposite chair. The furniture was arranged for conversation. I commented on the fact and expressed the hope that he would be open and honest with me.

"Of course," he said, "but what's this about?"

I was surprised that he hadn't begun by demanding warrants and threatening lawsuits. He wasn't stupid. In some ways I wish he had been. The more adept he was at denying involvement the longer it would take to discover his actual role in the terrorist operation.

"This discussion is part of an ongoing investigation," I said. "I'd like to begin with something more general."

He looked at me quizzically.

"Please describe your profession." I was being generous; I could have said *occupation*.

"I'm an attorney."

"And what is your specialty?"

"Corporate law."

"You'll have to excuse my skepticism, Mr. Willets, but most corporate attorneys have offices that are closer to their client base."

"That's true," he said, not volunteering anything more.

"But you don't."

"No, I don't."

"Why not?" I asked, feeling like a dentist doing a complex extraction.

"I do all that I can to preserve confidentiality."

"But the attorney-client privilege provisions would hold regardless of your place of business."

"That's true," he said.

"So why do you live sixty miles from your work?"

"I have a residence in the Adirondacks. As you can see," he said, pointing with his left hand to the dining area table and the computer and paperwork there, "this is my office."

"Yes, but the point is that you don't have an office in Manhattan."

"No, I don't."

"Normally this would not be seen as *reassuring* to your clients."

"No, it wouldn't."

"I'm sorry, but I don't understand," I said. "Attorneys file papers. They talk to bailiffs and judges. They talk to other attorneys. They huddle together near city halls and city courthouses. You don't."

"No, I don't."

"So you don't actually litigate."

"No."

"You consult?"

"Of course."

"In what area?"

"Career development."

"I don't understand," I said. "You're an attorney, not a human resource specialist or corporate recruiter."

"True."

"And what are the specific career development issues on which you advise?"

"I advise on career transitions."

"You mean when people retire or are fired?"

"No, when people are transitioning from one organization to another."

"I see. Tell me more."

"When individuals in positions of considerable authority—particularly individuals in possession of professional information that might be termed *transformational* —relocate, it is a matter of some concern to the organization from which they are departing. From the moment that there is any suspicion concerning their intentions they are at risk. Their office locks can be changed; their computers can be confiscated and their email and data files subjected to investigation. They are treated like spies or saboteurs. The organizations of which they have been a part bring down all of the corporate force that they can muster to secure any information that might be lost to the company and neutralize any effectiveness that the individual who is departing might have in the receiving organization. The departing executives are pariahs, cast out on an ice floe or relegated to the dark spaces beyond the warmth of the corporate village. There are cases in which their homes have been invaded and their property been taken."

For someone who spoke in monosyllables he was suddenly speaking in paragraphs and platitudes. For a moment I felt as if he was pitching his services to me.

"When a person anticipates finding himself in such a situation, he seeks (if he is cautious and wise) to mitigate ill effects, maximize new opportunities, and avail himself of a knowledge of the laws that govern his impending condition. In short, he requires expert advice. I provide such advice and I do it in such a way as to minimize any attention that might be drawn to myself or to my clients. I meet with them in informal, non-business settings. I maintain as much anonymity as possible. In some cases I work through other, trusted individuals."

"Such as your clients' personal attorneys."

"Yes, or their spouses."

"But you could live anywhere, so long as you didn't maintain an office and so long as you continued to meet in what you termed non-business settings."

"Yes, that's true."

We were back to the monosyllables. "But you don't," I said. "You live sixty miles away from your potential client base."

"My mother lives in Cornwall," he said.

"That wasn't in our files."

"She uses her maiden name."

"Sterritt?"

"Her name's not Sterritt; it's Sterrittson. There must be an error in your files."

"I'll have to check," I said lamely. "You have a client by the name of Malawi."

"Malawi? I don't know anyone by that name," he said.

THIRTY-THREE

I took out my cell phone, pulled up Malawi's picture, and showed it to him.

"That's Mr. Quattar. He's a Jordanian oil executive, working for a division of *British Petroleum*. His actual specialty is natural gas and he was trained as a geologist at Imperial College, London. He's considering a position with *Texaco*, but his knowledge of the middle east fields is invaluable and *BP* would be most upset if they knew that he was taking that knowledge to a competitor."

"And did you check on him at all, Mr. Willets?"

"Why would he lie about such a thing? Why would he pay me if he didn't need my services?"

"And you bill at…?"

"Eight fifty an hour."

"And to date you have billed how many hours?"

"Around thirty."

"That's not much money to him, Mr. Willets. By the way, his name is Karras al-Malawi. Malawi is a Saudi national and a member of the Abbas Al-Madi terrorist cell. His family made a fortune building roads across the desert; his specialty is blowing them up."

"I simply can't believe that. He's an educated man, a sensitive and thoughtful man."

"Surely you don't want me to go down the list of poets and composers idolized by the Nazis, Mr. Willets…"

"No, that isn't necessary. And your name is…?"

I was struck by the fact that he spoke so directly and so innocently without demanding to see my shield and credentials and study their every detail. Either he was an honest dupe or a highly-skilled operative. "I'm Special Agent Harrison," I said, "from the New York field office."

Instead of responding he shook his head from side to side. After a few moments of that he asked if he could have a glass of water. "There's *Evian* in the refrigerator," he said. "You can have some too."

I opened a fresh bottle and filled two glasses. After he took a drink from his I took a drink from mine. He put down his glass with his free hand, turned to me, and said, "Agent Harrison, you are free to go through any of my records and any of my property. I assure you that you will find nothing implicating me in a terrorist plot. What I don't understand is why Mr. Quattar or Malawi would pay my fee and take up my time."

"Neither do I, Mr. Willets," I said. "That's what we have to find out." I wanted to maintain my edge with him, particularly when he was so forthcoming with regard to waiving the need for a warrant and throwing open his home to the FBI. One possible reason for Malawi's actions was obvious. It was all mystification to distract us. The *Huis-clos* plot was bogus, cover for something else, probably something much bigger. While we chased around after people like Willets, the Al-Madi cell was busily planning something altogether different. From the beginning I had doubts about the explosives that had been found. It had all been too easy—fool's gold in mines salted by experts. I needed to talk to Salva immediately. As I looked at Willets, appearing to be searching his eyes for information, I felt my cell phone vibrate in my jacket pocket. "Excuse me," I said, knowing that Willets wasn't going anywhere. I opened the sliding door onto the tiny slab of patio behind his townhouse, walked outside and closed the door behind me. I looked at the incoming number, hit the green receiver icon and said, "Hello. I've been waiting to hear from you."

THIRTY-FOUR

"How are you?"
           "I'm fine, Richard. What's wrong?"
"Nothing."

"Are you in Washington yet?"

"No, that's been changed. I *will* be in Washington, but on a different assignment. Have you got a few minutes to talk?"

"Not really. Sorry, I'm on a case, questioning a suspect."

"Call me later?"

"Yes, of course," I said, "the moment I get a chance."

I rang off and looked at my watch. It was 2:00 a.m. in Kansas City. Richard didn't call in the middle of the night unless there was something important he needed to discuss.

I went back inside and told Willets I would have to take him to the city for further questioning. He balked at first, but then agreed. He asked if he could first shower and shave and I said yes. He had been forthcoming, so I agreed to be forthcoming as well. However, I searched his bathroom and bedroom for possible weapons, borrowed his toolbox, and nailed the bathroom and bedroom windows to their frames with multiple finishing nails before removing the cuff. It was melodramatic, perhaps, but until I was certain that he was not a member of the Al-Madi group I was determined to take all of the regular precautions. I waited for him outside the bathroom, in the upstairs hallway, with my weapon in hand. He was agreeable to those arrangements, got ready in a little less than twenty minutes, and did not complain when I cuffed him to the doorframe in the back seat of my car.

We arrived at the field office in an hour and fifteen minutes and though it was not yet 5:00 a.m. there was conspicuous activity in every room. I drained and watered Willets, put him in an interview room, removed his cuffs, let myself out and locked him in, using the coded security pad.

The AD was out. His night secretary patched me through to him on a secure phone.

"What's up?" he asked. "I'm in transit."

"I brought Willets in. I finished the initial interrogation and wanted to keep him incommunicado until we could verify that he was clean."

"Clean?"

"Yes, sir. I'll give you all the details when we have time to speak at length. Bottom line: I think his business is legitimate and that Malawi has been using him to distract us. Willets offered to throw open his home and all of his records to me. On the drive into the city he volunteered to take a polygraph. He said he'd do anything we wanted. I think we should take him up on the offer, just to be sure."

"Go ahead and arrange it. Anything else?"

"Nothing factual. I'll wait until we have a chance to talk about the entire situation."

"OK. You should know that evidence has surfaced about additional targets. I'm on the L. I. E., driving to the end of the north shore."

Plum Island, I thought. The animal-disease laboratory. Live foot-and-mouth disease virus. Perpetually quarantined. Scientists go in and out by boat, changing their clothes, their glasses, and other personal items each time they enter and leave.

"Can we talk later this afternoon?" he asked.

"Of course."

"I've got to go to Fort Tryon Park after I get back from the island."

Fort Tryon Park. *The Cloisters.* Two million works of art, many of them priceless.

"I'll be here," I said.

"I'll be in contact with Janice," he said. "I'll ask her to give you my ETA."

"Thanks," I said, and rung off. Between Manhattan and Orient Point were two and a half hours' worth of hard miles, but the AD still could have made the run to the north shore, come back to West 190th and then returned to the field office by early afternoon. There may have been other stops along the way that he hadn't mentioned.

Special Agent Charlie Dolan, our polygraph guru, was out of the office, but scheduled to return within the hour; I caught him on his cell phone and gave him a quick rundown on the case. I then returned to the interview room, told Willets we were grateful for his cooperation, noted that we wouldn't be able to do the polygraph for an hour or so, offered him some magazines to read, and told him I'd be back as soon as possible. He smiled politely. He still hadn't asked for the opportunity to call his lawyer. Maybe he didn't need one.

I left the office, grabbed a tall black coffee from a sleepy street vendor, and found a vacant bench near the fountain in City Hall Park. There were plenty of choices at that hour. I wiped the moisture from the seat, flipped open my cell phone, and called Richard.

THIRTY-FIVE

After five rings I heard the rollover click and was given the leave-a-message prompt by a robotic female voice. It was the middle of the night in Kansas City, *if* he was in Kansas City. He hadn't said earlier and I hadn't enquired. All that I knew was that he wasn't in Washington. I left a brief message, asked him to call me, and went back to sipping my coffee.

An elderly man wearing a red flannel shirt beneath a dark green, waxed Barbour jacket approached the fountain with two bull terriers in tow. He reached into the fountain, pulled out a floating paper cup, deposited it in a trash bin, and said something to the dogs which seemed to catch their attention. They pulled west but he walked east and they followed. I straightened up as my phone rang.

It was Alice, the night secretary. "Special Agent Dolan is on his way; he should arrive in approximately ten minutes," she said.

"I'll be right there," I said, slipping my cell phone back in my pocket, but leaving it on *vibrate*. For the next five minutes I compulsively felt for its presence with my forearm. I continued to wonder why Richard hadn't returned my call.

I met Charlie Dolan in the hallway outside of the Willets interview room. Charlie was scrupulous with regard to his equipment but—by Bureau standards—comparatively unkempt in his person. He could wear gray wool and starched shirts, but his ties never quite matched his suits and his glasses were continually smeared with dust. The copper fittings attaching the nose pads to the lenses were green with oxidation and the arms sat unevenly on the tops of his ears. The first time I saw him I thought the lenses were much thicker than they actually were, since his eyes appeared blurred behind them. There were errant tufts of hair at his ears and nostrils. I wondered if the AD had spoken to him about it or was simply happy to trade off his personal appearance for his technical skills.

Perhaps it was all part of a ploy to trap the self-confident—to breed a false sense of security as he went about the business of interrogation. Anyone smart can beat the machine and anyone at all can beat the machine when it's operated by someone like this. Or so they might be led to believe. They could see him patting his pockets searching for pens or watch him cleaning his glasses with a wrinkled handkerchief or used tissue. He may have used his appearance and his disordered gestures like an anesthetic, taking away whatever edge his subjects believed they had and then probing their hearts and minds like a skilled surgeon.

"Let me get this straight," he said. "The AD's suspicion is that the subject is involved with the Al-Madi cell, through a Saudi named Malawi who the subject believes to actually be an oil executive named Quattar."

"Correct."

"But you believe he may have been duped and that Malawi is using him to decoy us while he pursues other—as yet unknown—activities."

"Exactly."

"And his job is to effect smooth professional transitions for executives whose personal knowledge can swing whole companies into the black or onto the trash heap."

"Yes."

"Did I miss anything? Oh, I mean besides the fact that he lives way the hell up in the Hudson valley?"

"In Cornwall, on 9W. He told me he lives there because his mother does."

"Sterrittson, but the Bureau file says Sterritt."

"Yes, exactly."

"I'll smoke him out and let you know what I turn. It shouldn't take too long."

"Many thanks," I said.

As he opened the door to the interview room he started to undo his tie. "Well hello," he said, in a friendly voice, "and how are you today?" He sounded like Mr. Rogers giving away ice cream to a playground full of wide-eyed children.

I went back to my desk, removed my cell phone from my pocket, and called Richard. He didn't pick up. I left a second message, my anxiety increasing by the minute.

Thirty-five minutes later Charlie came into our bullpen. The knot of his tie was back in place. "An altar boy," he said. "I don't think he's ever lied in his life and that's saying a lot for a lawyer. The only trouble was that I was asking yes or no questions but he kept wanting to give me essay answers."

"If you asked essay questions he would have given you monosyllables," I said.

"That's right!" Charlie said. "After I unhooked him I tried to tease out some extra information but he suddenly turned into Mr. Yes or Mr. No. Either way, I don't believe he was playing me. The thing is—he's got a highly developed sense of honor but little or no sense of humor."

"That was my feeling too," I said.

"You know what else he said?"

"What's that?"

"He said he'd be OK with it if we wanted to keep him here for awhile, even if the machine cleared him. He said that he could understand our concerns and knew that the security of the city was more important than his personal convenience."

"Almost too good to be true."

"Yes. I'm still chewing on that, but there's always an outside chance that there are still some decent, public-spirited citizens out there. If there are, he's their poster child."

I smiled just as my cell phone twitched on my desk blotter.

"Did I wake it up?" Charlie asked.

"If so, thanks," I said. "I've been waiting for a call."

THIRTY-SIX

It was the AD. "Are you available at 11:00?" he asked.

"Of course," I said. "I'm at the field office now."

"Do you know the David Burke restaurant in *Bloomingdale's?*"

"I can find it."

"Yes. Meet me there at 11:00 sharp."

It's actually called *David Burke at Bloomingdale's*, a tad pretentious considering that they offer takeout as well as dine-in. I went for the "Juicy Burker," reputed to be the best burger in the city. "Make that two," the AD said, "medium rare." The waitress left with our orders and the AD leaned forward, speaking quietly.

"So Charlie thinks Willets should get a medal rather than a set of cuffs."

It was a statement, not a question.

"Right."

"And you agree."

"I do, though I defer to his judgment on the polygraph. I'm just going on instinct."

"I've been chasing wild geese all day."

"Threats that proved unfounded?"

"Uh-huh."

"A snipe hunt, maybe."

"Keeping me busy and distracted. I know that's what *you* think."

"I'm bothered by the fact that the devices we've found were all so easy to locate."

"You always find the easy things first. I'm more worried about what we haven't found," he answered.

"The sites with the devices that we've found must be searched on fixed schedules," I said.

He didn't respond to my comment, so I continued. "There are only two ways to have a clear idea of those schedules—have concealed agents at every possible site in Manhattan keeping records of the inspections and their cycles or…"

"Or?"

"Or have somebody on the inside."

"You think they may have an operative within our organization or the city's?"

"That wouldn't come as a great surprise, would it?" I asked.

He didn't respond. As the pause lengthened and became uncomfortable I spoke up again.

"Assuming we caught all of the devices we were either very lucky or unconsciously playing along with their plan."

"You shouldn't discount the possibility of luck, Gwen."

"I understand, sir. What do you want me to do?"

"I don't want to make any moves that could tip Al-Madi to the fact that we're suspicious. I want you to check out Leon Donovan. He's a known Malawi-contact. Lately he's been sitting in Southold, contemplating the cosmos. He walks out into his three-season room in the morning with a cup of coffee and the *Times*, spends the afternoon reading and falling asleep on his couch, watches the evening news, goes to bed early, buys his groceries at the *Handy Pantry* in Mattituck, still rents a DVD every now and then, and occasionally picks his nose, but we haven't detected anything more serious than that. An hour ago he was sighted in Penn Station, heading south."

"For Washington?"

"Yes. The Director has somebody waiting for him there. The D.C. agent will hand him off to you when you get there later today."

"You think Donovan's a serious player?"

"Not really. I think he's a dupe, but we might learn something by following him. It could be tricky. Photographers are sneaky; they know how to ingratiate themselves and how to become invisible if they have to. He'll have a good visual sense and an awareness of his environment. At least he should have, if he's worth a damn."

"I'll stay on him."

"I know you will. That's why I want you there and not somebody else."

"Thanks."

"Forget it. There's probably nothing at stake beyond a nuclear device and six and a few million lives."

III

HUNTING GROUND

THIRTY-SEVEN

It took me a little over thirty minutes to pack a bag and get to Penn station. The next train out was a start-and-stop local, but I was already in contact with the agent in Washington—a man named Beehler, who had the situation there in hand—so I got on board, mentally prepared for the extra hour of travel time. Donovan had paid for his ticket with a credit card and his destination was a matter of record, so he was either innocent, stupid, or planning (like everybody else) to hide in plain sight. He had also sprung for the club car, so he would be fortified with lunch and a glass or two of wine as he headed south.

I opted instead for the quiet corner of a second-class car and a pre-packaged bagel and cardboard cup of coffee. As I futzed with the packet of cream cheese and miniature wooden knife I looked out at the bleak landscape, the littered yards and the rusting rails, and thought about the old days, actually the old, old days when the prairies were dotted with corpses and whole generations were lost in an afternoon.

It wasn't all that different from the current moment. Whatever their dress, demeanor, or protestations you could never really be sure who the enemy was. Today's trading partner or neighbor might be tomorrow's attacker. In its way the prairie was like the desert; at any moment your enemy might appear, silhouetted against the horizon, prepared to butcher every member of your party. Surprise and shock were mutually-reinforcing goals and there was no sure and certain place in which to hide. Gathering in groups might simply make you a better target. Peeling off in an attempt to escape attention could mark you as the confused faun or aging stag that ultimately drew all the wolves. Brutality and fear were constants, civilians and noncombatants always at risk. Promises were empty, treaties lies, life nasty, brutish, short, and blood-soaked.

The dangers were more elusive now. Surrounded by the props of civilization and mighty architectural works of man the proximity of the predator was easily forgotten. The absence of clubs and stones and sharpened steel masked the violence of the weapons that had replaced them and the reddened hands and electric brains of those who wielded them. The smell of lifeless flesh brought it back quickly but that was in another place and time, or so we liked to believe, in the antiseptic shell where we cultivated our delusions.

Suddenly a vivid memory: my mother had always told me to ride facing the direction in which the train was traveling. "You'll get sick otherwise," she would say. Somehow it didn't work that way for me. I liked to watch what had already passed. It helped me think. It taught me lessons and offered me reminders. I like to see what we've survived and I want to be reminded of whatever's still out there haunting us. I need to look at rusted bridges and junked cars, at weeds among discarded, creosote-stained railroad ties and sparse woods that had been forests before they became hobo jungles, at faded signs on the walls of crumbling warehouses and small cottages with tar paper roofs and mismatched shingle siding. Most of all I need to look out at the people who've continued their lives amid the weight of the past and the pain, taking their children to and from school, carrying groceries in plastic bags with thin-stretched handles, patching up their homes and their lives, unaware that there were people preparing to deprive them of their futures and their dreams. I read once that no matter where you stand in the streets of London you are never more than ten feet away from a rat. It isn't a particularly comforting thought, but seeing just one in an unexpected place instantly reminds you of the invisible legion.

I tasted the remaining drops of cold coffee staining the edge of my cup, found the vendor's cart in the adjoining car, purchased a refill, and returned to my seat. The other passengers inhabited a separate world. Some read newspapers; some stared at spreadsheets on their laptops, hoping for inspiration; some slept, their chins tucked against their chests or rhythmically listing to the side with the movement of the train.

In the next car I had seen a mother with her three children. Two were asleep; the third was playing intently with a *Pokémon* game boy. All were dressed for a visit with grandma and grandpa, a week in the country with slow, sleepy mornings and comfortable evenings around the fireplace. Mulled cider and homemade soup, ripe red apples covered with caramel and heaping bowls of popcorn. Happiness is a warm, twelve-pole tipi with thick blankets and a dry smoke-hole set amid a sea of stars. With talk and quiet and love and companionship, the ponies fed and resting, the infants nursed into silent sleep, the elders leaving their sons and daughters to their urgings and desires. Paradise. Until you're attacked.

As we pulled out of Philly and passed the rubble at the edge of the Penn campus I thought about the divide that separates the civilized from the savage. It wasn't so much a line of demarcation as a tightrope on which we balanced or to which we clung desperately. I never believed that there was a thin line between madness and genius but more and more I had come to see that we are surrounded by both and the ascendancy of one or the other can be a matter of simple luck, with each of us doing what we can to tilt the odds ever so slightly toward the sunlight.

When the announcement for Baltimore came I began to gather my things and my thoughts. At New Carrollton I called Special Agent Beehler.

"Harrison," I said.

"I was just going to call you," he answered. "There's been an interesting development."

THIRTY-EIGHT

"He arrived on time, but had a drink at Union Station. I thought perhaps he was waiting for someone to meet him, but after he had his drink he left the terminal, walked to a local Irish bar, and had a couple more. I figured if he wanted something that only the latter would have he should have gone there first, since all he had at the Station was bar scotch."

"And did anyone meet him at the Irish place?" I asked.

"No. He just sat there, sipping his drinks."

"Maybe he thought he was being followed and figured he could check you out by leaving the Station and seeing who stayed on him."

"Could be, but I've got a team of three—one in a car, one on foot, and one on a messenger's bicycle. If he has any brains at all he'd know that we travel in groups and don't carry flags or wear uniforms. If he wanted to lose us on the other hand…that'd be easier."

"But also more obvious," I said.

"Yes, well, there's nothing very obvious about him. After his second drink at the bar he went back to the Station, caught a cab to the New York Avenue Hertz office, picked up a rental, and drove out to the hunt country."

"The *hunt country*?"

"The hunt country."

"Maryland or Virginia?"

"Virginia. Middleburg."

"That's, what, forty miles?"

"Forty three from Union Station, give or take a few yards."

"And what is he doing there?"

"He just ordered a second lunch. Caesar salad and a crab cake sandwich."

"Where?"

"The *Red Fox Inn*."

"No peanut soup?"

"Nope."

"He could have gotten the salad anywhere and better crab cakes closer to the bay. Did he meet someone there?"

"Not yet."

"I'm just coming into the District," I said. "They've got a car for me in the lot behind the station. I'll be there as fast as I can."

"He's not hurrying," Beehler said.

"Good," I answered.

Middleburg is the base of operations for the rural Virginia chic. Robert Duvall and Sissy Spacek drop in from time to time, as did the late Jack Kent Cook, Senator Warner, and other current hunt country celebs. The *Red Fox Inn* dates from 1728 and is smack in the middle of the village, in the shadow of the Blue Ridge and Bull Run mountains. Technically a bed-and-breakfast, most come to the inn for the drive, the atmosphere, and their signature peanut soup. The *Inn at Little Washington* has better food, nicer rooms and prices to match. It's the terminus of choice for the foodies and those celebrating an anniversary, while the *Red Fox* offers atmosphere, quaintness, a nice drive, and a chance for a celebrity sighting. There was no reason why a person like Donovan would be there, unless he had plans and motives that had so far escaped us. I said as much to Beehler and he agreed.

"Unless he's here for a battlefield tour or a meeting with somebody, there's not much reason to drive eighty miles round trip for a sandwich."

I pulled out of the lot and headed toward Constitution. "Tell me some more about the Irish place," I said.

"It's called the *Celtic Cross*," he said. "Standard fare. Harp and Guinness on tap, shooters of Black Bush, green beer on St. Paddy's Day…corned beef…cabbage…a bartender named Brendan and a pet cockroach named Kevin."

"And Donovan was absolutely not there to make contact with anyone…"

"He walked straight to the bar, had his drinks, and walked straight out again. No one approached him while he was there. He spoke to Brendan, but all he did was order his drinks."

"And he drank…?"

"Jameson, neat. And yes, we did check his bar napkins after he left—nothing underneath, nothing tucked between the folds."

I wanted to say "Good work," but I didn't want to sound patronizing. "How about at the *Inn*?"

"So far he's been alone. No trips to the toilet. He's actually reading while he eats."

"The *Qu'ran*?"

"Sorry, no. He's reading the new book by the *Da Vinci Code* guy."

"I hear it's not as good as the earlier stuff," I said.

"Yeah, me too," Beehler answered.

"I've got a thought," I said.

"Shoot."

"Why don't you send somebody into the men's room and check it out. I know it's a long shot, but what have you got to lose?"

"Actually I've got a guy in there now," Beehler said.

"Great. You're way ahead of me."

"It all goes back to the Corleones," he said. "You reach around behind a toilet tank and you never know what you might find. And don't worry…if there's anything there you'll be the first to know."

"Thanks," I said. "I appreciate it."

Five minutes later as I was crossing the Roosevelt Bridge, looking at the Kennedy Center on my right and the river below, my cell phone rang.

THIRTY-NINE

"Gwen?"

It was Richard.

"How are you?" I asked. "I was worried about you."

"I'm fine. I was incommunicado for awhile. New assignment."

"Where are you now?" I asked.

"Los Angeles."

"What are you doing there?"

"It's part of my new gig. I'll tell you about it when we meet."

"How soon will that be? I'm in Washington."

"That's where I'm headed," he said. "I'll be there tonight."

"I'm on assignment," I said, my anticipation rising. "What time will you be in?"

"A little after eight, eastern time. I'm on the 1:00 United flight to Dulles."

A second call came in—from Beehler. "I've got to go," I said. "Call me tonight when you arrive. If I can't pick you up then I'll call you at the first opportunity."

"Go," he said. At least he was alive and well, I thought, as I hit the button to accept Beehler's call.

"Harrison…" I said.

"Great minds travel along the same path," he answered.

"What did you find?"

"I'm not entirely sure yet, but there was a note in the men's room. It was in a plastic slipcase, inside the toilet tank."

"What did it say?"

"You'll have to see it. There's a map, some letters and a set of numbers. The location is not explicitly identified."

"Anything obvious?"

"Just with the numbers; there's a date—Thursday the 11th."

"That's the day after tomorrow."

"Yes, it is. Where are you now?"

"I'm just getting on 66."

"Donovan just ordered some cobbler and a cup of black coffee."

"He hasn't retrieved the message yet?"

"No. There's something else too."

"What's that?"

"There were two latents on the slipcase. A thumb and an index finger."

"That makes me a little nervous. I don't like it when things seem easy or obvious."

"I thought you might say that," Beehler answered. "But sometimes we *do* have luck on our side."

"I like what Knute Rockne said about luck and divine providence," I said.

"What's that?" he asked.

"He said that God's on the side of the team with the biggest tackles."

"Hopefully that's us."

I clicked off and pressed harder against the accelerator. I crossed over Glebe Road; a few minutes later I passed Lee Highway, driving along the edge of Falls Church. The traffic slowed as I approached Leesburg Pike, below Tysons Corner, but as I got closer to the beltway I was able to do some broken-field running. I had only been gone a few months and was struck by the density of the traffic and the new construction that was filling in every available square yard of earth. The kiss-and-ride dropoff at the Vienna metro station was congested even in late afternoon and the approach to the Chain Bridge Road interchange between Fairfax and Oakton was a half-mile-long parking lot.

As I headed further west the civil war names appeared—Mosby Woods, Antietam Ave, and Route 50—the Lee Jackson Memorial Highway—which I took into Middleburg. Suddenly it began to sprinkle and then rain more heavily, the initial windshield smears obscuring my views of the landscape. By the time I approached Middleburg the rain had stopped, though occasional drops fell from the trees and the wide-wheeled SUV's dotting the highway continued to kick up a combination of moisture and grit.

I talked to Beehler briefly. He promised me the full use of his team and informed me that Donovan was paying his check. "He'll probably just be getting in his car when you arrive. I'll put all of my men on him; they'll tagteam him, so he'll have no inkling that he's being followed. I'll brief you on the current details when you arrive." He also told me to leave my car behind the building, with the keys in the ignition. One of his people would drive it back to the city for me.

As I pulled in front of the stone building housing the restaurant Donovan's Taurus came into view at the corner. He eased his way through the stop sign, turned left and headed east. There was a dark sedan behind him. I looked in my rear-vision mirror and saw a second car pulling away from the curb, a few hundred feet ahead of him. I wondered where number three was.

Beehler caught my eye as soon as I walked through the door. He had asked me what I was wearing, so that he could project a sense of familiarity to anyone nearby who was watching. He himself was out of Bureau uniform. He was wearing beige cotton slacks, cordovan loafers, a tattersall shirt, reddish-brown sweater, and tweed jacket. Captain Preppy comes to the Hunt Country.

I gave him a blow-by kiss to complete the scene as the waitress approached. He ordered cobbler and coffee; he told me later he'd been anxious to try it after watching Donovan eat his. I ordered tea. The waitress offered a basket of brioche on the side and I took her up on it. She also brought homemade jelly and butter.

"I always liked this place," I said, as I surveyed the room as inconspicuously as possible. The full array of hunting pictures were still in place, including my favorite, a drawing of a fox sitting comfortably in a leather, Queen Anne chair, in a room with wide-plank hardwood flooring, small brass candelabras and dark plaid wallpaper. There was a glass of sherry on a table beside the chair. The picture was entitled "Sly Boots."

"I saw him leave," I said. "Your guys had him surrounded."

"*Your* guys now," he said. "The New York AD asked for full cooperation and we're happy to provide it."

"Much appreciated," I said. "Where do we stand?"

"I faxed the latents downtown," Beehler said. "No response yet. We lit up his Taurus with a Bureau bug that looks like a standard LoJack device. It'll never raise any questions on a rental and it will appear to be inactivated if he checks. Just in case, I put a backup device on the battery. It's smooth to the touch and undetectable—assuming he's brave enough to touch something that could give him a shock. If he leaves the car we can still track him. I put a thin coat of clear compound on his accelerator and break pedal. He'll get some of it on his sole and a good bit will adhere to his instep and the edge of his shoe. Microscopic particles are visible with the proper optical instrument. It'll be like breadcrumbs in the forest, except that no one but us can see them."

"What was on the drawing?" I asked.

He reached into his inside jacket pocket and removed his digital camera. "I'll blow this up as soon as I get to a printer," he said, "but there's not a whole lot here." He hit the power button and then the button next to the LCD screen. He handed me the camera and I looked at the image. There were two lines that appeared to be borders and some space in between, an X, the letters TR, and the date Thursday—11.

"Roosevelt Island?" I asked.

FORTY

"Interesting thought," Beehler said. "There's not much there to blow up except for the statue of T. R., but a lot of interesting things would be in range...the White House...the Kennedy Center...the Pentagon... stop me when I mention something that's *not* an attractive target.

"I figure Roosevelt Island to be about 100 acres," he said. "The vegetation is dense—lots of cover and concealment."

"Some solid ground, but also marsh and swamp," I said. "You can only access it from the northbound lane of the GW Parkway, and then you have to get onto the island itself by way of a single wooden bridge. One machine gun could keep a lot of people at bay if they were looking for a pitched battle. On the other hand, they could fire off a few rounds and then exit on the river. At night...with scuba gear...they'd have a fair chance of escaping unscathed. The island's closed then and with its awkward location it would take our side five or ten minutes to realize that we were under fire, locate the likely source, and dispatch troops and vehicles to the point of origin. Under those circumstances that would be an eternity. A skilled crew could already be on shore and changing into fresh clothes. They could also come in and get out by boat. Maybe use a combination. Feint with one route, but take another. The possibility for diversions would be nearly endless. They could also block any possibility of entry except by boat or helicopter—take out Key Bridge, Memorial Bridge, the 14th Street Bridge..."

"Or just make additional mischief—take out the Lincoln Memorial, the Jefferson Memorial, or Reagan National," he added.

Beehler was now fully engaged; he called over the waitress. "We've got to make some phone calls," he said. "We'll be right back to finish our food."

"I'll warm your coffee when you return," she said.

We hurried to his car and he booted up his computer. "Ladies first…" he said. I googled *mortars*. "They would need a high trajectory," I said, "if they wanted to go for all of the sites we discussed.

"Here we go," I said. "The old reliable 4.2 inch. No longer in our active inventory, but there are plenty around."

"Mechanized, usually," Beehler said. "That would make it harder to bring in."

"Hard but not impossible."

"What does it weigh?"

I moved to another site. "A lot," I said, "626 pounds."

"What if you break it into component parts?"

I surfed to another site. "Seven pieces," I said. "The largest is 158 pounds, the sighting equipment only 4 pounds."

"Becoming more doable," Beehler said.

"Pick your ammunition," I said. "A high explosive round is effective for more than four miles. "White phosphorus will go nearly that far. Imagine people on the mall with burning bits of the stuff in their flesh. You have to dig it out with knife points. Putting it under water doesn't stop the burning process."

Beehler nodded in agreement. His mood was somber now.

"The rate of fire goes down the longer you shoot, but the standard rate is 18 rounds per minute for the first 60 seconds. How much damage could you do from Roosevelt Island with 18 mortar rounds?"

He didn't answer.

"It gets worse," I said. "Just a little reminder—the weapon was first developed to deliver chemical agents."

We passed on the remaining coffee and tea and headed toward the city. I continued to work the computer. The island consisted of 91 acres;

Beehler was close. T. R. died on January 6, 1919. The island was purchased in 1932 and with the glistening speed of the federal government, congress approved funding for the memorial a mere 28 years later. It was finally dedicated in 1967. They'd have to move a whole lot faster if the Al-Madi cell decided to set up operations there and use the nation's capital for a mortar range.

FORTY-ONE

While we drove I worked the computer and the phone. The agents following Donovan reported that he was making a brief visit to the Virginia wine country.

"What?" Beehler said.

"A place called *Volterra*," I said. "Known for its sparkling wine. Donovan bought two bottles. He's at a place called *Naked Mountain* now. Their specialty is Chardonnay, if you're interested. Any messages?"

"They don't need much direction. They'll keep an eye out for anyone he might meet there. Ask them to give us a call when he's moving again."

"Will do," I said. I then called the Director's office. He returned my call in four minutes and I briefed him on Donovan's movements. He asked if Beehler had given the latent check the highest possible priority. I told the Director that he had and that we expected the results any minute. He cleared us to visit Roosevelt Island, asked for hourly updates, and clicked off.

The call on the latents came on Beehler's phone. He snapped it off of his belt and told them to talk to me. The tech's name was Carol Taylor.

"No match," she said. "Sorry."

"How about points for possible comparison?"

"Plenty," she said. "There was simply nothing corresponding in any of the databases. Nothing even close."

I thanked her and then informed Beehler.

"I'm not surprised," he said. "Anyone with prints on file would have been more careful."

"Probably," I said, though I still wasn't convinced that we weren't being set up.

It took us another thirty minutes to get into the city, get onto the northbound segment of the Parkway, and park in the lot on the western side of the river. As we walked across the bridge and onto Roosevelt Island I put my hand around Beehler's arm. You can never be sure where the prying eyes are and whether or not they're on you, so I decided to keep up the act.

We had made our plans before arriving at the island, since there was always the possibility that we were under auditory as well as visual surveillance. It wouldn't take anything more than a simple stone age-technology mic to overhear our conversations.

The air was thick on the island, the humidity spreading down through the trees, hanging over the footpath, and seeping into the soft and moist earth. The compensation was the rich green of the surrounding vegetation. From the Potomac, suddenly, to Puget Sound.

"I'd like to just walk in the woods awhile," I said, as preplanned.

"Let's meet back at the statue in twenty minutes," he answered.

I made my way through the trees, trying to project an awe in the presence of nature while actually looking for possible gun emplacements or potential storage areas for weapons and equipment. The foliage was thick, but at night, with the island deserted, a small stand of trees could be felled quickly and a vertical field of fire created. The traffic on the bridge and parkway created a hum that would diminish at night but not completely disappear. It would be useful in masking any sounds of activity on the island. It was also safe to assume that any terrorist worth his hire would be equipped with night-vision goggles, so that the likelihood of any tell-tale lights amid the darkness was virtually nil.

I looked for shoreline that could be used for an amphibious landing and departure and there was more than enough of it to meet the needs of a small team. I'd seen fifty-foot motor yachts in the waters above Key Bridge, so a large vessel would have no problem coming by the island, unloading people and cargo, and leaving a smaller vessel behind, one capable of evading easy detection in the darkness. I was thinking maybe a rubber raft with a battery-powered electric motor. Run silent, run quick.

Some tender soul from the National Park Service had installed a succession of bird feeders with squirrel baffles along the main path leading to the memorial. They were each doing a brisk business. Cardinals, jays and flickers were all vying for feeder space, with sparrows and grosbeaks doing their best to stay in the game. I heard some noise along the ground and remembered the presence of snakes in and around the water, but when I looked more closely I saw a gray squirrel, intent upon an activity involving either the burial or retrieval of nuts.

There were more tourists in the area than I expected. All on the monument circuit. Most were simply walking to and from the memorial, snapping their pictures of the giant bronze of T. R. before getting back on the parkway. The path really wasn't designed for much more. The soldiers from the Pentagon who spent their lunch period jogging along the river seldom came up this far and the picnic crowd generally stayed closer to the Mall. It was so close and yet—in its way—so remote. A perfect place from which to attack.

After I rallied with Beehler and we got in his car he nodded a dispirited 'No' to me. Neither of us had seen any evidence of suspicious activity but I took the gesture to also be an expression of frustration at the dangers implicit in the site and the ease with which they could be exploited.

I checked in with the Director and briefed him while Beehler drove back into the District, taking Key Bridge to the Whitehurst Freeway and on into the stone, brick and cement jungle of activity that was central Washington. The FBI building had been sited in the old peep show district broadly described as '14th Street' but most of that trade was now gone. Bureaucracy trumps sex, especially in Washington. For some the two are commensurate.

The people and equipment in the headquarters building probably wouldn't help us very much, but we thought we might stand a better chance of shaking some information loose if we were in the belly of the beast, closer to the super computers and the army of staff and special agents that at least shared our goals and our anxieties.

We treated ourselves to two cups of recently-brewed coffee and some not-so-recently pre-packaged sandwiches. I went for the cheese and tomato; Beehler selected something that looked vaguely like beef. They were easier to open than cd packages, but not by much. After Beehler took his first bite and fought back a grimace he turned to me and said, "There's something I just don't understand..."

FORTY-TWO

"What's that?" I asked.

"Leon Donovan," he answered. "Why him?"

"He looks like a time-warped hippie in an academic uniform," I said. "Maybe this is his way of settling old Vietnam scores. A lot of people from that generation never got over it—people on both sides of the issue."

"I'm been over his file a dozen times," Beehler said. "He was rousted a couple times when he was in college—sit-ins, demonstrations, the usual—but nothing big, certainly nothing involving any overt violence. The dean of students bailed the groups out on each occasion and little Leon went back to class, completed his work, and graduated. He never joined the Weather Underground or any other such group."

"And he was fingerprinted, so if he pulled anything later we'd have a rap sheet and a paper trail."

"Oh yes. They all were, basically just to make a point, let them know that they were now 'in the system' and that the big bad government would be keeping its eyes on them."

"What college did he attend?"

"U-VA."

"Not exactly a hotbed of radicalism," I said.

"No, there were still a lot of 'gentleman C' types there in those days. As far as I can tell he was just indulging in some rites-of-passage stuff; he was hardly alone at it. Demonstrations were a great place to meet women, for example; at least that's what I've been told."

"I don't think of Virginia as a big arts place, though. Literature, maybe. Language. Foreign affairs. And yet he was able to make a living as a photographer…"

"Right. He actually majored in English. A few years after he graduated he took the New York School of Photography course. Pricey and legit, not a fly-by-night 'draw the pirate' kind of arts school. He started out in retail sales jobs, but he must have reached a point where he decided he wanted to do something else."

"He inherited money recently," I said. "What was the source of that?"

"Insurance. His father actually owned a title insurance company. His mother sold it when the father died. Leon inherited a tidy share of the profit when she passed and he'll be the beneficiary—ultimately—of her policy as well."

"What do you mean, ultimately?"

"It's a gift deal. She sold the company for $12 million, gave Leon half and various and sundry charities the other half. Her own life policy—worth $2 million, was given to her college as part of a trust. They get the income for ten years and then he gets the corpus at the end of the ten-year period."

"Which school?"

"One of the eastern girls' schools. Smith, I think." He thought about that a second and said, "Sorry, *women's* school."

I smiled. "So he gets the 2 million in deflated dollars, but has plenty to tide him over in the meantime."

"Right. There are also some significant tax advantages, I guess. Anyway, the good news is he doesn't have to take pictures of corporate headquarters buildings and smiling executives for the stockholders' magazine any more. He's now a card-carrying member of the idle rich and can take pictures of flowers and sunsets instead. If he feels like it. He can also just sit around and stare intently at his navel or trim his toenails unless and until he decides to blow up a building or a city. Which brings me to where I started. I still don't understand why he'd want to do that. Life is good, or at least it *should* be for him at this point."

"Always hard to say. It could be a personal vendetta or possibly a long-simmering political thing. He might also just be a nutcake."

"Not likely that they'd trust a nutcake with an important role in a major operation, though."

"No, though it certainly wouldn't be the first time. They always seem to be able to find people willing to strap explosives to themselves… and I'm pretty sure they're not promising the women the roster of 42 virgins they're promising the men. Maybe he's a dull guy looking for a little excitement and some very bad guys glommed onto him and told him they were going to make him a star."

"Maybe he's a groupie, like the 60's New Yorkers who wanted Black Panthers at their cocktail parties."

"Hard to say," I answered. "Before we can put him on a shrink's couch we'd better take him off the battlefield. I don't want him to have the chance to celebrate with that wine he just bought. When we finish here I'll nose around and see if I can find any points of additional contact between him and the Al-Madi cell. He's obviously in bed with them. I'll try to find out how and when the courtship started."

We worked through the available databases and briefed the director again on what we knew and what we didn't. In the meantime I got a voice mail message from Richard, telling me that his plane was now scheduled to arrive at 8:45. I tried to tease any information I could from the fingerprints on the *Red Fox Inn* message, came up dry, and checked in with the surveillance team. Donovan was holed up at the *Key Bridge Marriott*, dining on some room-service risotto and a tiramisu. Interesting spot—well within range of a mortar aiming west/northwest from Roosevelt Island.

FORTY-THREE

By 7:30 Beehler had left to check in with the surveillance team. Sometimes there are minor details that take on major proportions when you chew on them long enough; you don't know until you've talked them through with those who are actually on the front lines. Meanwhile I stopped trying to tap the dry well of fingerprint data and instead ran a basic search on Donovan's father's company, wondering if anyone had put the information on his son's newly-obtained wealth together with accounts of his past bouts with political activism. It was a stretch, but I didn't have any other drawers to open or buttons to push.

The company was called *Hearthstone Insurance*. Based in Cincinnati, it was once linked with a chain of S & L's, called *Hilltop Savings*. The loan officers at *Hilltop* tried to steer borrowers to *Hearthstone*. In turn, *Hilltop* and *Hearthstone* were linked with *Country Lane Realty* and a legal firm by the name of *Hubble and Brand*. The firm was started by old man Hubble (Charles W.), who came up with the notion of a seamless circle of service—developing property, selling it, holding the mortgage on it, insuring it, and then selling it again and again and again. All quite legal, of course.

The only slight element of a conspiracy against the public concerned the fact that Ohio has a provision for registering certain parcels of real estate and then guaranteeing the title. The county recorders' offices then maintained two sets of records, one for regular property and one for registered land. In examining the title of a normal parcel, the attorney was required to check some fifty years of records, searching for possible liens and any glitches in the chain of ownership. This would always take hours and could take days. With registered land, however, the state certified the title and the registry books carried a single page per parcel. The title examination took minutes. The attorneys' charges, however, were based on the value of the property rather than the ease of the examination. In dealing with registered land—wherever possible—*Hubble and Brand* got maximum fees for minimal efforts. Again, it was all quite legal—a strategy based on an initial investment for newly-developed property resulting in a lifetime of easy pickings, assuming that the initial investment was made up in large volume later.

This would be true in spades for high-end deals, since boondock property generally involves a higher proportion of slips and snags. When Zeke and Zeb sell land adjoining Dogbreath Creek the country lawyers aren't as careful as their city counterparts would be in handling property on Versailles Lane or Blenheim Boulevard. *Hubble and Brand* stayed on the boulevard whenever possible and old man Hubble's college chum, Barnard Donovan, proved to be a beneficiary of the plan when he was cut in for a share of the action.

The only people who went to Smith and Amherst in the 30's and 40's were the progeny of old-money scions, for whom the later acquisition of an insurance company would be a classic case of the rich getting richer rather than one of up-from-poverty bootstrapping based on pluck and luck. The first surprise in all this was the fact that their bouncing baby boy attended a public institution, though U-VA's gentlemanly reputation placed it above the garden-variety schools that expanded in reaction to the GI Bill and, later, the Sputnik scare. The second was the lad's downscale career choice. Even Karsh and Bachrach were probably seen as tradesmen by the membership of Barnard Donovan's club.

I searched and surfed some more and turned a little additional information. Donovan had had a brief flirtation with print journalism and short stints with the *Baltimore Sun* and *Chicago Trib*. One of his photographs made it into a yearbook of memorable shots compiled by the University of Missouri Journalism School—an image of Pat Nixon lighting up a cigarette. That small success apparently led nowhere, since he surfaced next as a photographer for the 3M corporation, Xerox, and IBM. I wondered if daddy's connections had been tapped when other opportunities evaporated.

Donovan was married, briefly, in the 70's. His wife Carol Dalton (I was expecting a Muffy), was the daughter of the owner of a chemical company specializing in industrial resins. The elder Daltons were prominent fixtures within the Chicago society scene, with a multimillion-dollar lakeshore residence in Winnetka and a snowbird retreat in West Palm Beach. No children from the Donovan/Dalton marriage and no specifics on the reasons for the breakup. I aligned the dates; he was working at the *Chicago Trib* at the time of his wedding. Perhaps his own family connections were sufficient to counterbalance his workaday employment when he and his wife were in black tie and gown.

The more I combed the less I seemed to find. There was no apparent or even plausible prior connection between Leon Donovan and jihadist terrorism and nothing in his past to suggest a basis for such a relationship. I couldn't deny what I had seen with my own eyes, however, and the absence of any further evidence was proving to be increasingly frustrating.

I came at him from the other direction, running searches on Al-Madi and his organization, but the closest I came to a Leon Donovan was a Leonard Dunstar, a retired state department official twenty years Donovan's senior. Eventually I looked at my watch, realized that Richard would arrive in a little over an hour, secured my car, and drove west toward Dulles.

The building had acquired an addition in the 90's which maintained Saarinen's original design—adding a new set of supporting hooks to the expanded, curved concrete roof. Some described the roof as a giant hammock supported by a row of parallel trees. The light glowing through the sheets of glass below is always a special sight as the access road turns and the structure comes into full view. Not quite Stonehenge on Salisbury

Plain, but close. Stonehenge has the benefit of the burial barrows leading the eye to the monument; perhaps the Al-Madi cell had plans to add some bodies to the earth around Dulles some day.

My Bureau credentials enabled me to go, unticketed, to the arrival gate area in the pertinent midfield terminal. The 'mobile lounge' bus (increasingly rare, as Dulles' gates and concourses metastasize) was sparsely populated; the traffic was coming in the other direction—toward the main terminal. I got to the pertinent area in five or six minutes, checked the arrivals screen—his flight was still on schedule—looked at my watch, and saw that I had a fifteen-minute window in which to make myself look presentable. I touched up my makeup, did what I could with my suddenly-unruly hair, slipped an Altoid into my mouth, and walked toward the gate. Except for an elderly attendant with a wheelchair, I was the only one there to greet the plane. I wondered what would happen when we met, wondered what he might say, wondered what he might do.

FORTY-FOUR

As I leaned back in the black, vinyl-clad seat I suddenly felt movement under my arm. For a second I had forgotten that my cell phone was set on *vibrate*. I removed it from my pocket, checked the number on the screen, hit the green telephone icon, and said "Hello," trying not to sound overly eager. Old teenage habits die hard.

"Gwen?…Richard," he said.

"Hi. Did you just land?"

"Yes. We just got the *all clear* from the cell-phone police. Where are you?"

"Waiting for you at the gate. Check that. Waiting *expectantly* for you at the gate."

"Great," he said. "We should be there in a few minutes. How are you?"

I liked the sound of the *great*. "I'm fine," I said. "I'm looking forward to seeing you. Have you eaten?"

"No, I passed on the mini-snack. You?"

"I've been waiting to join you."

"Excellent," he said. "Oh, here we are. We didn't have to taxi hardly at all. Let me get my things together; I'll see you in a couple of minutes."

As the passengers filed out of the plane, turning left and proceeding in the direction of the mobile lounge bay, I gave them enough room to pass while I watched for Richard. It took him nearly ten minutes to appear at the top of the jetway. When his eyes caught mine he was smiling. Carrying an attaché case and a thick garment bag, he hurried toward me.

I held out my arms, wondering if he would accept the invitation. He came in close and kissed me on the mouth without a second's hesitation, then held me in an extended hug. I kissed him back and said, "Hey, I like that greeting."

"I really missed you," he said.

"I've missed you too," I said. As we turned and walked toward the mobile lounge stop, he reached around my waist, still holding the attaché case, which bounced off of my right hip.

"Sorry," he said.

"Here," I said, taking the case and holding it in my hand. He tightened his grip and I felt his fingers against my waist.

He had no other luggage, so we were able to go directly to my car. We stood close together on the mobile lounge, leaning into one another as the driver accelerated and then eased his foot against the brake. With each movement of the bus I felt more and more that we were actually becoming something like, well, a couple.

"That was lovely of you to meet me that way," he said. "I guess our credentials do come in handy for some things."

"I know that the airport's safer this way, but it's not the same," I answered. "It's good to be greeted."

"I didn't know if you'd kiss me back," he said, suddenly, "but I figured it was worth a try. If I hadn't I would never have known."

"Never?" I said, taking advantage of the lurching bus and moving against him. "That doesn't sound very optimistic."

"I was scared to death," he said.

"Really?"

"Not scared of you. Scared of the wrong answer."

"No need," I said, looking straight into his eyes.

He leaned forward and kissed me again. "I may just keep doing that," he said.

We walked over to my car in the short-term lot. Dulles continued to feel like a work-in-progress, with plywood ramps and elbow-level tape indicating the pathways between the terminal, the taxi lanes, courtesy bus pickup points, and adjoining parking areas. When we got in the car I asked him where he wanted to go for dinner. "Just a second," he said, as he leaned across the seat, slipped his hand around my waist and kissed me more deeply. Finally he sat back and said, "OK...dinner?"

"Dinner," I answered.

FORTY-FIVE

We made it to McLean by 9:25; my restaurant of choice didn't close until 10:00 and at this comparatively late hour we wouldn't need reservations. *Cafe Tatti* is a tiny European restaurant in a strip mall on Old Dominion Drive. There for nearly four decades, its name is Italian, its menu eclectic, its owners Greek. We were directed to a corner table which offered as much privacy as *Cafe Tatti* affords. After a glass of wine we each suddenly realized that we were famished.

I had soup and fish, Richard salad and lamb. After the second glass of wine he was reaching across the table and holding my hand.

"I've never been here before," he said.

"Nice, isn't it?" I said.

"*Very* nice. Soft lights, good wine, perfect company."

"So what have you been up to?" I asked, not letting go of his hand.

"Actually I've got a completely new assignment. I'm working as a liaison with the Secret Service. Part of the Homeland Security reorganization. They want the agencies to talk to one another more and it's my job to make sure that the Bureau and Secret Service stay in close touch."

"Presidential detail?"

"Yes."

"That's very interesting," I said, my curiosity suddenly at war with my desire to keep his attention focused on my hand and my eyes instead of on our respective work.

"I was just in your old neighborhood. The president was visiting Mount Rushmore with the new British P.M. I was in the advance party and I squeezed out an extra day and a half to take a tour of my own."

"What did you see?"

"Geological sites. Very, very old rocks. The Wind River Valley. Battlefields. Massacre sites…"

"Little Bighorn?"

"Yes, and the sites around Sheridan."

"How did the P.M. like the Black Hills?"

"A lot. I didn't realize how rich the area was in natural resources. Not just gold and silver, but beryl, mica, feldspar and other things. We saw a sign that described the area as the richest place on earth."

I could see where this conversation was going and was touched by his desire to connect with me, though I was hoping for a different topic and a different direction.

"The Congress awarded $105 million in compensation," he said. "I wonder what the net worth would be of the literally millions of acres taken from the Sioux."

"Hard to say," I answered, "but a whole lot more than $105 million."

"What's that," he asked, "the cost of one 737?"

"I'm not sure," I answered, "but I appreciate your thinking about it."

"It's hard not to, once you know the facts."

"I know," I said, "but thinking about it too much can make you sad and there are too many happy things that might be forgotten in the process. So how's your dinner?"

"Excellent," he answered.

"How long will you be here?" I asked, regretting it the moment the words slipped out. I was starting to sound like my mother when I arrived for holidays or school breaks.

"A week," he said. "How about you?"

"I'm not sure," I answered. "At least a couple days."

He reached out with his other hand and said, "Let's use it wisely."

"Sounds good to me," I answered, wondering how I would ever be able to do that and still spend time with him.

FORTY-SIX

As we made our way through dessert and coffee I wondered where the evening was headed.

"Where do you stay when you're in D.C.?" I asked.

"*Key Bridge Marriott*," he said. "The Bureau gets a special rate."

And neighbors like Leon Donovan, I thought.

"How about you?" he asked. "Where are you staying?"

"I haven't checked in yet," I said. "I've got a reservation in Crystal City."

"At the Hilton?"

"Yes."

"Good buffet," he said.

"So I've been told," I said. "Also location, location, location. Actually I came here to check on somebody. He happens to be staying at the *Key Bridge Marriott*."

"Want to be close to him tonight?" Richard asked.

"I'm not sure that's a good idea," I said. "I've followed him before. I don't know what kind of memory he has but I don't want to risk jogging it."

"I understand," he said.

"It's nothing about you," I said. "This is potentially very big and I can't afford to take any chances."

"Possible terrorist event?"

"Yes," I said.

"I thought the likely target was New York."

"Some still think so, but I think they're wrong. The AD's letting me follow up on my intuitions. We have a record of a previous contact between the guy at the *Marriott* and a major New York cell—*in Washington*. Now he's back."

"I'm amazed we haven't heard anything," Richard said. "It makes no sense at all—especially with the President and British P.M. together. Needless to say the terrorist opposition hasn't been very happy with the previous cooperation between us and the Brits. If they had a chance to obtain revenge for Iraq they'd take it. Big, big headlines."

The reality started to sink in. "Maybe there *is* a connection," I said. "When will they be here?"

"Thursday," he answered. "The 11th."

"That's the day we're concerned about," I said. I had paused briefly before saying it. In moments like this you have to trust someone, even though the possibility remained of an inside figure within the Bureau or Secret Service who was keeping information from the presidential detail. If the action really was to take place in Washington, the New York AD and Bureau Director should be clean; otherwise they wouldn't have permitted me to sniff out the situation and offer me the Beehler team in support of the operation. Still, you can never be sure. Perhaps they thought I'd be unable to do anything anyway and allowing me to come to Washington would serve as cover for them later. Either way I decided to roll the dice and share the information with Richard. In an instant I had thought of him as a possible lover, then a possible assassin, and suddenly, again, as my most trusted confidant.

"Is the P.M. going to be in Blair House or the White House?" I asked.

"Neither," he said. "The two are flying in from the coast late Thursday morning on Air Force One. They're landing at Dulles and going directly to Vienna to attend a performance at Wolf Trap. Immediately after that the P.M. will return to Dulles and fly to London. The President is going to Camp David for a long weekend; that's the current plan, at least. They're not going into Washington at all."

I thought about that for a moment, remembered the scant but precise documentary evidence with which we had been working, thought about it some more and saw the picture emerge—all very loud and very clear. We had been wrong, completely wrong, life-and-death wrong.

FORTY-SEVEN

"We've followed our suspect around the northern Virginia countryside and turned a document," I said. "It carries the date of the eleventh and includes a diagram that appears to be a central locus between two lines that appear to represent borders. There are also the letters *t* and *r*. We assumed that the *TR* referred to Teddy Roosevelt and, hence, Roosevelt Island, in the middle of the Potomac, with the borders being the respective shorelines or, possibly, the highways beyond the shores."

"Great place to set up shop," Richard said. "Rich targets all within easy range. You'd need something with a high trajectory. You couldn't bring in a large artillery piece very easily, but you could move in a mortar without too much trouble, particularly if you were doing it at night. With all those woods you could even move it in months in advance and bury it in parts, then reassemble it quickly when you were ready to begin shooting."

"Exactly what we were thinking," I said. "But while you would be able to hit the White House, Blair House, the Pentagon, and dozens of other attractive terrorist targets, it's a long way to Vienna or Dulles. We didn't find anything on Roosevelt Island that looked suspicious. It looks as if we've been wrong from the get-go. The t and the r could refer to the toll road."

"You've got the Dulles toll road on one side of Wolf Trap and Leesburg Pike on the other," Richard said. "There's even a Wolf Trap exit off of the toll road that's used during concerts. It's close, very close. Close enough for them to erect walls that insulate the facility against the noise from the access road and the toll road."

Washington bureaucracy: the Dulles access road is controlled by the FAA and restricted to airport traffic only. On either side of it are the eastbound and westbound lanes of the Dulles toll road. Police patrol the airport exits, trolling for cars that evade the tolls by using the access road. The toll road itself was paid off decades ago, but the charges continue—a fat cash cow that helps swell the Virginia tax coffers. Day by day the traffic increases as the Dulles corridor expands and the remaining land is built out with subdivisions, corporate headquarters, and the strip malls that provide support for them—a nearly endless vista of ingress and egress points with tollbooths and palms into which you drop handfuls of quarters.

"What a sweet target," I said. "They could kill the president, the British prime minister, and thousands of innocent bystanders."

"They like to kill innocent bystanders," Richard said, "but most of all they like to grab the headlines. Changing the New York skyline in striking the trade center had both imagistic and symbolic value, but we've tended to forget their desire to hit civilian targets in Washington. To most people the Pentagon is a military target, but they planned to strike the civilian government as well. They always like revenge and they always like to make the point that they're actually capable of accomplishing what they set out to do. It gives their supporters heart."

"Maybe this is their second try at a strike on the 11th," I said.

"Maybe this time they're better prepared," Richard answered.

"Or at least believe they are," I said. "The name of their operation in New York—that is, the operation we thought would be in New York— was *Huis-clos*. No exit. We thought they were sealing the city by taking out its bridges and tunnels, then exploding gas lines and raining down fire of various kinds on the people trapped inside. Perhaps the operation is much more literally titled."

"Fire in a crowded theatre?"

"Yes, and with no possibility of escape."

"I've got to call my people," Richard said.

"What if one of them is on the other side?"

"You think that's a possibility?"

"Somebody had access to the security cycles in New York and put explosives in place prior to the sites' being checked. Putting the explosives there was no mean feat, so it's not as if they're completely incompetent. By the same token, they were able to install them in such a way as to enable us to find them and hence believe that we had prevented them from succeeding."

"It could be somebody in New York—somebody in city government."

"It could," I answered, "but it could also be somebody in Homeland Security, somebody at the next level."

"So you think we should lone wolf it?" he asked.

"I think we should go on a picnic tomorrow—just be a couple trying to find a little time alone. Maybe we'll see something in the process. If we do we can decide who we want to tell."

"Even if there *is* a mole and he tips off the terrorists so that they shut down the operation—that would still be a form of victory," Richard said.

"I agree," I answered, "but what if we could shut down their operation and catch them as well?"

"Better still," he answered, in a tone of understatement, "but I still have another question."

"Yes?" I asked.

"Where are we going to spend the rest of the evening?"

FORTY-EIGHT

I knew that I would have to stay in constant touch with Beehler as well as convince him that I was doing something productive on my own, but I didn't mention that to Richard at the time and risk spoiling the moment. We bagged the *Marriott* and the *Crystal City Hilton* and took interconnecting rooms at the Tysons *Crowne Plaza*. Though newly renovated it was a little downscale for the occasion, but I wasn't really sure I was ready for the *occasion* quite yet. He had just kissed me for the first time, after all. I figured the interconnecting rooms were a nice compromise. Besides, it would give me the opportunity to check in with Beehler without turning my necessary duties into a distraction for Richard. I was trying to be faithful to both my life and my work, figuring that if I didn't pay serious attention to the latter the former might cease to exist. Again I was concerned that I might be indulging in melodrama, but I was enough of a professional to realize that the worst I could imagine was probably not too far from the terrorists' intentions and aspirations.

That didn't mean that I was ready to risk my life—particularly if there was very little of it left anyway—without creating a memory or two, so after I talked to Beehler (Donovan was still tucked away for the night) and told him and eventually the AD and Director that I wanted to follow a hunch tomorrow (promising always to stay in immediate touch, should anything develop), I showered, slipped on a nightshirt, knocked quietly, and opened the door to Richard's room.

He was lying on the single, queen-size bed, wearing a grey tee shirt and white boxers. "Well, at least we've got the briefs or boxers issue sorted out," I said.

"I agonized for a few minutes," he said, "and then did the right thing—I picked out whatever was clean."

I walked over to the bed, sat beside him and then curled over into his arms. We kissed deeply, several times, and I put my face against his shoulder and my arm around his waist.

"Now I'm really conflicted," he said.

"In what way?" I asked.

"I've been thinking about people who want to kill us and now you've suddenly given me something else to think about—something much more attractive. On the other hand there's always the ugly possibility that their plot might actually succeed."

"You're reading *my* mind," I said.

"There's a really good side though," he said.

"What's that?" I asked.

"Now we have something to live for. In addition to all the other things, of course, but something big and something personal."

"That's right," I said, pulling him toward me and kissing him again.

"I'm very, very happy," he said.

"Why?" I asked.

"Because…you're comfortable with me…like this."

"I've always been comfortable with you," I said. "Just because we had more clothes on…"

He smiled. "When you met me at the plane I wasn't sure what would happen. Now I'm reassured."

"About what?"

"About…about the fact that you must have been thinking of me as more than just a friend for some time now or we wouldn't be here like this so quickly."

"Maybe I'm just easy."

"I don't think so," he said. "Reticent, maybe. Guarded, maybe. Careful...but not easy."

"Like you said earlier—maybe we don't have all that much time and we should use it wisely."

"I wouldn't be here like this," he said, "unless I believed that you would want to be here beside me, regardless of the external circumstances."

"Right answer," I said, as we kissed again, this time longer and deeper.

FORTY-NINE

As we wended our way through the industrial forest of Tysons Corner and its back- and frontage roads, heading toward Leesburg Pike and Wolf Trap, I summarized for Richard what I had been able to find that morning on the internet.

"It was a gift from Mrs. Shouse, originally Ms. Filene. Hence the main performance facility is the Filene Center. Quite an interesting woman. President Ford bestowed the Presidential Medal of Freedom on her and the Queen made her a Dame Commander of the British Empire. She got similar forms of recognition from France and Germany. A dog breeder, club woman, author—you name it, she did it. Very big in democratic party circles. A trustee or overseer of more boards than I could count and she knew every president from Woodrow Wilson to William Jefferson Clinton."

"She was pretty old then when she died," Richard said.

"Ninety eight and a half. Her husband was Jouett Shouse, a Missouri native but a congressman from rival Kansas. I think that's my first 'Jouett' ever. He was a pal of Harry Truman's. Truman used to visit him at Wolf Trap; they hunted together there."

"It was a farm, wasn't it?" Richard asked.

"Yes, an actual working farm. Mrs. Shouse's retreat from Georgetown. They grew corn and wheat...alfalfa...oats...you name it. They raised chickens and ducks, turkeys...cows...horses. Their kennel produced champion Boxers, miniature Pinschers, and Weimaraners. The property really *was* a haven for wolves, but that was in the eighteenth century.

They were all gone by the time Mrs. Shouse purchased her 168 acres. I wouldn't even want to think about what a parcel of that size would be worth today. When the government accepted her gift in 1966 the congress appropriated $600,000 for its administration. That might get you a small house in the neighborhood in the current market."

"If the kitchen hasn't been updated," Richard said.

"Right," I said. "It hasn't been a very lucky place. The inaugural season had to be delayed because the Filene Center was destroyed by fire before it could be completed. The same thing happened in 1982 when a fire of 'undetermined origin' destroyed the Filene Center for the second time. And how about this little wrinkle—the Foundation determined that the 1982 season would still take place, so the acts performed in a huge tent, termed the Meadow Center. Its previous site had been in the United Arab Emirates. The Saudi government actually footed the tab for its transportation to Wolf Trap."

"So it's burned twice but without any loss of life. Maybe the terrorists hope that the third time will be the charm. They may also want to send a message to the Saudis in the process, noting their disapproval of the previous help they provided to the great Satan."

"I think that may be a fair assumption," I said.

"I've never actually seen the structure," Richard said.

"Vast," I said, "at least from the pictures on the internet, and again, all wooden. Douglas fir with a ceiling made of yellow pine. The wood is supposed to be fire-retardant."

"Sounds like a tinder box."

"Yes, I'm afraid it does."

"How many people does it hold?" Richard asked.

"There are just under 4,000 in-house seats and room for just over 3,000 on the lawn."

"Twice the toll of 9/11."

"Potentially."

"In an area of a little over 100 acres?"

"The Park Service gives an official number of 117 acres of national park land. And don't forget the set of adjacent parking lots," I added. "Plenty of fuel and potential shrapnel there."

We let that all sink in as Richard drove my car between the auto dealerships facing the pike and turned onto the main highway. The traffic was dense in each direction. We passed the exit for the Dulles access road and drove west toward Leesburg. The highway was dotted with developments, most with stratospheric price tags. A few minutes later we turned left into the development which adjoined the park. Termed *Shouse Village,* it was bordered by a decorative wall with a concrete image of a minstrel-like figure playing a musical instrument. The streets were named in cutesy musical fashion—Sibelius Drive, Trombone Court, etc. Veering to the left and bypassing the remainder of the development we drove down into the park area.

"Hunting ground," Richard said.

FIFTY

We parked the car and walked up the slow incline into the park. We were holding hands, but I wasn't faking anything this time. The park was deserted except for some grounds crew and they went about their business, paying little attention to us. When we got to the Filene Center we were struck by its size. A multi-storied expanse of wood and lights and fabric, it dwarfed us as we entered.

"This is huge," Richard said. "It's cavernous. The largest hall at the Kennedy Center has fewer seats than the orchestra alone and there are another thousand seats or more in the balcony." He shook his head in frustration. "Where do you begin?"

"It's an absolute security nightmare," I said. "It's bad enough that so many things can be hidden in the performance facility proper, but here an assault team could come out of the woods as well or begin dropping things from the sky. Let's not even talk about the fact that mortars could be driven to the subdivision above in a delivery van or on the back of a pickup truck. All they'd need to do is slit the family's throats and set up shop in their backyard. With the concert and other background noise the audience would be in a fool's paradise until they saw the flash and the blood splatter."

"And look at the easy escape routes," Richard added. "You're a minute from Route 7. You could slip into McLean and all the back roads, head up to Tysons and get on the beltway…take 66 toward the District…head toward Dulles…or take Chain Bridge Road into Vienna and Oakton, pick up 66 in the opposite direction…it's completely porous."

"Right," I said. "And the seats are so exposed. Where would they put the principal VIP's—in the front of the balcony or the front of the orchestra? Either way they'd be an easy target for a sniper."

"Lincoln's Ford's Theatre box wasn't all that safe," Richard said, "but this is much worse. It's like that old Hitchcock movie with the scene at the Royal Albert Hall. Pick your sniper's nest. There are plenty of good ones available."

"We've got to bring the Bureau into this," I said. "There's no way we could check this out alone. We'll need dogs and detection devices. There's no security here at all. Someone could have buried a device on the lawn just beyond the covered seats. They could have done it weeks ago. Or even months. Roadies are in and out all the time, with crates and boxes and cables."

"Think of the nooks and crannies," Richard said. "In addition to all the dressing rooms and public toilets you've got an orchestra pit with a lift platform, catwalks, cyclorama pits, ratholes for microphone cables... it just goes on and on."

"I'll call the Director," I said.

"I've got to call the Secret Service," Richard said. "I wouldn't be much of a liaison if I kept them in the dark."

"What if we let the Director do that?" I asked. "He's got a good relationship with the AG and with everybody else at the top. They *should* know and the fewer who know the better."

"You're right," he said.

I took out my cell phone and called. An hour and fifteen minutes later the park was covered with agents and technicians with every manner of scanning and detection device. Six trained dogs were sniffing everything in sight and a command center van was in place, equipped with computers with oversized screens on which to examine the park and the Filene Center's blueprint data. The coordinating agent was a woman named Elaine Sanchez. With her earpiece, microphone, and attractive hair and eyes she looked like a rock diva. The principal difference was that rock divas didn't carry Sig Sauer sidearms and have direct cell- and computer lines to the Director of the Federal Bureau of Investigation.

"I won't mince words," she said. "I'm not happy about this. The presidential detail did a routine sweep several days ago, but this place is a security disaster area. The president insists and everybody salutes. His people don't talk to us and they don't welcome second opinions. He made up his mind and that was that. All because he loves the damned history."

"What do you mean?" I asked.

"WolfTrap, the *history*," she said, as if I was deaf. "For the bicentennial the Scottish Military Tattoo performed here. It was a gift from Great Britain. Prince Philip even came over for the performance. Now with the P.M. in the country, the president considered it the perfect place for a celebration. I need hardly remind anybody here that the bicentennial was pre-9/11. Somehow the White House refuses to remember that fact. I don't know what the two of you have learned, but if there's any chance at all of a terrorist event we have a grave situation on our hands. Pun intended."

Before proceeding she held up her right hand and clicked on her microphone with her left. "I understand," she said. "Check it again and then check it a third time. I *know* we have a lot to cover. Have you ever seen the results of a high explosive device in a congested area?… No? Well, I don't think you'd enjoy it. And get into every corner of the loading dock area. That's the quickest and easiest place to install a device. The slots for the vertical doors are naturals and all the surrounding steel would create some nice shrapnel effects. Who's under the stage?…Have the dogs been there yet?…Why not?…Get them there ASAP."

She turned to us and started in again. "They believe that all they have to do is set up some metal detectors the day of the performance and check out the people who walk through the front gate. It somehow never occurs to them that these people plan in advance. Anyway, you two could be helpful…"

"What do you need?" Richard asked.

"You could start with a visual check of all of the surrounding buildings—toilets, souvenir stands, food service facilities, whatever. Look for anything out of the ordinary, anything that looks newly patched or painted. Look in areas where people don't like to stick their hands. Nasty places. Smelly places. Look at any objects that could contain a device the size of a shoe box. See if they're legit. Look at anything that's bolted or nailed or screwed down. See if there are any signs of recent alterations. Establish an inspection pattern so you don't miss anything. Let me know if you see anything that looks suspicious and I do mean *anything*."

She paused for a second and looked at me more closely. "You're Harrison, right?"

"I am," I said.

"We checked Roosevelt Island thoroughly after your run-through. It's clean."

"Good," I said.

"It's *not* good," she answered. "If we had found something we would have known we were on the right track. Now the clock is ticking and we're standing here with empty hands staring at one another."

I hesitated a second before speaking but then decided to do it. "Agent Sanchez?"

"Yes?"

"By any chance did the Director say anything to you about New York?"

"What about New York?"

"About the devices found there."

"Amateurish, in my opinion."

"The devices?"

"The scattershot approach. And the target."

"Why do you say that?"

"New Yorkers are resilient. Half the time the city doesn't work. The lights go out, the air conditioners shut down, the garbage isn't picked up. The real New Yorkers just sit down on the sidewalk and have a bagel and latte. This is a much better target. They start the schooldays late here when there's a heavy rain. A single prediction of snow flurries and the grocery store shelves are emptied. If your purpose is to terrify people, this is the place to hit."

"Especially when the president is in town."

"Start looking," she said.

Before I could respond she was on another call.

FIFTY-ONE

The park grounds were vintage pastoral. Despite the on-site food services, many still came to Wolf Trap to sprawl on the lawns and picnic, a fact encouraged by the imagery in the park's promotional brochures and their on-air ads. Local groceries and eateries offered pre-packaged baskets for those on tight schedules and judging from the offerings in the Leesburg Pike restaurants leading to the park the business was brisk. In addition to some rich food it was also a safe bet that many of the people attending the concerts were fortified with two, three, or four glasses of wine each. In the comfortable and slightly-blurred minds of those stretched out on the grass at sunset the possibility of a terrorist attack was remote in the extreme. The manicured lawns dotted with copses of trees amid the rolling hills added to the effect; Wolf Trap offered a sweet evening in the country, even if you were only a few minutes away from the strip malls, bustling hotels and noisy watering holes of Tysons Corner. With a little more green space I could imagine ghostly images of the hunt country types riding to hounds, but with the backdrop of dense woods it was easier to imagine Harry Truman and Jouett Shouse stalking the local game with rifles or shotguns.

Isolated trees were a long shot as a sniper's perch, but I checked them anyway before proceeding to the woods to the south. The surrounding subdivisions had been built four or five decades before and the incursions of civilization—particularly the sounds of traffic on the Dulles toll and access roads—were clear. Still, I saw an isolated deerstand in one of the trees. The ladder was long gone and the seat itself was little more than a rusted outline, but it was there nonetheless. It was also bolted in place and facing in the opposite direction and hence of little use to anyone seeking a position that would provide a good sight line to the Filene Center.

Aside from some isolated beer cans and bottles there was no significant evidence of recent human activity within the adjoining woods. The fresh deer pellets among the leaves and along the trails indicated that enough still roamed the woods and countryside to call attention to themselves. I wondered if they feasted on the red, pink, and white azaleas and other plantings that characteristically decorated the upscale suburban residences in the area. The local woods were always thick with white and pink dogwoods and the impatiens, hasta and pachysandra within the subdivisions must have advertised themselves to the deer as a vast and inviting smorgasbord.

I had turned off the ring signal on my cell phone but I felt it vibrate in my jacket's inside pocket. I looked at the i.d. for the incoming call; it was Richard.

"Find anything interesting?" he asked.

"Just some deer poop," I said. "How about you?"

"Nothing specific. A few Secret Service types just arrived. They're throwing their weight around, trying to convince Sanchez that they're in charge now. She just smiled and took an incoming call."

"Where are you now?" I asked.

"Checking out the *human* bathrooms," he answered. "I started with the ones on the hill, near the concession stands. I'm going to work my way down to those at the base of the Filene Center."

"I'll check the back of the facility and work my way around to the east, in your direction," I said.

The back of the Center was swarming with agents. By now half were clambering on the loading docks and half were on the ground below, going over every square foot of soil with metal detectors and surveying the grounds with binoculars. The phones were ringing and the dogs sniffing. I didn't see any visual cues to suggest that anyone had actually discovered anything, but it was clear that they were looking intently.

I found Richard coming out of the men's room beneath the orchestra area. When he looked at me I thought I saw something in his eyes other than simple recognition.

"Find anything interesting?" I asked.

"I found a lot of places to hide bombs," he said, "but there was nothing in them yet."

"That's good," I said. "What's happening inside?"

"The dogs are going over the covered seating area. They seem pretty interested, what with the remains of old food spills and the human smells lingering on the seats…I'm glad I'm not a dog. I wouldn't want to be aware of all the things that they're aware of."

I smiled in agreement. "When they smell something really suspicious they let you know."

As we walked along the side of the Filene Center, toward the seating area, I would have taken him by the hand, but now that we were surrounded by agents we kept a professional distance. Most of our counterparts were doing their best to look serious and efficient and I didn't want to draw any unnecessary attention.

Once inside the Center proper we had a closer look at the orchestra and balcony areas. The sides of the facility were open and the air blowing through the auditorium was heavy and warm. The volume of wood surfaces was striking. The acoustical shell ceiling and wall pieces were in place, as were the lights. The stage was ready for action; the only missing pieces were the performers, the audience, and those preparing to destroy the facility and all within it.

FIFTY-TWO

While Richard checked out crawl spaces and dark corners I called Beehler.

"I was starting to get worried," he said. "Hadn't heard from you in awhile."

"I'm fine," I answered. "What's up with our friend?"

"Nothing momentous. He slept in this morning and had a heavy breakfast. He's at Tysons now—at a camera shop."

"What's he buying?"

"Nothing yet," Beehler said. "I think he's just killing time, windowshopping."

"I need a favor," I said.

"Name it."

"I want you to send me a digital image of the map you found in the toilet at the *Red Fox Inn*."

"I'll send it to your iPhone," he said. "I have an enhanced computer image. I'll send that rather than the image in my phone. It'll take a couple of minutes."

"Thanks," I said, and gave him the number. He didn't ask me where I was. He must have figured I'd tell him if he needed to know. After I received the image I went to Sanchez's command van.

"What have you got?" she asked.

"The document we found that suggested this site to us."

"Digitalized?"

"Yes," I said. She directed her tech to download it from my phone and put it on screen.

"The two lines are the Dulles toll road and Route 7—Leesburg Pike," Sanchez said.

"That's what I figured," I answered.

"If it's a crude drawing it won't help us very much," Sanchez said, "but if it's drawn to scale it might."

"Like an overlay," I said.

The tech diddled with a map of the area, changing its scale to fit the drawing. She didn't talk while she worked, but she altered the screens, anticipating Sanchez's questions. Once she had the roads in place she pulled in a map of the Wolf Trap grounds, then an outline of the Filene Center.

"It looks pretty accurate," Sanchez said. "See the X?"

"The right side of the balcony, toward the front," I said. "Where would the President and P.M. be most likely to sit?"

"They'll sit in the center of the balcony, in the first row," Sanchez said. There was no hesitation in her voice.

"So this would provide an excellent line of sight to them."

"Yes, but it wouldn't be a very attractive position for a sniper. Too exposed. Too obvious."

"And you never know where the Secret Service might be," I added, "but they'd be around and only too ready to take away your weapon and break an arm, wrist, or set of fingers in the process."

"Unless the weapon was some sort of plastic device with plastic projectiles it would never get past the metal detectors," Sanchez said, "unless, of course, it was already here."

"But we haven't found it yet," I said.

"No."

"Let me check out the site," I said. "I want to get a better look."

"I'll come with you," Sanchez said.

The end seat on the right side of the first row of the balcony was approximately twenty-five seats from the center. Patrick Mahomes could have made a grenade throw at that distance, but it was doubtful that Leon Donovan could and any near misses could easily fall into the orchestra area below and leave the occupants of the balcony unscathed. The angles were tight and any person aiming a rifle from the end-seat position would risk hitting one or more of his seatmates on the bridge of the nose with the barrel. There was no way that it could be done without revealing his intentions. Most serious of all, the side seats in the balcony row were accessible by a nearby aisle but enclosed on the far sides, so that the person in the end, interior seat was trapped and would have to get past three seatmates to get to the aisle. From that position there were no easy exits.

"This just won't work," I said to Sanchez, "unless…"

"Unless what?" she asked.

"Unless the person is not there to kill the President or P.M."

"Why *would* he be there, then?"

"How about to take their picture?"

FIFTY-THREE

"He *is* a photographer," I said.

"Keep talking," Sanchez said.

"Maybe he's there to record the event. Assuming he's got a phone/camera with an internet link he could broadcast the event to the world."

"It's the sort of thing they'd aim for," Sanchez said. "Big headline, big splash, big publicity. They may want to go back to living in the middle ages but they know that they need modern technology to get them there."

"He couldn't operate a weapon and take pictures at the same time though, unless he was cuing the detonating device and then going up in smoke with everybody else."

"Tough mission," Sanchez said, "but it wouldn't be the first time."

"What if he's a stooge?" I asked. "He takes the pictures while somebody else sets off the bomb."

"And it's all broadcast live."

"You wouldn't need much time," I said. "I can hear the voiceover: 'The following executions are brought to you by your friends at Al-Quaeda.' Cut to the picture of the President and P.M. sitting comfortably in their seats enjoying the show. Suddenly a red blast with fire and wood and blood everywhere. Then, fade to black."

"And any confirmations of an event in the Filene Center would reinforce the visual messages that had already been spread across the world on the internet."

"Yes," I said, "and Donovan could be completely circumscribed with regard to the event. He has absolutely no idea what's really happening. He's been told there's going to be a prank or joke, maybe something that will occasion embarrassment...whatever. But nothing that puts him at risk. He's simply on the scene, getting the scoop. A marginal photographer with some political leanings...no big wins in years...an ego to be stroked. Somebody from the terrorist cell approaches him, offers him a chance to be famous, tells him he has to keep a secret or the event will be compromised, offers him a couple of bucks and all the copyright and intellectual-property assurances he needs."

"He presents himself as a tabloid publisher or a website owner. Offers Donovan some references and bona fides to hook him."

"Right," I said, "and the event could be innocuous—a pie in the face, a political sign, a crude gesture...the case would be easy to make. The tabs'll pay serious bucks for a picture of an actor buying broccoli or one of an actress walking around with her hair uncombed. They're always on the street—pockets filled with walking-around money—trolling for opportunities."

"And he has no idea that his body is going to turn into red mist in the process. He's told to start shooting pictures at a certain time; the terrorists make sure the feed is working and then set off the device."

"It's at least plausible," I said.

"Yes, it is," Sanchez said. "Let's find that bomb."

There was nothing under the balcony structure and no perceptible alterations in the seats, flooring, or surrounding areas. The dogs sniffed until they were bored and confused, looking to their handlers with quizzical expressions. The imaging devices turned up nothing. It looked like a day at the beach, with slackers with metal detectors walking endlessly through the sand, trying to find something—anything—of value. Sanchez had more than twenty agents and techs examine the site and every one of them came up dry.

Richard had joined me and the two of us went over the site at least a half dozen times. We tested other ideas and hypotheses—a directional device spraying shrapnel; catwalk perches; the possible uses of lighting for maximum media effect…nothing jumped out at us as obvious or even plausible. Any interior sniper's perches, for example, would have been scoped out by the Secret Service on their first pass and there would be an army of agents in the Center on the night of the performance, guarding entrances and exits and access to dark corners.

There would also be a set of special rules in place during the time that the President and P.M. were in the hall. Once in their seats the members of the audience would be required to stay there and there would be last-minute walkthroughs, clearing the facility before anyone was allowed to enter. If the terrorists were able to learn that the President and P.M. would be in the audience for this performance they would be smart enough to figure out that there would be serious lockdown procedures in operation. They would also know that there would be F-15's in the air and special satellite surveillance. Their best chance was to have a device in place, well in advance of the event, a device that would be difficult to detect.

I asked Richard when the decision had been made for the President and P.M. to attend the concert.

"I don't know," he said. "I was told four days ago. I wouldn't be the last to learn about it, but I wouldn't be the first either."

I went through the Director's office and found out that the event had actually been scheduled months earlier and that the program had been adjusted to fit the occasion in the last forty-eight hours.

"That's characteristic," Richard said. "They had to be given advance notice in order to book the event, but the Secret Service would give them minimum notice of who would be there, so that all security issues could be locked down. The White House chief of staff and his Downing Street counterpart would know, but again, they'd keep as few people in the loop as possible. There have been no public announcements, no doubt at the insistence of the Secret Service. From their point of view it's nothing

more than a media event—glue the audience in their seats and hope that
they're smiling and clapping wildly whenever they're on camera. Show
the president waving and the first lady looking radiant. Then get it the
hell over with. The important thing is the videotape. That recreates the
moment and makes all America feel warm and gushy, but nobody sees it
until *after* everyone has left and the site is secure."

"*If* they get a chance to leave," I said.

"Right."

I went over to Sanchez. She had just clicked off her phone and
returned it to her jacket pocket. "Any idea when the decision was made
for the President and P.M. to come here?"

She paused before responding. "We just learned a few days ago," she
answered.

"And there were no indications of a possible terrorist attack until
my report?"

"No. Not even any abnormal chatter. What are you thinking—that
there hasn't been much of a time span in which the terrorists could obtain
intelligence of the event, plan an operation, and then bring in a device?"

"Yes. And even if New York is a diversion, they've been working on
that for what was probably a longer period of time."

"Who said it was a diversion?"

"You yourself said that you liked Washington as a target much more
than New York."

"Yes, but I didn't say New York was a diversion."

"What are you saying?"

"I'm saying (and I said) that, in my opinion, the New York operation
was amateurish. The fact that they may lack good judgment doesn't mean
that they don't have hostile intentions. On 9/11 they hit both New York
and Washington. Why wouldn't they try to hit both again this time?"

"But we discovered the devices. They installed them before the
routine sweeps were made."

"Did the New York AD tell you that?"

"Not exactly, but he didn't deny it."

"He didn't deny your supposition but he didn't confirm it either?"

"No, he didn't."

"Agent Harrison, there are no routine sweeps of core New York infrastructure. The sweeps are always unscheduled. We would never risk compromising security in that way."

"So how could we get that lucky?" I asked.

Sanchez just stared at me.

"Never mind," I said. "I get it."

FIFTY-FOUR

So let's assume (I said to myself) that the AD has an informant in the terrorists' organization. He would protect the person's identity at all costs, certainly to the point of not mentioning the fact to me. But if the decision to have the President and P.M. come to Wolf Trap was announced only recently, how would the terrorists know of it in time to mount a significant operation? Perhaps the AD had fed something vague to his informant, a *quid pro quo* for all of the intelligence the informant had given him, a putative act of faith or trust. Perhaps he feared that the informant was actually working both sides and hoping for a tidbit here or there that could be put to use. The informant's cell could then turn their attention in that direction and that *would* make the New York piece of the operation a diversion. The *real* plan was to let the Bureau find out about New York and then get comfortable. It wouldn't have cost them much. There was plenty of C-4 to be had and plenty of people willing to make their way through the city, leaving little piles and stashes of it in their wake. The key thing was to work the Bureau, make them think that the plan was to seal off Manhattan for awhile and wreak a little havoc, while the real goal was to assassinate the President and P.M. in an act of epic revenge.

But why would the AD tip the informant about something as big as the President and P.M. being together in the unspecified future, even extraneous details concerning such a meeting? Perhaps he was baiting some traps, hoping to come in at the last second, call timeout as the clock clicked its way toward 0, and grab the whole damned group of them.

A counter-counter move. In the meantime he had turned me loose in an attempt to provide some mystification for the spotters on the other side. Maybe I was *our* diversion, my actions an indication to them that the Bureau was flailing in multiple directions, uncertain of the terrorists' ultimate plans. Maybe he was giving them enough time and opportunity to cast their net as far as possible, involving a major share of their network in the operation. Dream big dreams; make big bombs, then go down together in a heap. Instead of just putting the Al-Madi cell members in the dock and on the gallows, he'd put a whole army of terrorists there. The world would be safe (for a moment at least) and his career would be made. *We'd* have the media event.

But if so, where was the bomb? This couldn't all be faked. What was Donovan doing in Washington and what were he and his confederates up to in that toilet in Middleburg? This had to have a point to it, but, again, where was the bomb? We had picked our way through the Wolf Trap woods, the parking lots, the outbuildings, and every square inch of the Filene Center and found exactly…nothing.

I rejoined Richard and told him my thoughts. "I don't have time to play Spy versus Spy," I said, "and try to figure out who's up to what. We've got to stop second-guessing and searching for ultimate motives and find whatever's here."

"We're running in all directions," he said. "Let's start with some rational assumptions." He quickly realized what he had said. "You know I didn't mean to imply that you're being irrational," he added.

"Of course not. Let's hear them," I said.

"OK. We haven't detected any metal, so the bomb is probably plastic."

"Right," I said.

"And the dogs haven't smelled anything, so the bomb material is probably odorless."

"Agreed," I said.

"And nothing's looked out of place, so…"

"So we've probably been looking in the wrong place," I said. "What the hell have we been doing?" I asked. "Instead of trying to cover every square inch of this piece of Northern Virginia we should have put ourselves in their place to begin with and started there."

"Keep talking," he said.

"The whole structure of the Filene Center is supported by a set of pillars that keep both the balcony and the roof in place. If you blow the pillars the whole place collapses and everyone inside is trapped."

"No exit," Richard said.

"And if the blast is big enough you'd shred everybody near it and cover the rest in smoke and flames."

"We need a ladder," he said, "and a socket wrench."

Fifteen minutes later a tech from the bomb detail was carefully removing the bolts of the steel plate that masked the point at which one of the support pillars was attached to the roof. When the bolts were loosened the plate failed to fall away from the bottom of the roof and top of the pillar.

"Be very careful," Sanchez said. "It could be booby-trapped."

We were standing next to her, on the grass to the south of the structure. The bomb tech attached a rod with prongs to the sides of the plate and climbed back down the ladder, extending the rod as he did so. Our hearts stopped and we forgot to breathe for a moment as he locked the extended pieces of the rod and tugged gently on the plate.

Nothing.

He tugged again, this time using both hands, and one side of the plate came free. I was watching with a small pair of binoculars I carry in my purse. Attached to the edge of the plate was a gumlike substance that stretched and elongated as the tech pulled on the rod.

I handed the binoculars to Richard. "That's not insulation," I said.

FIFTY-FIVE

I could see Sanchez's lips pronouncing the word.

"*Semtex*," Richard said. "Pliable, odorless, and twice as powerful as TNT. Very, very stable—part *RDX* and part *PETN*—and with an indefinite shelf life. The Libyans used it to blow up Pan Am flight 103 over Lockerbie. Three pounds of it are enough to bring down a two-story building."

"There's probably a pound of it around the top of that pillar," I said. "More than enough to blow the pillar and most of the roof and balcony to shreds."

"Since Lockerbie they've changed the appearance and recipe to make it more detectable. The Semtex used industrially is a bright red-orange color and the inventor's added some metal components and a distinct odor to make it more noticeable. Unfortunately, thousands of tons of it were sold before the changes were made."

"Who bought it?" I asked.

"The usual suspects," Richard said. "Iran…North Korea…Iraq."

By now Sanchez was speaking insistently to the bomb tech. "Talk to me," she said. "Have you found the det cap?"

She paused for his answer.

"How's it rigged?" she asked.

After the next pause, she said, "That's what I thought. Check another one. See if they're all set up the same way."

I looked at her, indicating I'd appreciate the information.

"The det cap's attached to a receiver. The device could be set off by a cell phone. I'm sure they all are, so they all can be blown at once by a single call."

"But probably not the photographer's," I said.

"No. He's the fall guy," Sanchez said. "He takes pictures of the President and P.M. and while the last one's being fed onto the internet his pals make the call that launches him on his one-way trip to meet Allah."

"His seat is right under one of the pillars," I said.

"Right," Sanchez said. "They don't want him around after the dust settles and the last flame goes out. It's not their way. They probably put an extra few ounces around the top of *his* pillar, just to make sure."

"Can I say something?" I asked.

"What's that?" Sanchez asked.

"We better not get comfortable."

"I agree," she said. "We've got to find every bit of plastic in this place. Just because we've found some doesn't mean we've found it all."

"I was thinking of something else too," I said.

"Yes?" she answered. There was a hint of impatience in her voice.

"If we lock this place down and keep the story quiet we might be able to catch the call when it comes in tomorrow night, plot its source, and intercept the caller."

"That's a long shot," Sanchez said, "since they'll almost surely be in motion and anybody in motion around here is in motion in dense traffic."

"I understand," I said, "but what do we have to lose?"

"Nothing," Sanchez said. "You know, of course, that that's also what they're trying to do in New York—catch whoever it is who makes the call trying to set off each of the devices in the city simultaneously."

"I figured so," I said. "Even with the devices disabled, the AD would have to protect any possible informant by ordering the expected countermoves. And even if there *is* an informant *and* he or she is working both sides and the terrorists learn that the Bureau intends to shut down their operation, each side would still go through the standard motions, so that the go-between was temporarily protected."

"That they would," Sanchez said.

"But what if there *is* no informant," I said, "what if we've just gotten lucky on two occasions?"

"It's very seldom *all* luck," Sanchez said. "Sometimes the work actually pays off. But," she added, "that doesn't mean it's time for us to start congratulating ourselves."

FIFTY-SIX

"I'm not comfortable with this," I said to Richard. "This is the second time we've gone down the same road."

"What do you mean?" he asked.

"It's the second time we've scoped out the plot and the second time we've found the devices."

"I agree with you that we shouldn't get comfortable," he answered, "but don't you think it's possible that we might have actually worked the case successfully?"

"It's possible," I said. "I'm not saying it's too good to be true. I'm just saying that it's working out very neatly."

"You're thinking that somebody's dropping corn kernels on the path and we're greedily picking them up, just the way they want us to."

"Right."

"Maybe it's time for a second opinion."

"I think so too. I'm going to call the AD."

It took ten minutes to get through to him on a secure line. "I was just about to call you," he said.

"You've been talking to Sanchez?"

"She reports to the Director," he said. "The Director brought me up to speed."

"I felt I should talk to you. It's just an instinct or maybe a hunch, but I wanted to tell you something..."

"Yes?"

"It all seems awfully tidy to me," I said.

"That's your usual hunch."

"I'm sorry, but that's the way I feel and I wanted you to know it."

"I appreciate that," he said, "but there are some things you don't know. The first is that I'll be joining you soon. Who's with you?"

"Richard Ingle."

"The Secret Service liaison."

"Yes."

"And you trust him?"

"With my life," I said.

"Anyone else?"

"No."

"And your judgment isn't being clouded by your personal relationship with him?"

I wondered what he knew and how and when he knew it, but answered promptly. "No. I've trusted him from the beginning."

"I'm at Andrews now," the AD said. "I just landed."

He didn't provide any more detail, but he didn't have to. He was telling me that the Washington scenario was sufficiently plausible for the Director to instruct him to put New York in other hands and focus on Wolf Trap. In a routine situation the Washington office would have played it solo, but the Director had decided to pull in his top talent.

"I understand," I said. "The Director is taking this very seriously."

"Special Agent Harrison…Gwen…"

"Yes, sir?"

"There's something else you need to know."

"Yes, sir?"

"There *is no* Bureau informant in the Al-Madi cell. Sometimes we do good work and sometimes we just get lucky. Either way, we'll take it."

"Understood, sir."

"That's history now anyway. You know what they say—we're like goalies. You can make a thousand saves but the only shot that anyone remembers is the one that gets past you."

"Yes, sir."

"There's something else."

"Yes, sir?"

"Special Agent Sanchez has not shared everything that she's learned with you."

"Yes, sir?"

"When they removed the bolts from the plate covering the Semtex at the top of one of the support pillars…"

"Yes, sir?"

"There was some rust on the bolts and some insect evidence…"

"Yes, sir?"

"The Bureau and the Secret Service have only been aware of the President's plans for this meeting with the P.M. for two weeks. Sanchez believes that the Semtex was installed at least a month ago."

FIFTY-SEVEN

My mind raced through the possibilities. None of them were encouraging.

"So you believe that they have someone on the inside, sir."

"They have access to information that they could put to very dangerous use. At this point we don't know how they obtained that access."

"May I ask another question, sir?"

"Of course."

"Is it fair to say, sir, that you believe they're replaying 9/11 and seriously targeting both New York and Washington?"

"Certainly the body count would be comparable or worse," he answered. "New York is a very rich target and they have a significant collection of operatives there. With the concentration of media in New York, it's very hard for them to resist an attempted strike. I believe they're anxious to succeed in Washington as well. In some ways they failed last time. United 93 was headed for the Capitol or White House, not Shanksville, Pennsylvania. There's also some reason to believe that they were unhappy with the Pentagon strike."

"Yes, sir?" I let him continue.

"American 77 struck the west block, but the area was under renovation at the time. One possible target was the Army's logistical command. They had been relocated during the renovation. These are the people who put the tanks on the ground for Operation Desert Storm."

"Do you believe that they were targeted specifically?"

"I haven't seen definitive proof, but the terrorists certainly would have seen them as an attractive target."

"But not as attractive as the President of the United States of America and the Prime Minister of the United Kingdom."

"No, not as attractive as them."

"What do you want me to do, sir?"

"Stay at Wolf Trap. I'm coming in by government sedan. The Director is always under observation; he doesn't want to tip our hand by appearing on the scene, so he's asked me to be his eyes and ears. Sanchez could do it, but she already has her own three-ring circus. The Director wants someone at my level who can come in relatively unnoticed from another jurisdiction."

"I understand, sir."

"You'll be *my* eyes and ears," he added. "I'll be communicating with the Director while I stroke the heads of the other agencies and keep their egos soothed. You'll be my person on the actual field of play."

"Will do, sir."

"And Ingle can work with you. I'll clear it with the Secret Service. Not that it's stopped you so far…"

"Thank you, sir. And Beehler and his team?"

"We'll pull them in if and when Donovan appears at Wolf Trap. In the meantime they can continue following him. You haven't heard anything lately, have you?"

"Just a report on his breakfast and a shopping trip to Tysons."

"Did he buy anything?"

"No. He just windowshopped at a camera store."

"Staying in character. Perhaps he suspects he's being followed. Or maybe he doesn't suspect anything and he's just killing time."

"We consider him part of the target," I said. "He'll take pictures that are fed onto the internet and then he'll be eliminated."

"Vaporized is probably closer to the truth," the AD said. "Somehow they always seem to be able to find people like Donovan."

"Yes, sir. We'll see you soon."

"Right. And Gwen…"

"Yes, sir?"

"If they knew the President and P.M.'s plans before we did, give some thought to what else they might know."

FIFTY-EIGHT

We always seemed to be working on multiple fronts—taking the war to the terrorists, watching our flanks and maintaining equilibrium within the federal bureaucracy, dodging political missiles, protecting the public without riling or misleading them and trying to separate the intelligence wheat from the disinformation chaff. If I tried to psych out the ultimate realities of our situation and continued to weigh the range of possibilities in every aspect of our current case I could tie myself in some grand, Gordian mental knot and overlook the real task at hand. On the other hand, if I pressed on without thinking through each and every permutation and implication I could end my career and possibly my life in a single, naïve step. How do you run through a minefield which hasn't been surveyed when standing at its boundary and gaping is no longer an option?

Richard was a great help and support. He was working closely with Sanchez, offering her his military expertise and helping facilitate the succession of searches that followed the discovery of the Semtex. He was also keeping her at arm's length from me so that I had more room to maneuver and greater opportunity to aid the AD, who was due to arrive within the next few minutes.

Meanwhile the traffic on the Dulles Access Road was heavy and noisy, despite the sound walls that had been installed to mute the engine noise of the stream of cars, trucks, SUV's, and motorcycles that raced west to the outlying suburbs and exurbs. In Washington, when you build it, they come. The beltway, the Access Road, Lee Highway, Leesburg

Pike, Route 66, Glebe Road, Arlington Boulevard, the GW Parkway—
the whole panoply of concrete and asphalt strips covered with hurtling
steel vehicles—constituted a sclerotic network that could close up in
an instant, suffocating and strangling the sprawl of humanity between
Baltimore and Richmond and beyond.

I wondered if that had been part of the Al-Madi plan. If they wanted
to add gridlock to death it would require little additional effort for them
to do so. The action would have a direct impact on the lives of over six
million people, some of them the makers of policy, some of them the
profiteers who fed on the policy, some of them the media and think
tank chatterers who discussed and pontificated on the policy, many of
them the innocent bystanders trying to make a living, trying to get by,
trying to find opportunities for their families, trying to get home when
the traffic came to a dead stop and the sky was filled with fire and smoke
and screams.

Fifteen minutes later the AD arrived. He had called me first on his cell
phone and as I walked toward the parking lot I was impressed by the fact
that Sanchez had been able to move so many elements of her operation
away from the roadway and draw as little attention as possible to their
actions. Nothing happening here—just a few Secret Service personnel
running their usual checks and ticking off boxes on clipboard forms.

When the AD got out of the car there was no hooplah—no spear
carriers opening his door, no hypertrophied agents in tight suits talking
into collar mics, no one running toward him, stuffing reports or classified
documents in his hands. He got out of the passenger seat and was wearing
weekend clothes—twill slacks, a corduroy-collared jacket, and work
shoes. He caught my eye and walked toward me without any special
indication of urgency.

"We owe you on this one, Gwen," he said.

"Everybody here did a good job, sir," I said.

"Yes, but they didn't come up with the idea."

"Richard confirmed my suspicions," I said. "I couldn't have done it alone."

"Give him an attaboy from me," the AD said. "He'll appreciate it more coming from you." It was the most personal thing I had yet heard him say.

"Now," he added, "we've got to get ready for tomorrow night. Keep walking with me."

As we approached the Filene Center he spoke again. "Some old business first..." he said. "On Malawi's recent trip to Washington..."

"Yes, sir?" I said.

"He had breakfast at the University Club and a late dinner at the *Gold Room* with David Willets when he returned."

"Right."

"We've since gotten another piece of information. That same day there was a withdrawal from an ATM in the lobby of a midtown hotel. The person was using Malawi's bank card. The ATM photograph of the person conducting the transaction looked like Malawi. He was dressed in the same general manner and, of course, he had Malawi's card. And there have been no reports that the card was stolen. One big hitch—the man was wearing sunglasses: big *Maui Jim's* that covered a significant portion of his face."

"Malawi was establishing an alibi," I said, "in case there were ever any allegations that he had been meeting with Donovan in Washington."

"Yes," the AD said. "This would square with our assumption that his relationship with Willets was phony and that he was using it for other purposes. We thought initially that he might be meeting with him to mislead us. It now appears that his relationship with Willets could also be used to help build an elaborate set of alibis if he were ever investigated, arrested, and indicted. Willets is a standup guy. Discretion and honesty are his watchwords. Without them he has no business. With him testifying that Malawi was a client and producing elaborate records of their meetings, the case for his defense would be reinforced immeasurably.

Lawyers keep records of every personal transaction, billing you for every minute and every second. Willets would be introduced as the go-to guy for unimpeachable honesty and then asked to produce an array of documents which would square precisely with Malawi's accounts and timetables. His story would acquire instant plausibility, particularly for a jury that thought the Bureau was becoming too aggressive and intrusive. All very clever..."

"I agree," I said. "What is Malawi doing now?"

"Interesting that you ask," the AD said. "He boarded a plane for San Francisco this morning. He paid by credit card. I should have mentioned that when you followed him to Washington he must have paid cash, since there was no record of a credit card transaction. He's also booked a room in Pasadena for later in the week; he guaranteed the reservation using the same credit card."

"He didn't want anyone to know he was going to Washington; he wants everyone to know that he's going to San Francisco, particularly with something big going down tomorrow night."

"Right. He'll be establishing his presence at the *Top of the Mark*, sitting near a television monitor and sipping $20-a-glass scotch when the Filene Center explodes."

"That's his plan," I said. "And I assume that we've got people following him to see what he does and who he calls when there's no network break for an emergency special report."

"That we do," the AD said. "We'll know exactly when the devices are to be detonated, since we'll intercept the signal designed to activate the caps. Malawi will be checking his watch carefully. He may even be tied in to the feed from Donovan. I doubt that he's the person directing the setting off of the devices. They'll do that from a secure location with full internet access and multiple screens for monitoring network reports. From their bunker they'll notify somebody in a mobile location, who will make the actual call. Still, he'll be tied in in some important way and the instant we know that the attempt was made to detonate the devices we'll move people in closer to Malawi to watch his movements and overhear his conversations. Actually, the more public the place in which he tries to draw attention, the better it will be for us."

"He could just stay in his hotel room," I said, "but it looks as if he's going out of his way to establish his presence as far away from the operation site as possible. Besides, he may want to watch the response of other people to the event. Relish it a little."

"The hotel room would be OK too," the AD said. "We could set up a full surveillance operation there in less than fifteen minutes. Now let's talk about our version of what's going to happen instead."

FIFTY-NINE

"Let's start with Donovan," Salva said. "We'll mic his area so that we can pick up any audible communications. We'll also have some minicameras on him, so we can see what he's doing with his camera phone or any other devices he brings in with him. Beehler's people will stay on him and see where he goes and what he does after he finds out that whatever action he's been expecting has been rescheduled for the twelfth of never.

"Sanchez's people will be covering the entire area, just in case anyone tries to bring in anything fishy at the last minute. They'll be reinforced by some agents from Quantico. We'll have all the cattle chutes and metal detectors in place at the entrances, of course, but they may try to sneak somebody in through the woods. I don't want any mystery guests. We'll keep the areas beyond the center facilities as dark as possible and have people with night vision goggles positioned in the trees and brush to keep an eye out.

"I'll brief the President and P.M. and inform them of our plans. They've already been informed concerning the general situation and have decided to proceed as if nothing untoward is expected. The Secret Service is bouncing off the walls, of course, but the President reminded them that we're at war and that that includes the commanders as well as the soldiers. He sees this as a significant opportunity to make some inroads and develop some new leads. He is confident of his safety. All in all it was a close call, but this is what he wants to do and so we're going to do it. We have special escape routes cleared if we need them, specially-reinforced presidential limos, including extra ones to be used as decoys, if needed, a set of F-15's and choppers at Dulles, fire-retardant suits, radiation suits, oxygen masks, and just about everything short of a time-travel machine and the 82nd Airborne."

"What do you want Richard and me to do, sir?"

"I want you between me and the President and P.M. I'll be coordinating and reporting to the Director. The President will have his full array of assistants and Secret Service staff buzzing around. I want you to hang back, in reserve, so I can plug you in wherever I might need you. Who knows? We could get lucky. You might even get a chance to enjoy some of the show."

A few minutes later I rejoined Richard. "He's sidelining us," I said. "He said he wants us to be in reserve so he can use us in reacting to any changed circumstances, but if we're right and we've scoped out all the details correctly there won't be anything unexpected to react to. We'll just be standing around and waiting."

"Really, what else *could* he do with us?" Richard asked. "You don't want to be narrowcasted and stuck behind a camera or pair of binoculars. Beehler's whole team is available to keep tabs on Donovan. We've pretty much got things covered. If he's keeping you in reserve for something unexpected you should consider that an indication of trust. I can't think of what else might happen, but I can't imagine that it would be good. Think of yourself as the clutch hitter or the closer he's counting on to save the game."

"You're sweet," I said, squeezing his hand.

"I'm serious," he answered.

"I know you are," I said. "I just want to be doing something."

Just then my cell phone twitched. I answered; it was Sanchez.

"Just had a thought. Why don't you take a ride through the neighborhood?" she said. "See if anybody's snooping around, checking us out."

"Will do," I said.

Sibelius Drive was a large circle; the south side of which stood on a crest above Wolf Trap. It would not have been easy for an observer to pass between the houses there and set up an observation post in one of the backyards. There were no vacant houses on the market in that part of the development and there were a number of women and children in the driveways and on the sidewalks. The lots offered privacy to the rear, but the houses were close together as well as close to the street. The curving street afforded clear lines of vision to multiple sets of neighbors, so that a stranger could be observed from different angles by different people.

In addition, the neighborhood association operated a watch program and as luck would have it the watch was in operation that afternoon, driving around Trombone Court and Sibelius. The driver was an elderly man in an aging, black Taurus with magnetized rubber signs attached to the doors on both the driver's and passenger's side of the car. They read: *Shouse Village Neighborhood Watch*, and, on a second line, *Mobile Patrol*. I imagined the old man had a cell phone, a clipboard with log sheets, and a deep desire to say "10/4" to someone. We followed him at a distance and noticed that he stopped at a house with an open garage door, knocked on the front door, and pointed in the direction of the garage, doubtless counseling the owner to close it, lest a potential burglar be tempted.

A foreign agent would have hesitated to approach a house and risk being recognized as a ringer. Who knows? He could be knocking on the door of the neighborhood association president or sergeant-at-arms. Reassured, we drove around for a few more minutes, and then explored the other side of the road (Towlston, becoming 'Trap' Road) that wended its way through Shouse Village and Wolf Trap. We saw nothing of interest except a long ranch home, probably built in the 50's, that now served as a church for disaffected conservative Catholics. It offered Latin masses each Sunday.

We returned to the main parking lot and Richard turned off the ignition. "Talk to me about what they knew and when they knew it," I said.

"The terrorists?"

"Yes."

"New York's an ongoing target," he said. "They could plan an operation there anytime. This, on the other hand, is special, what with the President and P.M. coming to the performance. Of course, it'd always be a decent target for them—kill a couple thousand people, some of whom would almost surely be Washington movers and shakers... including some administration people who they'd always like to see die. On the other hand, I wouldn't see it as a target of choice."

"Too remote," I said, "and not sufficiently grand. The Filene Center has already burned a couple of times. It's basically a huge open cabin in the woods. I figure they'd like the Kennedy Center a lot more. Bigger splash. Better imagery. You've got the Watergate next door, the T.R. Bridge, a lot of nice things nearby. Lots of symbolic overtones. Turn that big bronze bust of J.F.K. to twisted metal, flash the picture across the internet...they'd love to have some images to counter the pictures of the Saddam statues falling into the town squares."

"So they're here because the President and P.M. are," Richard said. "And since the decision was made only recently they've had much less time to plan the operation and get their Semtex in place. The huge thing is that they somehow knew about the presidential decision and invitation before the agencies knew. That means they've either got somebody on the inside or they've found a way to intercept presidential communications."

"They could have gotten lucky," I said. "They could have intercepted something on the Wolf Trap end or maybe something on the performance and talent end. Maybe a civilian who works for the Marine Band, for example. Maybe they've got somebody at the Park Service and in each of the other agencies that supervise performance venues in the metropolitan area. You never know...an aide may have made a call...or even the

President himself. He likes to do that. Every Washington agency is like every airport or train terminal. Somewhere there's somebody working for minimum wage who would see a handful of thousand-dollar bills and agree to cooperate, particularly if the person didn't know the dimensions of the operation he was supporting."

"Easier to be a one-handed juggler than keep an open society secure," Richard said.

"Right, but let's assume that the screws are tightened a bit when the President and P.M. of the United Kingdom are involved. This isn't like the President suddenly getting a yen for some ethnic food and dropping in on one of the restaurants in Adams-Morgan. Let's say that they were careful, dotting all the i's and crossing all the t's. Everything on an ultra need-to-know basis. How did they penetrate all those levels of security?"

"Very good question," Richard answered. "And you know the followup."

"Yes. Like the AD said, if they're capable of doing that, they're capable of doing other things that we haven't yet anticipated."

SIXTY

We continued to mull over the possibilities while we tried to kick back and eat a quiet dinner. *Rocco's* is a McLean mainstay, with all-you-can-eat specials and oceans of cheap, house wine. By the time we got there the dinner crowd was long gone and there was no competition for quiet, corner tables. The thick, vinyl red and white tablecloths had probably each been wiped clean at least five times that evening and the wait staff had earned the right to sit down and enjoy a cup of coffee and a few minutes of decompression.

Richard humored me as we ran down a seemingly-endless litany of terrorist intentions and opportunities and sorted through a punch list of details to be checked before the arrival of the presidential limousine the following evening.

"I know I'm obsessing," I said, "but I keep thinking we're overlooking something important."

"You're not obsessing," he answered. "You're just doing your job. If I were the president I'd sleep better knowing that someone like you were worrying about me."

"The more we talk about it, the better I feel," I said. "Sanchez is on top of things. That reassures me. I also feel better now that Salva is here. The bomb squad is excellent. If there's any more Semtex there, *I* certainly don't know where it would be. And anything detectable by dogs would have been found. Those German Shepherds went over that place at least ten times."

"I think it's interesting that they got the Semtex installed so expertly in the first place," Richard said, "but the more I think about it the more I realize that it wouldn't have been all that difficult."

"Right. All they'd have to do is loosen the bolts and squeeze it in. They could have had phony roadies do it during the day or slip in a guy at night. I'd probably do it on the cusp—have some roadies doing their standard gig, then pull the security guys together, thank them with some food and drink or whatever, while one last guy installed the explosive. They could have had some special spotlights in place at the top of the pillars. While they took those down they were also installing the Semtex. What would a skilled person need—thirty or forty minutes, max? Meanwhile, the rest of the crew is on its way to the parking lot, thinking about hitting the local bars before calling it a night. Besides, the easiest things to do are always the things that you'd least expect."

"When this is over we'll identify the moment at which the presidential decision was made and then check all of the crews with access to the Filene Center after that point," Richard said. "It'll be a finite number and the Bureau has a big computer."

"Right," I said. "The roadies for the big acts often travel with them for years. It would be very hard to slip in a new guy without everyone noticing the fact. I imagine also that most of the stage guys must be unionized, so there would be elaborate past records on them and on the people for whom they've worked. And the security people work for services that are well-organized and well-known. You don't entrust a high six-figure concert involving thousands of people to Bozos off the block. We should be able to sort out any suspicious names fairly easily. I'll start on that first thing in the morning, when the Wolf Trap people are back at work and they can guide us through their files."

"How's your food?" Richard asked.

I hadn't really thought of it. I had been focusing all my attention on the situation. "It's not bad," I said. "The sauce has a kind of sweet taste to it, that goes with the garlic and other stuff."

He lifted his glass to me in a mini-toast. "I'm glad you're enjoying it," he said.

We passed on coffee and drove past Wolf Trap before returning to the *Crowne Plaza*. I don't know why, but I wanted to feel that the place had been safely put to bed for the night. There were still some cars in the parking lot as we drove along Trap Road and I saw what looked like the flicker of a light in Sanchez's headquarters. It made me feel better.

We continued to drive toward downtown Vienna, passing the "Barns at Wolf Trap," a smaller venue used for chamber music and other limited-audience events. Some cars that looked like federal sedans were parked just off the road. That made me feel better also.

It was nearly midnight when we returned to the *Crowne Plaza*. Richard fell asleep with his arm around my waist and his forehead buried in my hair. My eyes were still wide open, staring intently at the pebbled ceiling, looking at the patterns there for something to investigate or someone to follow.

SIXTY-ONE

We arrived at the Filene Center at 7:00. A buffet table with coffee and bagels had already been picked over. The cattle chutes had all been installed and the metal detectors were already being tested. The conveyor belts were now rolling beneath the imaging devices and the techs were being counseled by both Bureau and Secret Service types on the kinds of objects they were most likely to encounter. Each car entering the facility's lots was subjected to a full inspection, complete with dogs and mirrors. In fact, there were so many dogs walking through the aisles of the Filene Center that the venue looked like a casting call for a remake of *The Adventures of Rin Tin Tin.*

The communications net was in place and functioning. Flesh-tone earpieces and dark lapel mics were everywhere and both Sanchez and Salva were chattering to the troops. A new bank of computers had been added to Sanchez's command center and there were security signs detailing instructions and ground rules everywhere. The doors on each of the toilet stalls had been replaced by half-doors and the facility's stores of wine and beer were replaced with club soda, bottled tea, and bottled lemonade. Better a park full of teetotalers than the occasional staggering drunk.

There were agents everywhere—scouting positions in the woods, checking sight lines, and poking around backstage, looking for hidey holes, nooks, crannies, observation points, and spare equipment that could be considered dubious or explicitly dangerous.

A tree service had been brought in to trim any limbs under which the President and P.M. could conceivably be imagined to walk or drive. This was standard procedure. In the District—where tree-trimming and pruning occur every second or third leap year—this would be a major portion of the security detail's masterplan. The last thing any of the agents wanted was to have an embarrassing accident result in an injury to a dignitary and the end of several careers. Decades earlier, when Reagan had visited Georgetown for an honorary degree they had trimmed trees over an area eight blocks in length.

Special clothing had been ordered for those operating concessions; the tops were color-coded to indicate the security checks which they had cleared and the degree of mobility which they were permitted. Supervisory personnel wore enameled pins that appeared to be routinely patriotic, but actually indicated their level of seniority and their permitted latitude of movement—eagles for those at the executive level, flags for middle management, and crossed red, white, and blue ribbons for the foot soldiers.

All foodstuffs had been subjected to a primary and secondary inspection and then sealed in locked containers. The grass had been freshly (and closely) trimmed, probably at first light, since no lawn equipment was now in evidence. All trash receptacles had been removed and been replaced by transparent drums with ventilation holes to facilitate canine inspection.

The toilets were being inspected for the third time, with checks and rechecks of all tanks, soap- and towel dispensers. A military helicopter circled the facility just above the treeline and canine units patrolled the perimeter of the grounds.

The "Barns" section of the park had been completely locked down. The buildings were occupied by S.W.A.T. teams that could be brought into play, as needed, and some all-terrain vehicles were positioned behind the "Barns" for rapid deployment in the event of traffic gridlock. Richard noticed some other niceties that had been kept in their cases: a supply of concussion grenades, a set of light anti-tank weapons and (very low-keyed) a selection of surface-to-air missiles. When the President comes to town and brings the Prime Minister of the United Kingdom with him the troops try to insure that a good (and safe) time is had by all.

I went into the command center, greeted Sanchez and the AD, and asked the AD what he wanted Richard and me to do. He took me outside without speaking. I was sure that he trusted Sanchez absolutely, but everything with him was on a need-to-know basis and his preferred discussion model was always one-on-one.

"What do you hear from Beehler?" he asked.

"I talked to him at 5:30 this morning," I said. "All quiet. Perhaps even suspiciously so. Yesterday afternoon Donovan returned from Tysons without making any purchases and went straight to his hotel room. Since then he's been living on room service. Steak and frites and chocolate mousse last night; crepes, tea, and melon this morning."

"He ate that early?"

"No, Beehler had one of his people check the order on the hangtag on his door."

"That does all sound suspicious," Salva said. "Who goes to Washington, drives to and from a suburban shopping mall, and then holes up all afternoon and evening in a hotel room? What about phone calls and fax messages?"

"Virtually nothing. The room sensors picked up the keying of his cell phone last night. He didn't speak. Beehler's people think he called for today's weather report."

"He could have gotten that from one of the local TV stations—more detail too."

"He only turned on the set once," I said. "He listened to CNN for a few minutes and then MSNBC."

"And no visitors, I assume."

"No, sir, no visitors."

"Maybe he's going through a meditation sequence—getting himself in a proper frame of mind for his little job of work tonight."

"Could be. There are no books in his room beyond the magazines and guides provided by the hotel. No ipods or game boys or anything like that. Beehler's people went through the trash from his room. He didn't do the *Times* crossword puzzle. He didn't write on the paper… nor on the desk pads next to the telephones. He hasn't used any of the complimentary stationery. Nada."

"Let me know what he does today. My guess is that he'll clear out his room and put everything in his rental car. After tonight his part of the operation will be finished; at least that's what he believes."

"Yes, sir."

"OK. Now I've got something I'd like *you* to do."

SIXTY-TWO

"I want a sense of the rhythm of the performance tonight."

"The *rhythm*, sir?"

"Sorry. I didn't mean to be cryptic. I want a sense of how the whole evening is supposed to play out. I want to be able to imagine it—step by step and note by note—in my mind. Talk to the musicians. Go through the set list and the order in which the pieces are going to be performed. Check with the lighting people. I want to know what kinds of equipment they're going to use and how the performance will look and feel. Is this going to be like a rock concert or a chamber music recital? I know; it'll be something in between, but I want to be able to envision it and hear it in my head in advance. And most important—see if you can find out when the final set was determined. Surely they've been practicing for awhile, so it would be virtually impossible to keep the set list a secret. You wouldn't even need to coopt a member of the ensemble. All you'd need is a single guy with a broom sweeping the hallway outside their practice facility."

"I haven't had a chance to check out the public ads for the performance, Sir."

"See what they say. Do they actually list the music to be performed or do they keep it vague?"

"You mean like 'the Marine Band will perform a medley of patriotic songs'?"

"Right, exactly."

"Could you tell me more, sir?" I asked. "I'd like to have a sense of what you're getting at."

"Sure. I'm thinking about that old Hitchcock movie. You know… it's set in England and there's the guy with the cymbals and the assassin hiding in the shadows. He's targeting some dignitary in the audience and he's waiting for the guy with the cymbals to crash them together. He's planning to shoot at that moment, so that the sound from the gun is muffled by the sound from the orchestra."

"*The Man Who Knew Too Much.*"

"Was that the title?"

"Yes. It was set in the Royal Albert Hall, the circular venue, in London."

"Right."

"James Stewart and Doris Day in that version. Their child was kidnapped. Doris kept singing 'Que Sera, Sera'."

"I didn't know there was another version."

"There was an earlier, English version. I saw it in a film course in college. Hitchcock did that a lot."

"Did what?"

"Remake the same movie."

"Oh, right. Anyway, you see what I'm thinking. They're looking to make a big splash. Maybe they've figured the whole thing out down to the moment. We'll be watching Donovan closely, but I'm trying to get a leg up on this, anticipate what they might be thinking."

"I understand. I'll get right on it and report back whatever I can learn."

"Good," he said. "Go for it."

I rejoined Richard and explained what the AD wanted me to do.

"That's really interesting," Richard said. "It's sort of becoming a theme, isn't it?"

"What do you mean?" I asked.

"The movie stuff."

"Talk to me about that."

"Well, the New York thing has been done to death—take the whole island of Manhattan and isolate it. Turn it into an enclave or something. Sometimes the island becomes a maximum security prison. Sometimes it's the collective victim of an epidemic. Sometimes it's hit by a tidal wave. Sometimes there's a futuristic twist and we see Manhattan in a different century. Apes have even lived there. Whatever. It works for action/adventure, for sci/fi…anything. Everybody knows New York (and you've got a built-in audience in the city anyway), so you make a movie where the city becomes the subject of the movie, like one of the characters and not just the setting."

"Right," I said, "and the Wolf Trap thing is like *The Godfather*."

"Exactly," Richard said. "First they had the toilet handoff at the *Red Fox Inn*, then they segued to Wolf Trap. They're playing Sonny—outflanking the enemy by getting some inside information on the site for a meeting. They put their weapon there well before the meeting is supposed to occur. That way they can be searched and come out clean. Nobody thinks they'll know the site in advance, so nobody expects them to have a weapon there. Bang. They knock us off and escape scot-free."

"And our job is to outflank the people trying to outflank us."

"Just like the Little Bighorn," Richard said.

"I thought you might say that," I answered.

"Of course, that wouldn't be their version. That's actual history, not a movie."

"Right," I said.

"I like that *Man Who Knew Too Much* wrinkle," Richard said, "if, indeed, that's what they're thinking. Maybe the guy behind all this is a failed movie director or film buff of some sort."

"I don't know about that," I said, "though they picked the name of a French play for their operation. Maybe the notion of isolating New York or killing people in a crowded theatre is so obvious that people decided to make movies about it. They're just following suit."

"True," he said, "and there *have* been people killed in theatres before."

"You're right though, that whoever has been masterminding this is no doubt reaching for big headlines. If Malawi or his people aren't doing this themselves, they'd try to find somebody with a flair for the dramatic."

"OK," Richard said. "If they've hired this guy to be their director let's see what we can do to shut down his production."

SIXTY-THREE

In the next forty minutes I learned more about the Marine Band than I imagined possible. Their advance party—led by a public affairs specialist named Tina Connelly—had already arrived and was checking out the stage with the Filene Center technical staff. There were a lot of overalls and clipboards in evidence and nibbled pencils tucked above ears. Rolls of tape were hanging from most of the toolbelts and work gloves were extending from pockets. It looked more like a construction site than a performance venue. When Gunnery Sergeant Connelly finished with them she agreed to sit down with me. She talked about the Band as if it was a favorite relative. I knew it was old, but I didn't know it was established by an Act of Congress in 1798. That's *old* old. The Band's *seventeenth* director was John Philip Sousa. She spoke about him for nearly fifteen minutes. She also summarized the Band's early history and their relationships with the likes of Presidents Adams and Jefferson.

The military aspects of the organization were particularly interesting to Richard. Members of the Band have to audition. If they're selected, they then sign up for a four-year enlistment in the Marine Corps, but are guaranteed the assignment to the Band. No sudden bait-and-switch with a surprise announcement that they're actually off to Parris Island. They come in as E-6's. The director is a light colonel, the XO a captain, the assistant director a First John. The drum major is a master gunnery sergeant. "Gunnery" is an interesting word in the titles of these people, whose weapons include such items as the French Horn, Euphonium, and B-flat Clarinet.

Later I briefed the AD. "We're going to have a full stage," I said. "The band numbers over 140 individuals and that's not counting their stage managers, stage crew, and supply personnel. They also have a collection of library and public affairs staff. The set list is patriotic and was not advertised in advance. They'll start with 'Strike Up the Band' and end with 'America the Beautiful.'"

"Sounds very vanilla and white bread," he said.

"It will be," I answered. "They'll also do 'Hail to the Chief' and the national anthem, of course. The former is standard when the President is in the audience and the latter is standard, period."

"Any guest performers?"

"They have their own vocalist—a baritone by the way—who will do the Marine hymn and they're going to be joined for 'The Battle Hymn of the Republic' by a church choir from the District. They'll do the British national anthem in honor of the Prime Minister and 'Carry Me Back to Old Virginia' as a thank you to the local arrangers and some donors from Richmond. That's about it."

"And you have all this written down."

"Yes, sir," I said, handing him the list of the numbers to be performed. "Lighting will be very low-key. The stage will be illuminated, of course, and there will be spots on the vocalist and director, but nothing that could in any way distract. No strobes, no lasers, no flash pots—none of that stuff."

"What about fireworks?"

"No, the woods are too dry and the Secret Service gets too jumpy when they hear loud noises in the general area of the President."

"How will the whole thing begin?"

"The President, P.M., and their party will actually be brought in in the dark. They've got some portable floor lighting for the balcony; it's like those light strips on airplanes. And don't worry, before it's installed the dogs will be sniffing it and the bomb squad will be sampling its plastic casing. The audience will have been in place for at least fifteen minutes before the VIP's come in. When the presidential party is in place there will be some spots on them while the Band plays 'Hail to the Chief'. They'll stand, acknowledge the applause, smile and wave, and then sit back down. The spots are then turned off, the stage lights are brought up to full capacity, everybody stands up, they play the 'Star Spangled Banner' and then they finish the rest of the show. After the final applause the audience will be asked to remain in their seats and the presidential party will depart in the darkness."

"And no intermissions."

"No, no intermissions. The show is only an hour and a quarter long. If anyone is desperate to get to the toilet they'll be escorted there and not be permitted to return to the auditorium."

"What about the people sitting on the lawn?"

"Same deal. Once you sit down you're down for the duration."

"Tight ship."

"Yes. That's the plan."

"OK, Gwen, you've been over the whole thing. What jumps out at you, anything?"

"I think the move that they intend to make will come later rather than earlier. They'll want to establish something before they destroy it—get some images in peoples' minds…peace, harmony, patriotism, happy faces…then blow it all up. The government photographers will all be doing their thing when the dignitaries first enter. Some will send their pictures to their agencies electronically; some may even leave. Malawi's people will want to be able to get those images on the record along with those that they add—a kind of ugly *before/after*. They'll also want to give Donovan the chance to set up shop and send through some test pictures. They are also likely to want to hit us at a time when they're certain that the maximum number of people will be affected. That means they won't wait until the last minute. I'd expect them to act some time between half-way through and two-thirds of the way through the program. Donovan's probably on some sort of clock. The program begins at 8:00, so he's probably scheduled to do his thing at 8:30 or 8:45. They wouldn't have told him to do something right after a particular piece."

"Right. There's no way to control for that, since they don't know if the concert will start precisely on time, how long the applause will go, etcetera. If this is being coordinated with an attack on New York they'll be watching the clock closely."

"I figure this as their primary target," I said, "since their optimum time for striking New York would be earlier in the day—midday, for example, or during rush hour, not some time after 8:00 at night. There would still be plenty of traffic and plenty of people to hurt, but not for maximum effect. If they attack New York earlier in the day they know that the President will be whisked away instantly and everyone will immediately be on high alert. Their best shot is to hit all of their targets simultaneously."

"I agree," he said. "The only question now is whether or not we've anticipated their strategy correctly and, of course, whether we've actually found all of their devices."

"Right," I answered. "That's the question." Suddenly the reality of the situation went through my head like a steel spike. We could have swallowed their bait and still be surrounded by fifty blocks of lethal explosive. I decided two things: I wanted to be near Richard for what could be the last few moments of my life and I wanted to do everything I could in the meantime to push those moments as far as possible into the future.

SIXTY-FOUR

We received word of the progress of the presidential motorcade as soon as Air Force One touched down at Dulles. The limos met the entourage on the tarmac and the area was secured before any one appeared at the top of the portable stairway. Sanchez was observing the scene on a television monitor within the headquarters facility and informed me of each step as it occurred.

The President's miniature bull terrier, Bella, wandered out onto the stairway platform—her usual practice—and sniffed the air and inspected the scene. She was quickly picked up—all thirty pounds of her—by a fit presidential aide and carried to the second limo, an indignity which she tolerated as well as could be expected under the circumstances. The President and P.M. did their best to appear together arm-in-arm at the top of the narrow stairway, waved for photographers, and then hurried down the stairs and into their waiting limo. A few seconds later a surrounding line of stretch Cadillac XTS's pulled away and headed toward Wolf Trap.

Richard was now in constant communication with the Secret Service, briefing them on the actions of the Bureau and local law enforcement. Salva was in parallel communication with the upper reaches of the participating agencies. He had a brief conversation with the Vice President, who was part of the presidential motorcade, assuring her that every conceivable possibility had been anticipated and addressed. Doubtless upon Salva's prompting, the Vice President asked to speak with me, expressing her thanks for my work. We spoke for no more than fifteen or twenty seconds, but it was a nice gesture.

I appreciated the flurry of last-minute activity, since it took our minds off of other, darker possibilities, if only for a few moments. Ten minutes before the estimated time of arrival of the motorcade the audience were in their seats and the security personnel were at their posts. The inspections had been conducted efficiently and without long lines, principally because the Wolf Trap audience tends to arrive early, to allow time to acquire the best positions on the lawn and enjoy a picnic dinner prior to the event. With 2600 orchestra seats, 1100 balcony seats, and the capacity for 3000 patrons on the lawn (slightly reduced because of security requirements), the fact that the gates opened at 4:30 ensured a smooth process and an array of smiles and largely-unruffled egos.

All of the members of the audience were given a security tag after their inspections were satisfactorily completed. They seemed to welcome the acquisition of what would instantly become a souvenir that they could display for envious friends and relatives. It would compensate for the confiscation of their wine.

Donovan appeared at 7:00. As soon as he was spotted I received a cell phone message from an agent in eye contact with the official who was assigning arriving members of the audience to different cattle-chute lines. I kept Salva apprised of his movements. After visiting the toilet at the top of the hill and buying a small bottle of water Donovan proceeded to his expected seat and quietly flipped through the evening's program. At 7:30 he received a call on his cell phone. He spoke with the caller for no more than six or seven seconds and returned the phone to his inside jacket pocket. At 7:45 he removed the phone and went through the motions of turning it off in anticipation of the beginning of the concert. It took him longer to do so than was necessary. I checked with the agents who had him under telescopic surveillance and was informed that he had checked the quality of the images that were appearing on the screen of the camera phone. I was reassured by the fact that his anticipated actions were actually coming to pass and so-informed the AD.

"Sometimes we get it right," he said. "We can't underestimate our adversaries, but we shouldn't dig our toes in the dirt and consider ourselves the second team."

I thanked him and continued to work my way through the shadows, observing the audience and the empty seats in the balcony which would soon be occupied by two of the most important people—and richest terrorist targets—in the world.

When I stopped for a moment and surveyed the seats adjoining those that would be taken by the presidential party I thought about how far I had come and how little time it had taken me to get there. My parents remained skeptical of my choice, but had expressed the hope that it would make me happy and reassured me of their willingness to continue to support me, no matter what choices I might make.

I hadn't spoken to them within the last week and reminded myself to do so as soon as the opportunity presented itself. I didn't like talking to them when I was unable to inform them of my actual duties. It somehow seemed, I don't know…pretentious, even though I was simply following standard operating procedures. I preferred to keep our relationship a warm, familial one, not one punctuated by a set of reasonable questions that I was unable, indeed, forbidden to answer.

Lately I had sent some greeting cards as a substitute, trying to let them know that I was thinking about them and wishing them well, even if I had to keep a large part of my life a secret. I thought about this job as a long-term commitment and wondered about its potential long-term effects. Perhaps I could work out a code with them, a guide to generic messages that would tell them I was doing things I was unable to disclose, but thinking of them lovingly and wishing them all the best. I wanted them to know how important they were to me, even if the surest indicator of closeness and intimacy—the sharing of private thoughts and activities—was impossible.

Then, suddenly, something clicked in the back of my head as the house lights began to dim. I moved to a greater vantage point, wondered if Richard would be able to join me, checked on my sidearm, caught Donovan in my line of sight and waited for the program to begin.

SIXTY-FIVE

I watched the entrance of the President and P.M. with my night-vision miniscope. Surrounded by Secret Service agents, they seemed to be talking constantly—fast friends out for a night on the town. Actually a night in the woods, but their enthusiasm was palpable and their close personal relationship a matter of record.

After a strong rendition of 'Hail to the Chief' and the national anthems, a tidal wave of applause and miscellaneous smiles and waves, the VIP's settled in for the rest of the concert. My scope shifted between Donovan and the President. The former seemed squirmy, his chin and neck uncomfortable within his starched collar. He moved from side to side, seemingly trying to free his throat from the collar's grasp. He hadn't taken out his camera phone, but he was tapping his pocket, as if to reassure himself of its presence.

Richard was unable to stay with me during the concert. He was in the communications center with Sanchez and Salva, who kept asking me for updates. I continued to tell him that there were no new developments and he continued to answer that that was fine; that was what he wanted to hear.

The Band soloist's version of the Emma Lazarus Statue of Liberty poem brought the audience to its feet. It was 8:31. I focused on Donovan, who was applauding politely but unenthusiastically. I shifted to the President, who was saying something to an aide, who was leaning over the President's shoulder. The P.M. was whispering something to the Vice President, while all continued to applaud.

When they sat down the Band played an up-tempo version of 'Yankee Doodle Dandy' with alternating flute and piccolo solos. It was 8:35 and Donovan was checking his watch. At 8:40 he had his camera phone in hand. I checked with the agents scanning his moves with telescopic sights. He was photographing the President and P.M. and sending the pictures. They couldn't read the numbers he was punching in because he pulled the camera phone down to chest level in order to be able to scan the keypad. I called Salva.

"He's sending pictures," I said.

"Squirming too," he answered. He must have been receiving parallel reports. I didn't take umbrage at that; I figured that two or three heads are always better than one when you're trying to read a situation through gestures and body language.

"I think it's time," I said.

"I agree," he answered. "Elaine…" he said, calling Sanchez.

I couldn't hear her reply.

"We're watching the dismantled det caps," he said. "We've got them wired so that we'll see if and when they receive a signal." Then I heard him say, "Higginson…"

He was working multiple phones. Gerry Higginson was a bomb tech in New York. He must have been assigned to watch the dismantled devices there and report when they were activated.

Suddenly his voice was clearer and louder. "What's he doing now?" he asked.

"Still taking pictures," I said.

"Has he spoken to anyone?"

"No. He's just transmitting, not receiving. Wait…he's checking his watch again…he's craning his neck…looking for something…expecting something to happen. He looks frustrated. He's moving around in his seat, trying to get a better view. The people on the other side of the aisle are looking at him, wondering why he's not watching the performance. He doesn't seem to care."

"It's 8:45, coming up on 8:46," Salva said.

"Maybe his watch is fast," I said.

"You're probably right. American flight 11 hit the North Tower at 8:46," Salva said.

I heard Sanchez's voice. It was animated. "There they go," she said. Then I heard Salva's voice. "Higginson…"

Then I heard nothing but the sound of a shrill blast as the night sky erupted in a flash of red, white, and yellow.

IV

NAKED MOUNTAIN

SIXTY-SIX

The northern sky was filled with smoke and light as the audience screamed in shock and turned from side to side in search of answers. The President, P.M., and Vice President were covered with Secret Service agents, all talking into their collar mics. The realization that we had escaped something terrible washed over us slowly but surely. I felt my neck and cheeks flush and realized that my hands were suddenly stiff and clammy. The next thing I heard was Salva's voice.

"I'll get a report as soon as possible. The sound came from the north. It wasn't close; I'd say a matter of three or more miles."

"The Cabin John Bridge is about five miles, I think," I said.

"We checked and rechecked all of the bridges in the metropolitan area," he said. "They were clean."

"Right," I said, "but if the device was mobile…"

He paused for a moment before responding. "They could have parked on the side of the road and watched the clock," he said. "Checked the traffic flow…then slipped out into the stream…hit the middle of the bridge at 8:46. Put a finger on the button. Boom."

"All you need is something simple…a little nitrogen fertilizer and some fuel oil," I said. "Remember Oklahoma City."

"Right."

"Also, they could have easily escaped…towed the explosives in a cart or trailer behind their car, unhitched it, and simply driven off. The cars behind them would be playing Demolition Derby and jamming traffic trying to dodge the thing while the perps drove off the bridge, accelerated, and then detonated the device."

"Just a second…" he said.

The presidential party was now surrounded by Secret Service agents and moving quickly out of the Filene Center as ushers and miscellaneous agents cleared a path for them. Donovan was frozen in place. I was close enough to him to see his hands shake. Just above him I could see Beehler, moving into position to follow him when he left. Salva's voice came back on.

"It *was* the Cabin John; they also took out the Wilson," he said.

Even if Chain Bridge and the Memorial, 14th Street, and Roosevelt bridges were still in operation, shutting down the Cabin John to the northwest and the Wilson to the south would completely gridlock the city for hours. The Cabin John (or "American Legion" bridge) and the Wilson were the beltway bridges, the major access routes spanning the Potomac between Virginia and Maryland.

"How about civilian casualties?" I asked Salva.

"Too early to say. Each bridge has sustained major structural damage and some CB radio traffic indicated that several cars went into the river from the Cabin John." He paused for a second and his voice went lower. "That's a long drop."

"What about the President and P.M.?"

"Unless their cars can sprout wings like Chitty Chitty Bang Bang, they're not going to the White House or Camp David. The Secret Service would never put them in the air anyway, not during a terrorist attack. The P.M. hoped to fly back tonight, but that's not going to happen. They've already locked down Dulles and Reagan and they can't get to BWI or Andrews. Besides, we don't know what other surprises the terrorists may have in store. They'll take them to a secure location until we know more."

"Can I ask another question?"

"What is it, Gwen?"

"Did the devices go off in New York at the same time as the devices here?"

"Yes, they did."

"Sir..."

"Yes?"

"What do you want me to do? I want to help."

He paused for several seconds before answering. "I'm not sure that I have an assignment for you just yet," he said. There was a sense of loss in his voice, even a hint of bewilderment.

"Beehler has Donovan in hand; he's basically come down with a bad case of the shakes and a lot of questions on his mind."

"Let me check with Sanchez."

"Thank you, sir; I'll come to you."

I immediately called Richard. "Where are you?" I asked

"Still in the communications center."

"Did the Secret Service tell you what they're going to do?"

"They only said that they're going to transport the presidential party to a safe location."

"I'm coming to join you," I said.

"What does Salva want you to do?"

"Nothing, at this point. And I don't like it."

"What do you mean?" he asked, probably surprised by my statement, since he knew I wasn't prone to insubordination.

"This is the time when we're most vulnerable," I said. "This is exactly what they want to see—the full array of federal agencies chasing their own tails and trying to figure out their next step. They would anticipate this. It would be part of their plan. We've got to clear our heads and plan the next step carefully."

"I agree," he said, "but we've got to get some reports first. What else have they targeted? What else have they hit? What about the people covering Malawi and the other members of the cell? What are they likely to do next?"

"I'll be there in a couple minutes," I said.

I circled around the outside of the Filene Center and made my way up the hill to the communications center. Beehler checked in with me while I was en route.

"Donovan's moving," he said, "but not very briskly. It's as if he's as confused as anyone else. Of course, this could be a dodge. He may have a set of orders he's acting on. They certainly didn't tell him that he was going to be shredded by wood chips or turned into red vapor. They probably sketched out a scenario to maintain plausibility. We'll follow him anyway, of course, but I think he's on a snipe hunt."

"I agree," I said. "Let me know if anything happens."

Richard was standing outside the communications trailer when I approached it. When I reached him he kissed me. Then he squeezed my arm, straightened up, and returned to his more official demeanor.

"Where are they taking the President?" I asked.

"To the Mountain," he said.

"We've got to talk to somebody before they do that."

"What about?" he asked.

"Trust me, Richard," I said. "I don't have time to explain now. We simply have to do it."

SIXTY-SEVEN

The "Mountain" is the site on the eastern side of the Blue Ridge to which presidential-level officials are taken during severe attacks. A heavily-reinforced command center secure against all conventional and nuclear strikes, the facility is a mass of tunnels, situation rooms, sleeping quarters, and dining areas, with defensive military systems and miles of cement walls, rolled homogeneous and composite armour, state-of-the-art ventilation, heating, and cooling devices, and an array of communications technology enabling the President to maintain command control by radio, television, computer, landline, satellite and cellular devices.

"They'll be safe there," Richard said.

"But they have to get there first," I said. "Somehow, someone knew that the President and P.M. were coming to Wolf Trap. The information was passed to the terrorists. Whoever discovered those plans can discover these. Besides, the Wolf Trap visit was not anticipated or expected. This was not a matter of inference or guesswork; they had inside information. The situation now is worse. Given the fact that the city is now gridlocked, the logical expectation is that the Secret Service would seek to sequester the President, P.M. and Vice President in the closest, most accessible, most secure location. Everyone who wishes us serious harm already knows of this site's existence."

"And what are you saying, Gwen, that they will be planning an ambush of some sort?"

"What would you do?" I asked. "You've cut off their natural escape routes and offered them a single, logical alternative. Why?"

"But the original plan was to blow them up. Taking out the bridges could simply be their way of tormenting ordinary citizens by bringing the war to them."

"Yes, but the opposition is smart enough to know that we could have penetrated their plan and discovered the devices. Thus, they had a backup, one that guaranteed they would win, either way. They'd kill us at the Filene Center or kill us when we tried to escape."

"I don't have the kind of authority we'd need," Richard said. "I can't tell the Secret Service what to do."

"I know you can't," I said, "but maybe Salva can intervene in some way. He's got the ear of the Director and the heads of all the pertinent agencies."

"All he can do is say no," Richard said. "Let's propose it."

"Agreed."

We went inside the trailer and explained our concerns.

"I know where you're coming from," he said. "It's still Operation *No Exit*. We're deluded in believing that there still *is* one. We're being canalized."

"Exactly," I said.

"I'll try to stop them," he said, "but I don't hold out a great deal of hope."

I wanted to argue and persuade, but I knew it would only waste time. We stepped back outside and gave him time and room to work the phones. He emerged four minutes later.

"They didn't have any other options," he said. "They can't sit here. They can't drive aimlessly. They can't go into the District. The Pentagon is already encircled by gridlocked traffic and even if they could get to Ft. Belvoir or Quantico they don't provide the degree of security that they need."

"So they've already left?"

"They're just pulling out," he said. "What if we bring in some airmobile infantry and blanket the facility?"

"We don't know where they are, so we don't know what area to patrol," I said.

"Right. And we'd telegraph our own intentions and lose any chance of catching them. I know what I'd do if I were them…"

I completed his sentence. "*I'd* have a couple people, no more than that, and I'd have them armed with things like light anti-tank weapons and surface-to-surface missiles. Pick off the convoy of Cadillacs like tin ducks in a shooting gallery."

"Agreed," he said. "Maybe the Secret Service will go for this," he said, his mind rushing to possibilities. "They could drive to a nearby, secure area and put the VIP's in one of the sedans…keep the Cadillac convoy together…to keep the terrorists guessing…then drive to the Mountain by a circuitous route and give us enough time to get there first. If the terrorists have intercept teams along the way the President and P.M. will bypass them by taking a different route. You can then go directly to the Mountain and see what you can see."

"Sounds good to me," I said. "There's only one problem…actually two."

"Yes?"

"First you've got to get them to agree. Then you've got to keep it secret from nearly everyone involved. That won't be easy. It may not even be possible."

"Because you think there's a leak."

"I don't know what there is, but somehow the terrorists found out about the Wolf Trap event before anyone else did."

"I'll try to keep it controlled—get the VIP's in another vehicle and have them drive off to parts unknown. Then the agent in charge will tell the rest of the drivers to simply follow him, but not tell them where he's going. I think that's the best we can do."

"I agree. That sounds good. Richard and I will take off immediately and communicate only with you."

"I'll have Sanchez equip you with anything you need," he said. "You'd better get going. And Gwen..."

"Yes, sir?"

"Be very, very careful."

SIXTY-EIGHT

Technically the Mountain is in Markham, Virginia, on a road just off of route 66 on the eastern side of Front Royal. Blue Mountain is to the west and Naked Mountain to the right. Naked Mountain is the site of a vineyard.

"Donovan was visiting wineries after his lunch in Middleburg," Richard said.

"Could have been a coincidence," I said. "It's a natural thing to do when you're out in the hunt country, especially if you have time on your hands. Have you ever been there?"

"Once," he said. "About six or seven months ago. You're basically talking about a quiet country road that happens to be just off of 66. It's about fifty miles from here. Heavy traffic and craziness on 66 until you get closer to the piedmont, though there are still a significant number of people who commute to D.C. every day from Front Royal. When you turn off at the Markham exit things instantly get very quiet and very rural. It's nice. You were on the freeway for an hour and then you're suddenly in the woods and mountains. The average Sunday driver or wine taster is totally unaware of the fact that there's a major, underground government installation just down the road. That's the whole point, of course."

When we got to the car I booted up the computer as Richard drove out onto Trap Road. I pulled up the Naked Mountain site. "They're reputed to make the best Chardonnay in the state of Virginia," I said. "It's a pity we won't have the time to taste any of it tonight."

Richard nodded in agreement.

"The logical route to the Mountain is 66," I said, working the Mapquest site. "The back door approach would be via route 50—go through Middleburg on the way to Winchester and hang a left on 17, then shoot over to 688 and go into the Mountain area. We can get to 66 through Vienna and Oakton. We're already beyond the beltway and we can drive directly toward Front Royal. With any luck we'll have at least thirty minutes before the convoy of Cadillacs arrives. We can scope out the area and report back to Salva."

"I doubt that they'd locate near the entrance to the Mountain," Richard said. "The area is filled with sensors and surveillance equipment. They couldn't just set up shop in a pillbox on the side of the hill and wait for their targets to come into view."

"I agree," I said, "but they would probably anticipate the possibility of the convoy coming in by the back door. They may have a team on either side of the Mountain proper, most likely on adjoining private property. Let's see what we can see…"

I pulled up a satellite scan of the area through the Bureau's GIS system. "Here's something," I said. "The area around the Mountain is steep, with 90 degree outcroppings. Not a place from which to shoot a weapon that involves a significant backblast. Plus you've got the surveillance equipment to deal with if you try to climb and crawl your way toward a more workable location. On the other side of the road, however, it's more promising. There's a meadow with dense woods behind. You could slip out of the woods and move into position fairly easily."

"Private property?" Richard asked.

"Yes, I believe so," I said.

"That doesn't mean there wouldn't be sensors and scanning cameras."

"Right," I said, "but it's a matter of patience and planning. I'm sure there's constant motion in the woods with deer and other animals. If you're willing to go to ground and sit tight for a long period of time you'd have a good chance of going undetected, particularly if you were dug in."

"The dig would be easily detected," he said. "You can't move in with a backhoe and start building fortifications."

"No, but maybe you could do a little bit here and a little bit there over a long period of time," I said. "They could act like hunters or dog walkers or maybe even picnickers and prepare the position a few scoops of dirt at a time. All they'd need to do is locate the cameras and determine when they're scanning in their direction and when they're not. As the camera turns in another direction they'd dig frantically, then go back to eating and drinking as it turned back."

"If it was me I'd try to dig a trench just below the top of a hill," Richard said. "That way you could observe the road without breaking the line of sight. Put some camouflage paint on your face and some weeds and leaves on your head and just hunker down. Then, when you see the convoy coming, stand up and fire away, so the backblast of the recoilless rifle or RPG or whatever you're using would go over the top of the hill rather than into its side."

"Like a bazooka, you mean."

"Right. It would have to be something serious. The presidential limos are heavily armored. You can't just fire standard rounds into one. You'd need to inflict significant damage."

"And they'd need a small team to load the weapon and fire it."

"Depending on the weapon," Richard said, "but in this case maybe two or three teams to make sure they hit each vehicle."

"They'd probably go for the lead vehicle first, to break up the convoy," I said.

"Right."

As we turned onto route 66 the westbound traffic was surprisingly light. Traffic into the city was beginning to gridlock but drivers coming in from the west were getting off of 66 at 123 and either seeking alternate routes to their destinations or turning around and getting back on 66 to return to the far western suburbs and exurbs from which they came.

The cars in the eastbound lanes were also noticeably quiet—no heavy bass lines and rap music; people were tuned to the news, hoping for information about the explosions. The skies were clear; that could be in our favor if they were equally clear fifty miles to the west.

"I don't think I'm going to need the siren," Richard said.

"Just as well," I answered. "The less attention we draw to ourselves the better."

For the next ten minutes of the drive I settled back in my seat and gathered my thoughts. An odd sense of calm blew over me, since Richard and I had survived a potential threat as well as an actual one. Perhaps now it would be our turn to surprise the opposition. They would be counting on our lack of awareness of the final act of their play, imagining that we were lurching ignorantly into the sights of their weapons as they had successfully outsmarted and outflanked us.

As we drove on I remembered an event that had occurred years earlier. I was in high school and my family was in Washington for spring break. We were driving across Chain Bridge in the early evening when suddenly there was a flash of red, green, and white light in the sky above the Potomac. At first we thought it was a plane exploding, since they fly down the river to land at Reagan Airport, but the sound was that of a distant bit of fireworks rather than that of powerful explosives. Although the burst was sudden and followed by some separate bits of flame falling to the earth, it was not symmetrical like a fireworks display.

On the evening news that night we learned that what we had observed was actually a meteorite. The heat had come from friction with the air as it passed through the Earth's upper atmosphere. The airflow melts and then removes the meteorite's outer surfaces. Scientists later informed the curious populace that this had been a stony meteorite, a chondrite actually, chondrites being named after their most prominent features—tiny spherical bodies called chondrules. The chondrules were formed four and a half billion years earlier in the Solar Nebula, the cloud of dust and gas from which the Sun, the planets, asteroids and comets were formed.

Chondrules are not found in rocks on earth. They come to us from the very birth of the solar system. Sometimes, like this time, an explosion in the sky above a river can prove to be harmless in its effects and beautiful in its display. At other times it can result from torrents of anger and hate that have seethed for generations and suddenly been released in an act of singular violence.

Some commentators on 9/11 spoke of the attacks as, ultimately, a grand, if heinous, work of art. The imagination responds to form, whether it be associated with pure beauty or utter ugliness.

That was then and this was now. What we would need most in the minutes ahead would be clearheaded reason and the capacity to understand and respond, not sit with our mouths gaping in confusion or incomprehension. Perhaps we *had* been outflanked, but it was still a long way to the final act of their little drama.

SIXTY-NINE

My father used to talk about the drive from L.A. to the desert and how the cement and neon finally disappeared as the grit and rock came into view. The land forms and the climate really didn't change, but your sense of it all did. You felt as if you had crossed some border and left civilization for the waste beyond, though it was really all waste that had been irrigated or former scrub that had been cleared.

As you drive from the Washington suburbs to the exurbs the signals of change are the fresh plasticity of the strip malls, the increasing lengths and breadths of the townhouse developments (with their declining prices) and the number of buildings—abandoned service stations, farm houses, pre-chain motels—that represent the abandoned fragments of a past era. Beneath all these human markers, however, we were still traversing the same hunting ground that had persisted for millennia and beneath the calm and civilized exteriors of the men and women who had covered the land with monuments to capital and industry and development were the still-beating, ancient hearts of hunters and scavengers. The endless chain of corporate logos and predictable franchise architecture obscured the fact for a moment or two, but a single explosion brought it all rushing back. The underlying element was always one of struggle and survival.

The sky that hung above today's bedroom communities—outlined and divided by azaleas, yews, and sculpted boxwood—had arched over the same expanses when ancient predators walked there, just as the cold, bright moon fixed in the air above us had once illuminated battlefields covered with torn and splayed corpses. The blood and stench of the ages commingled in the soil and cries of horror and pain still echoed in remote crevices and corners. Maybe I was obsessing, but when I looked for symbols of civilization my mind kept turning to memories of barbarism. I didn't like the feel of it at all.

As the moonlit outline of the Blue Ridge came into view we talked about our next steps.

"Driving speed is crucial," I said. "I'm not trying to backseat you, but we'll have to pass through whatever gauntlet might be there at a plausible, normal rate. As far as they're concerned we have no reason to slow down and look around."

"Just a tired couple snaking our way through the dips and bends as efficiently as possible."

"Right. Anxious to get home, but not end up in a roadside ditch."

"I can do that," Richard said. "We'll come in from the south. You look east and I'll look west as we pass through the area around the Mountain. No rubbernecking, just a slow scan."

"Exactly," I answered. "And Richard…"

"Yes?"

"Be very, very careful."

"Always," he said.

"I know, but I've got a bad feeling about all this, probably because I've seen the sky light up once tonight and that was more than enough."

"Have you got any of your hats with you?" he asked.

"I've got one scrunched up in my purse. I'll put it on."

"Anything that makes you look less official," he said.

"Good idea. I should have thought of it."

"You were trying to stay beautiful for me," he said. "You know I like to have a clear view of everything."

"That's sweet," I said, giving him points in my mental ledger for trying to put me at ease and take my mind off of my obsessions and fixations. "You're a very thoughtful young man and I appreciate that, especially [putting on the broad, soft-brimmed hat] when I'm in my full southern belle mode."

I could see him smile from the muted light of the dashboard. He eased into the exit lane and turned off of 66.

"Here we go," he said. "Let's check this place out."

He was holding at 25-30 as we drove through the darkness. I reached into my purse and took out my sidearm, holding it on my lap and preparing to make my way through the woods and scrub in search of the would-be ambushers.

As we passed the sign for the Naked Mountain vineyards and winery I slipped two additional magazines of ammunition into my jacket pockets. I could feel the adrenalin level in my body rise. I was anxious to get outside, get some earth under my feet, track the people who hoped to do us harm.

The road jogged to the left and then to the right. As it began to straighten a car approached us. The high beams were on. "What do you think?" Richard asked. "Should I flash my bright lights also? It'd be the natural thing to do."

Before I could answer I saw an object extend from the driver's side of the approaching vehicle. A second later our windshield exploded, the car swerved, left the road, and began to roll as everything went black.

SEVENTY

I opened my eyes to a white room with blank walls, a shaded window, and shelves filled with monitoring equipment. There was no clock and no television set. An IV had been inserted in my left arm and I was aware of the presence of tape above my eyes and around my left ear. It appeared to wrinkle as I blinked my eyes. The AD had been sitting in a chair at the foot of my bed; when I scanned the room he rose quickly and walked toward me.

"How do you feel?" he asked.

"I'm OK," I answered. "How is Richard?"

"Holding his own," he said. "A lot of things are broken, but his vital signs are stable."

"Is he here, in this building?"

"No, he's at another location."

"Nearby?"

"I can't really say at this point," he answered.

"I don't understand."

"Above my pay grade," he said. "Homeland Security has the wheel now."

"But he's a Bureau agent," I said.

"Yes, but they're conducting the investigation."

"I don't understand," I said.

"The other side had to have known that we had changed our plans."

"Since the shooters were leaving when we got there."

"Yes."

"And the government thinks one of us tipped them off."

"No one knows how they found out. Everything's precautionary at this point."

"They've separated all of the agents involved and are interrogating them individually."

"Yes," he said.

"What did they find at the scene when they found us?"

"Gwen...I think you should rest now. There'll be plenty of time to go through this."

"I want to talk about it now," I said.

He looked as if he was suddenly carrying a great weight. Finally he spoke.

"Your vehicle was sprayed with a shotgun."

"Not a sniper's weapon," I said.

"A backup," he answered, "if you *were* shot by the terrorists themselves, which is the operating assumption."

"I doubt that it was anybody else. Things aren't yet so bad that private citizens amuse themselves by shooting strangers on quiet country roads. And even if they were, this would be too much of a coincidence."

"I agree," he said.

"Did they find anything at the scene?"

"Tread marks. After they shot, they accelerated. An SUV, possibly an Escalade."

"Where had it been parked?"

"Why do you ask that?"

"Do we know?"

"Yes. It had been parked a hundred yards or so down the road, to the north of where you were hit. Just off the highway. Under some scrub pine."

"Did they find a sniper's nest along the ridge line?"

"They're looking now," he answered.

"Can you check with them?"

"Gwen…"

"It would verify our assumption—that they were preparing to ambush the presidential convoy. Their car was hidden on the side of the road; they were off at the crest of the hill, positioning themselves to shoot. When they found out that all bets were off they returned to their car and started to leave."

"And then shot at you in anger and frustration?"

"I don't know. Something like that…"

"I'll see what I can find out," he said. "Meanwhile, you rest."

"With all due respect, sir, I don't think we have time for that. We've got to move."

"There's a full team in the field, Gwen," he said. "The last thing I want is to see you get out of here prematurely and end up bleeding all over my car."

I tried to form a smile. "Meanwhile," he said, "can I get you anything?"

"Thanks. I could use some juice. Something sweet and cold."

He went out in the hallway. A few minutes later a nurse in a starched, white uniform appeared at the door. She was carrying a cup with an orange fluid.

"Thanks," I said. "What is that?"

"Juice," she said.

"Anything else in it?"

"Just vitamins," she answered.

The cup had a very long, user-friendly straw. The contents tasted like out-of-date Tang made with iron-laced well water.

"It's kind of nasty," the nurse said, "but it's good for you."

"It feels good going down, so long as I don't have to think about the taste," I said.

She smiled.

"What have I got?" I asked. "Superficial stuff?"

"Yes. There were some glass fragments stuck between your left eye and left ear and damage to your left shoulder, but the airbag protected you from anything more serious on impact. The curves in the highway probably made the driver slow down. That would have helped too."

I hadn't noticed any tape on my shoulder, but when I moved it I could feel some bandaging grab against my hospital gown.

"Any word on the driver of the vehicle in which I was riding?"

"She or he wasn't brought to this facility. We weren't told anything about anyone but you."

"Where am I, actually?"

"Emergency Care, in Manassas."

"Like a miniature hospital?"

"Yes. Usually for people with heart attacks, but we also see accident victims."

"How long have I been here?"

She bent down and looked at my chart. "About three and a half hours," she said.

"Thanks," I said. "Any chance I could make a deal with you?"

"On what?" she asked.

"On some vitamins in other form, washed down by some real orange juice?"

"I'll see what I can do," she said, "but I wouldn't get my hopes up. If you get too comfortable here you might never leave."

"I understand," I said. "The insurance company's clock is ticking."

Ten minutes later Salva returned. He was carrying a bottle of orange juice from a vending machine.

"Much obliged," I said.

"The nurse mentioned it to me," he said.

It was watery, but better than the killer Tang.

"I've got a contact on the field team," he said. "They found a double foxhole along the ridge line. No evidence that it was occupied recently.

They missed it at first. Someone had thrown some branches and scrub over the top."

"They had to leave in a hurry," I said. "They didn't have time to fill it in."

"That would be my conclusion," he said.

"Then the only unanswered question is why they took a shot at us and made their presence so obvious. They could have packed their bags and RPG's or whatever and simply driven off into the night."

"Best guess?"

"Yes."

"They wanted to see *somebody* die."

SEVENTY-ONE

"There's one thing you can count on, Skip," I said.

"What's that?" he asked.

"It wasn't me and it wasn't Richard who tipped them. No false modesty—if they had an asset that valuable they wouldn't kill it off."

"Not likely."

"Particularly not when their current operation mostly went belly-up and they're likely to be hungry for additional revenge."

"I agree."

I paused before speaking, but then reiterated my request to see Richard.

"That's impossible, Gwen. Homeland Security wants first crack at him. Besides, he's sedated to the gills and won't be ready to talk for at least a day or two."

"Then let's you and I take a drive to the Blue Ridge and see what we can see."

He paused before responding.

"You can keep an eye on me," I said. "Make sure I stay out of trouble. I know that I'm not ready for full duty. I just want to see things. Walk around a little. Get a better perspective."

"I'll check back in a couple hours," he said. "Sleep in the meantime. By then it'll be light and we'll see what kind of shape you're in."

"OK, thanks," I said, closing my eyes, though my brain was whirring like an overwound toy.

He returned at 8:15. It had been light for hours. When I heard footsteps at the door to my room I opened my eyes. He knocked gently and I said, crisply, "Come in." When he entered the room I searched his eyes, looking for signals. Relief? Disappointment?

His eyes were flat. "How do you feel?" he asked.

"I'm ready to take a walk," I said.

"I'll check with the staff first," he said. "And with Homeland Security. Maybe we could do an hour or two and then let you rest some more."

"Why not just let me check out," I said. "A couple of pain pills and I'll be OK. There's nothing broken. The wounds are superficial. I'm a little sore but I can function."

He didn't respond; he just turned and left. Ten minutes later he returned. "OK," he said. "We'll try it for an hour and see how you do."

The Emergency Care facility insisted on taking me to the drive-up lane in a wheelchair. I slid into the front seat of Salva's sedan and slipped into my seatbelt. My shoulder was still very sore. He helped me click the buckle into place.

As he pulled out of the driveway I told him it wasn't really necessary for us to return right away to the scene of the shooting.

"Why not?" he asked.

"I trust the field team," I said. "They can find whatever evidence remains and start processing it. I just wanted to go somewhere where we could talk without fear of being overheard."

"OK," he said, turning right, toward the heart of Manassas. He was shaking his head slightly, in incomprehension. He was trying to do it inconspicuously, but I still noticed. A few minutes later he spotted a *Starbucks* in a mini-mall on Center Street. "They'll have juice too," he said.

"My turn," I said, getting out of the car. "You got it last time."

"Forget it," he said, as we entered. "What do you want?"

"Orange juice *and* coffee—black," I said.

"You got it."

I found a quiet corner booth and sat down, resting my shoulder against the wall. He returned in a few minutes with our drinks. "Now what do you want to talk about?" he asked.

"What really happened," I answered.

"Talk to me," he said.

"First," I said, "I think that the possibility that one of our people consciously tipped off the terrorists is remote in the extreme."

"I'd like to believe *that*," he answered. "I'd hate to think that one of our people was dirty, but, at this point, who knows? Answer me this— why did you say *consciously?*"

"Those are top people. With the exception of Richard and me they've been around forever. They've been cleared at the highest levels and I find it hard to believe that there's ever been anything in any of their records to cause anyone to be suspicious. They could, however, have said something that was overheard."

"The terrorists would have had to have had an agent on site," he said.

"Yes...?"

"If someone followed the convoy from Wolf Trap and then observed the principal dignitaries leave their limo and get in a sedan, they could have so informed the terrorists. But no...that wouldn't have happened."

"The switch was supposed to have been made at a secure site—in a garage or some other enclosed space, where it couldn't be observed."

"Right, and it was done just like that," Salva said.

"What you're saying is that they could have had a backup at the park—in the event that the bombs were detected and shut down. She or he overheard something or saw something that wasn't quite kosher. If so, it wouldn't have been Donovan. Too low level. Too much of an amateur."

"But possibly someone else..."

"Tough to pull off," I said. "We wouldn't let anybody get anywhere close to the vehicles. The place was crawling with agents...Bureau... Secret Service...it was like a convention. Wait a minute," I said.

"What?"

"It has to be…"

"What?"

I took a long drink of my coffee. "This is really good," I said. "I feel comfortable at last. That's it…"

SEVENTY-TWO

"What were you going to say?"

"I was going to say that comfortable's good, but not when you get *too* comfortable. All of a sudden it's so obvious; I could bang my head against this wall."

"I'm not following, Gwen. What's your point?"

I took another drink. "The real problem is not that the terrorists knew that the convoy wasn't coming last night."

"Yes…?"

"The problem is that they knew that the P.M. and President *were* coming to Wolf Trap and they knew it long before the agencies did. Last night was easy; all they had to do was have a car in the area, ready to follow the convoy of limos. The slightest change in protocols…the convoy turning off the road…the convoy taking a circuitous route… anything like that could have raised questions and forced them to abort. The real issue is that they knew something *secret*—something secret at the highest levels—before we did."

"I agree."

"My first thought was that they may have overheard something, but we do everything in our power to prevent that from happening. The President is shuffled from one secure facility to the next—no sound gets in and no sound gets out. His cars are the same as his office rooms; his environments *can't* be bugged."

"SCIFs—Sensitive Compartmented Information Facilities."

"Right. SCIFs. But there are SCIFs and then there are *SCIFs*. If you look at all of the presidential environments the limos are clearly the most vulnerable."

"Why do you say that?"

"First, because the other targets are so daunting. The Oval Office is under constant, intense surveillance. So is Camp David, in part because of the inherent threats posed by its location. The Western White House is on top of a mountain in Colorado and it's under constant guard by suspicious people with twitchy fingers and an arsenal of automatic weapons. Each of the room-sized SCIFs is crawling with Secret Service personnel. They're swept more often than the ice in a curling tournament. The cooks, wait staffs, and secretaries have been around forever and they're fiercely loyal. Air Force One is a possibility, but it has more cautious handlers than a Triple-Crown winner. There's also the fear that it could be brought down by a bomb or missile; that adds to the care and the caution. The limos—the 'beasts', the Cadillac Ones—are different. Think about it. They're used for awhile and then they're garaged. They're transported by aircraft. They're *out of sight* for long periods of time."

"But they're still SCIF's," the AD said. "The bad guys can't ride along with the VIP's to overhear their conversations and the limo phones cannot be tapped. All communications are encrypted through a system which changes frequencies two or three times a second. The messages simply *cannot* be cracked."

"Too much at stake," I said. "When the President travels he's got a military aide in the front seat with the Football. He's got direct lines to the Atlantic and Pacific fleet commands as well as the National Military Command Center. He's ready to go to war at any moment and his environment is absolutely secure."

"Has to be," Salva said.

"So even if they had a mole who was building or armoring the limos he wouldn't be able to bug the vehicle in such a way that the communications within the limo could be monitored by foreign agents."

"Absolutely not. And O, H, & E are above reproach."

"The armorers," I said. He tilted his head forward in recognition. I continued to be amazed by Salva's ability to call up precise acronyms and abbreviations. Success in a bureaucracy requires endless attention to bureaucratic detail.

"Right," he said. "O'Gara-Hess & Eisenhardt. It used to just be H & E, but O'Gara bought them out a few years ago. They have a sole source contract with the government. Nobody else touches the presidential limos. Saves a lot of hassle. If the government used other armorers their employees would all have to pass top level security checks and the clearance processes would all have to be vetted by the Secret Service. So they decided to avoid all the red tape and just stick with O, H & E."

"They're in the midwest, right?"

"Ohio. They used to be in Blue Ash, just outside of Cincinnati. I think they're still around there someplace."

"But what happens to the vehicles when they leave Ohio? This is very high tech stuff—special varieties of hardened steel...kevlar compounds... this isn't the same caddy that the funeral director drives."

"No, and the manufacturing processes are highly classified."

"So who looks after the cars when they get to Washington?"

"The Secret Service—Protective Vehicle Division."

"But something technical like that isn't part of a Secret Service career track. It's not like you're dealing with counterfeiting one day, presidential protection another, and then suddenly you're detailed for three years to the PVD and become a highly-skilled armorer."

"I don't know," the AD said, "probably not."

"I'm just guessing," I said, "but if I was responsible for the PVD and was looking to hire somebody I'd probably bring in somebody from the manufacturing operation, somebody who already had all the technical knowledge."

"Yes, and he (or she, I guess) would already have a security clearance."

"Right," I said, "but while they could join the Secret Service and be official and all that, it would still be a kind of short cut. Like a mid-career move...not a...*vocation*. And the technical knowledge would be key; that would be the sole reason for their being hired."

"They'd be like warrant officers in the military," the AD said.

"The short cut—it's a chink in the armor," I said. "No pun intended."

"But they still couldn't bug the limos."

"No, but a person like that...a person who had gained peoples' confidence over time...a person who was on call for special assignments; such a person could get past the security tape in an instant."

"And put a transmitter in a non-SCIF limo or sedan."

"Yes," I said.

"But that still doesn't mean that they could bug an armored limo."

"They wouldn't have to," I said. "If they were in the Protective Vehicle Division every day and everyone trusted them, all they'd have to do is find a tiny hole or crevice in the vehicles and slip in a voice-activated tape recorder—cold war technology, dinosaur stuff—then just check the tape every night when the vehicle was parked and see what the occupants had to say that day."

His face dropped. "And someone who had worked for the manufacturer would know the spots least subject to detection."

"Of course," I said. "It's all so simple in a way. Ultimately, it's not even a matter of technical expertise. It's simply a matter of gaining peoples' confidence...and then betraying it."

SEVENTY-THREE

"Tell me something, Gwen…" the AD said, as he finished off his coffee.

"Yes, sir?"

"What did you study in college?"

"Geography. Human geography, especially."

"People and the land, their interaction with the environment, that kind of thing?"

"We studied that, but that wasn't my primary interest. I did my undergraduate thesis on Victorian cities."

"In England?"

"Yes. I was always interested in things like the relationship between nature, land forms, economics, culture, that kind of stuff. You know why the west side of town is usually nicer than the east side of town?"

"Why?"

"Because the wind comes in from the west, so they put the tanneries on the east side, so you don't have to smell them. Then when the towns expand and become cities the expensive neighborhoods are in the west. The farther you could get from the smells the better."

"Not in New York, though," he said. "The east side is pricier than the west."

"No tanneries," I said. "When the economy changes it pulls a lot with it. It's like the comedian who walks through the audience and points to a nearby table saying 'Now these are the good seats.' Still, Mayfair is more attractive than Whitechapel."

"Fascinating," he said, sipping his coffee. "Here you are, a Native American woman, studying urban geography one day and then suddenly tracking terrorists the next."

"The reasoning process is the same," I said. "It's always a matter of identifying facts and eliminating possibilities. If you see tracks in the snow and it's 1985 you can eliminate a whole set of animals—mastodons, saber-toothed tigers, triceratops...if you're just outside of Bengal you have to be alert to possibilities that you can forget about if you're just outside of Poughkeepsie. You look at size and shape and the distance between the marks. You look at the foliage to the left and right and the foliage above...see what's been bent or broken...see what's still in place...you think about what you could possibly be up against...tusks, teeth, fangs, claws, venom, M240 machine guns.... The people who lived on the plains and in the mountains...those who survived and prospered...they were historians, naturalists, observational biologists...even nutritionists."

"And warriors," he added.

"Sometimes," I said.

"It has to be in the blood, at least to some degree," he said.

"What do you mean?"

"You," he said. "You're only a few months past being a rookie and already you're in the middle of a major case, maybe even a historic one. You're special, Gwen. It's a gift in some ways, but I have to believe it's also something in..."

"The tribe?"

"I wasn't going to say that."

I smiled. "It's not a bad term to me. You know what my grandfather used to say?"

He waited for my answer, clutching his empty cup.

"He'd say, 'Think about old Lewis and Clark. Off with their Corps of Discovery. Travelling through barely-known, barely-understood territory. Going upstream. Climbing mountains...and then finding more mountains...bargaining for horses...eating God knows what...

surviving the winter in the Columbia Valley with constant rain and the same diet over and over. Finally they're finished and this time they coast along the Missouri…back to St. Louis…a tiny place in those days…but a place with taverns and drink. They're sitting in those taverns, telling stories beyond all imaginings. And you know what the people said to them—the French, the Germans, sitting in those crowded taverns filled with smoke and beer and whisky—their mouths open and their eyes bulging. You know what they said? I'll tell you what they *didn't* say. They didn't say, 'Tell us about the Mandan; tell us about the Hidatsa.' They said, 'Tell us about the *Sioux*.'"

V

MILITARY ROAD

SEVENTY-FOUR

"We've got to pick up the track again," Salva said.

"Agreed," I said. "Can I make a suggestion?"

"Of course."

"We should do it very quietly. We don't know who's with us and who's not and we don't know whose communications are being intercepted or overheard."

"Correct."

"I'd like to see the personnel folders of all of the people at the Protective Vehicle Division and I'd like to see any records we could obtain with regard to telephone communications between them and potential cell members. It may be that all we could get would be calls between public phones or a mix of public and private, but I'd like to see a grid that might tell us something."

"Yes, we might find a call to Donovan, for example, from a number in New York, with repeating calls to D.C. or the Washington metropolitan area from the same source."

"Exactly," I said. "My mind is running to various possibilities. We might, for example, set up some sort of scam to draw them into the open, assuming they don't suspect us of having discovered their system (if we in fact *have*)."

"Right, but we'd need attractive bait or at least a commitment of significant resources and we're several steps away from that. We need to know more before we pitch something."

"Understood," I said. "How about Malawi? What's he been up to?"

"On the west coast, probably trying his best to distance himself and gain some deniability. He's never more than a phone call away, of course, but he's been seen in a number of public venues, public enough for us to assume that he's consciously leaving a trail."

"How about last night, say around 8:30?"

"Actually he left San Francisco and took the shuttle to Burbank. He was sitting on the verandah of a hotel in Pasadena, watching the smog on the palm trees in the San Gabriel Valley."

"And being watched," I said, "probably by design."

"Yes."

"That would suggest (as we thought) that the person in charge of the operation last night was a subcontractor."

"That's my guess," Salva said. "There was no great flurry of communications, even between 8:30 and 9:00. Malawi's cell phone was on the table while he was reading a book and sipping a drink. It's possible he was receiving text messages that we couldn't detect, but it's clear that he wasn't sitting in any command headquarters, issuing orders and managing countermoves."

"So where's the director of the operation—New York? Washington?"

"That's what we've got to find out," he answered. "Let's get started."

After we dropped our empty cups and bottle in the trash and recycling receptacles, the AD commented on his need to contact some 'assets'; these were likely to be agents like me—compartmentalized individuals with whom he could conduct compartmentalized business. I renewed my request to visit Richard and it was again denied. Then I asked what I could do besides sit around and heal.

"How do you feel, really?"

"Maybe fifty percent in my left arm and shoulder and close to a hundred everywhere else, so long as I pop an occasional aspirin."

"I'll get you a car," he said. "You can check with the team at the Mountain, see if they've turned anything."

Thirty-five minutes later we rallied with an agent just outside of Manassas. He didn't identify himself to me, but handed me his keys and left in Salva's sedan. I headed west. As I drove away from the strip malls and into the open, green spaces I began thinking about the local battlefields. Nobody at the time anticipated how bloody the actions would be. People from Washington would sometimes drive out to the countryside to see the engagements in the early portion of the war. Death as entertainment. Perhaps it was all a little unreal to them, much like our current situation. It was quite real to me though. Richard was wrapped up in a hospital bed somewhere—assuming he was still alive—and there was nothing I could do but maintain my focus and move on. I thought about the possibility of paying a visit to the person who had put him there; then I thought about how nice it would be to be able to introduce myself, mention my relationship with Richard and then give him some clear and unmistakable indication of how I felt about what he had done.

SEVENTY-FIVE

The crime scene techs were operating out of a modified van that had more pigeon holes and compartments than an alchemist's cabinet. They had taped off three principal areas within the general site and were proceeding square foot by square foot like a team of archaeologists on a long-term dig. They were finishing up with the segment of the highway that included the point from which the terrorists fired and the point at which we received that fire, but they were still working intently on the area where their vehicle had been parked and the area at the crest of the hill that circumscribed their foxhole.

When I drove up to the barricade that ran the width of the road I was told to park in the burn. The uniformed officer who had so instructed me called the supervising tech, who left the van and approached me. Her name was Evelyn Hallensby.

"Assistant Director Salva told us you were coming," she said. "How can we be of help?"

"I'd like to know what you've turned so far," I answered. "I know it's early but anything you have could be useful."

She took me back to the van and offered me some coffee.

"Several interesting things so far," she said, picking up a pair of plastic evidence envelopes. The first contained a tiny piece of paper with a burn mark along the edge.

"It's from a cigarette," she said. It was found in the area just behind the tree under which their vehicle was parked. It was found clinging to some weeds. It could have blown there from another site, of course, but the paper is very fragile and this is a large fragment. Also, it rained heavily yesterday afternoon, so the fact that the paper is fresh suggests that it was discarded some time between yesterday afternoon and this morning."

"Field-stripped," I said. "Military-style."

"Right," she said. "I think it's American and I doubt that we'll be able to pick up any DNA from it, but there's a small segment of a fingerprint—not enough to check for matches through our databases, but enough to verify and eliminate if we can identify a small group of possibles."

"Excellent," I said.

"This is interesting also," she said. The second envelope was larger; it contained some weeds, twigs, and assorted grit.

"This material is from their foxhole. There was a single large branch spread across the top and then grass, weeds, and miscellaneous junk strewn among the limbs. The grit is granite. And look here..."

She reached inside the van and took out a pair of plaster molds. "Footprints. Found next to their vehicle. The earth was soft after the rain yesterday. We got lucky there. Each was wearing boots with waffled soles. Size 9 and size 11 1/2. There was grit in one of the footprints next to the vehicle. Granite also. It matches the granite dust above the foxhole."

"He kicked the twigs and stuff across the top of the hole and some of the material that was caught in the sole of his boot broke loose and landed there."

"That's what we figure," Hallensby said.

"If there isn't any obvious granite in the area here, he must have brought it with him," I said.

"Right."

"A terrorist from New Hampshire?" I asked, rhetorically.

"Probably not likely, but I know a whole island of granite with a very big park in the center," she said.

"Fifty-ninth street and points north," I answered.

"It gets better..."

"The boots are military."

"They are indeed," she said. "Both pair."

"How about the vehicle?"

"Almost surely an Escalade. We'll know more after we go back to the lab. We'll also know more about the granite. If you give me your cell number I'll keep you posted. In the meantime, feel free to stick around. We're still looking for spit, urine puddles, that sort of thing."

"Much appreciated," I said. "Just one more question."

"Yes?"

"Which shoe had the granite?"

"Bigfoot's."

SEVENTY-SIX

Bigfoot. The mastermind, the person Richard called the Director? I had to admit that it made a certain amount of sense. A serious terrorist bent on killing the President of the U.S. and the Prime Minister of the United Kingdom was unlikely to send an assistant or functionary in to complete the operation. Unless, of course, there were people who were better assassins. In some ways, the most prominent terrorists were middlemen or brokers but ultimately they made their bones by terrorizing, not by administering. Also, if he was a failed subcontractor, whose attempt at demolitions had gone belly up, he would hesitate to send in the second team when the Malawi paycheck was still dangling in the air before him. At the least he would want to be in a position to supervise those who might possess greater technical efficiency, at least at crunch time. Placing him at the scene made sense; imagining his particular role there was still an open issue.

The granite in the boot waffling surprised me. A real pro would have been aware of our capacity to detect the presence of such material and would have taken the appropriate steps to frustrate our attempts. I also figured that the New York connection was a long shot. There was granite everywhere, after all, and it was unlikely that a pro would walk around Manhattan in Army boots, particularly if he was meeting upper East- and upper West-siders like Malawi. His first priority would be to fit in rather than stand out.

An hour later Hallensby approached me with an update.

"I've got something very interesting," she said.

"What is it?" I asked.

"In Bigfoot's boots—manzanita seeds. We couldn't identify them at first, but we took some pictures, scanned them, and sent them downtown. We just got back a positive i.d."

"California," I said.

"Probably," Hallensby answered. About fifty different species, ninety percent found there."

"It sprouts after fires. Used for watershed protection...erosion control," I said.

"Exactly," she answered. "Looks like he may be bi-coastal."

"Very interesting," I said, and thanked her for bringing me up to speed. I didn't share any other thoughts with her. There was no real need to. After watching our windshield blow apart I was more guarded... maybe compartmentalizing a little...like Salva. The fact that there were manzanita seeds in his boots *was* interesting, but it didn't mean that he was bi-coastal. There's plenty of granite in California. Again, there's plenty of granite everywhere, particularly these days, with the flooring and counter top industries featuring it prominently. He could be masquerading as a contractor or operating an import business as a front. He could also have a special collection of misdirection attire that he used to mislead evidence techs. I needed something much more specific and called Salva, first bringing him up to date on the evidence that Hallensby had turned.

"Sounds as if all of your intuitions were right," he said. "Let me rephrase that. Your *deductions*."

"*Intuitions* doesn't bother me," I said.

"They *were* going to attempt an ambush and when it was clear to them that that wasn't happening they tried to cover their tracks as quickly as possible and then got the hell out of there, stopping only to shoot at you. What do you make of that?"

"I don't know," I said. "It was incredibly stupid. The last thing they needed to do was call attention to themselves. What if they had missed and we had been in a position to call in reinforcements? What if we had been the advance party for a whole convoy of heavily-armed agents? It was unprofessional in the extreme."

"Agreed," he said. "On the other hand, consider their frustration. If they had been working on operations like this for years (as they probably were) and the whole thing fell apart like a bad suit (as it obviously did), they were very, very angry. You were handy, so they took it out on you."

"They might have thought that anything other than a pickup truck was likely to be a government sedan," I said. "There wouldn't have been much other traffic at that time of night. They saw us and acted impulsively. They wanted to blow up something and kill somebody and we presented them with a target. Still...it was very sloppy."

"Anger's a possibility," Salva said. "It's plausible at least. Maybe a little fear? That can screw up your head too."

"Because their employers were going to be very disappointed? Maybe even thinking about cutting their losses by severing their connection in some definitive way?"

"Not beyond the realm of possibility."

"He and his partner may go to ground fast."

"Assuming the partner's still among the living," Salva said. "In times like these everyone involved may be tempted to cut his losses."

"I'll keep you posted if they turn anything else," I said. "Anything new at your end?"

"Well, with Donovan sulking at his hotel I put Beehler on the Protective Vehicle Division personnel records. Nothing so far; they all look like squeaky-clean patriots. We made much more progress in another area. Something very promising," he said. "Based on one of your suggestions. I'll email you right away."

SEVENTY-SEVEN

I walked quickly to the Bureau sedan and booted up the computer. The encrypted email was already in the queue and downloaded to my inbox as soon as I entered my password. There was no message beyond an attached document, which I opened.

It was a map of the eastern seaboard with a superimposed triangle. Two of the lines were solid; one was dotted. I called Salva on my cell.

"Thank God for big and fast computers," he said. "A lot of people in New York call Long Island as well as Washington, but in this case the calls are both recent and suspicious. The Manhattan calls are from a public booth at Columbus Circle. There are calls *to* the other two points from that booth, but no calls *between* the other two."

"Malawi's at Central Park West, right in the neighborhood."

"Yes, and he'd pass this booth en route to any number of appointments in midtown, including his regular breakfasts at the University Club."

"How about the calls to Long Island?"

"Public phone; the North Shore Marina."

"In Southold?"

"Yes."

"Donovan. How about in Washington?"

"Two addresses—1855 Wisconsin Avenue and 4877 MacArthur Boulevard."

"Give me a second," I said, keying in the URL for Google maps.

"Already checked," Salva said. "The first is a public phone in a grocery parking lot."

"The Georgetown Social *Safeway*," I said, "the District Millenials' 7/11 and speed dating site."

"Bingo," he said.

"How about the one on MacArthur?"

"Addy Bassin's *MacArthur Liquor*."

"Right across the street from the Palisades *Safeway*."

"Yes," he answered.

"Top wine store," I said. "Another upscale stopoff point."

"Uh-huh."

"Each is on a major migration route, the first to the northern edge of Georgetown, then Chevy Chase and Bethesda, the second to Potomac, North Arlington and McLean."

"Right."

"Nice terrorist targets nearby," I said. "Dumbarton Oaks—a nice soft target...the Vice-President's house a little ways up the street...the National Cathedral..."

"Yes," he said, "and the Georgetown Reservoir over on MacArthur Boulevard. A chance to poison a high-profile part of the city's water supply..."

"Right," I said, "but when you think about it, the city is filled with terrorist targets. I like the migration route part better...and the fact that there are nice, large parking lots at each location. If you've scheduled an important call at a prearranged time the last thing you want to do is circle the block looking for a parking place."

"Or stand in the booth watching your car being towed," Salva added.

"And you could slip between the two sites very easily. MacArthur hits Wisconsin just a few blocks below the Social *Safeway*."

"Right, so you could mix it up a little if you were worried that you were being followed."

"Yes," I said. "Anybody seen any Escalades in the area lately?"

"Now that you ask, I've got people watching," he said. "Nothing yet. Of course, as you said earlier, they may go to ground for awhile, if they're not already buried under it."

"To my knowledge there's been no positive i.d. yet that it even *is* an Escalade," I said.

"No, and since they sell about 25,000 of them a year it's impractical to go door to door. We've run a quick scan for the area and are chipping away at it, but it's a long shot. There's no reason to expect that the vehicle would be registered in this area or even registered legitimately for that matter. We need something else."

"I agree," I said. "I'll check in with Hallensby; see if she's got anything new."

SEVENTY-EIGHT

"We've found a hair," she said, "up by their foxhole."

"What color?"

"Gray. Unfortunately there's no bulb, so there's no DNA."

"Probably none on file anyway, not if he's a real pro."

"Yes," Hallensby said. "It's not likely that we're looking at some street criminal who's been spreading blood and other body fluids for the last decade or two."

"How about the partial on the cigarette paper?"

"No word yet. We scanned it and sent it to the lab, but it was a tiny fragment. A long shot, I'm afraid."

I nodded in agreement.

"We need a break," Hallensby said.

"I'm sure if something's in the area you'll find it."

"Thanks," she said.

Her response was halfhearted; we both knew how steep the odds were. I got back on the internet, pulling up a detailed map of northwest Washington. I told myself that I had to somehow see past the clutter and envision the reality. So many streets, so many buildings. Constant activity. Pedestrian and vehicular traffic in all directions. Planes, trains, and automobiles, not to mention boats, crew shells and motor yachts.

And yet, what was at the base of it? Two tribes. A killing ground. An attempted ambush. A hunt of our own. A chase. I had to look beyond the human geography and see the human reality beneath. What would he do? Where would he go? What would his natural impulse be? How could we anticipate his moves and get there first?

I called Salva.

"Have we got somebody watching the phone booth in Columbus Circle?" I asked.

"Yes, of course," he answered.

"And a tap?"

"Yes."

"That's key," I said. "He's going to call *them*."

"I agree, but I'd like to hear *your* reason for saying that."

"Because he's become a target. They can't afford to have him at large. If he's awaited calls at his regular points then he knows they have the numbers and can identify the locations. Even if he's initiated the calls he knows that they have the capability of tracing them. Either way, those two phone booths are killzones and he has no intention of walking into a sniper's crosshairs."

"I agree."

"At the same time he'll want to be paid—if not for the job, then for his silence."

"He'll want the money wired, but Malawi is unlikely to agree to that. This guy would start a succession of transfers that would bounce across the globe and back like a ball in a Chinese ping pong tournament. Even with all of the resources and connections that Malawi could bring to bear, the guy would be able to stay a step ahead."

"And take the money and run."

"Exactly."

"So Malawi has to bring him into the open somehow. If we can intercept the call we have a chance to get there first. That could bring the big payoff."

"Meaning?"

"Malawi's shooter would be there as well. We could take down both of them and end up with two links back to the mother ship."

"Dueling confessions and dueling pleas for immunity."

I thought of the succeeding response, but didn't say it: *if one or more of them is still alive. And if I am.*

SEVENTY-NINE

I surfed the web compulsively, starting with information on Escalades and their navigation systems and moving on to hair analysis and DNA extraction. In between I pestered Hallensby, trying not to lean too heavily on her shoulder as I looked over it. I knew my problem; I hated the feeling of impotence and dependency and wanted desperately to be in the game. Donovan was little more than a sideshow at this point and he was holed up in his hotel, probably worrying over the room service menu. Malawi was still in the Langham Huntington Hotel, probably in a large bed in a large suite, dreaming of a morning dip in their olympic-size pool. The Washington traffic was still gridlocked and repairs to the Cabin John and Wilson Bridges were proceeding slowly. The city was moving at crawl speed and while some elements were working frantically the majority had put their lives and tasks on hold.

If Malawi was a compartmentalizer like Salva it was highly unlikely that he would permit one of his subordinates to take a call at the Columbus Circle phone and if he had any intention of taking out Bigfoot and his partner he would keep his own location a secret, dealing with them—if at all—through unregistered cell phones.

Except for Donovan and Malawi the other key players were faceless and anonymous, known only through their boot sizes and the scant evidence that Hallensby and her team had been able to turn. I had to face the fact that for the moment there was simply nothing that I could do but cool my heels, give my shoulder the chance to recuperate, and try to keep my mind from spinning out of control with nervous energy.

The good news was that we had largely averted the chain of catastrophic events that had been originally planned; the bad news was that their organization remained intact and now enjoyed the opportunity to lick its financial and public-relations wounds and plan its next operation. Their standard M.O. would be to take their time and plan something on a moderate to large scale—deliver a dirty bomb perhaps or explode a tank of liquid chlorine. They might release an aerosol anthrax spray or spread around some pneumonic plague or good old-fashioned foot and mouth disease. The possibilities were endless. They didn't lack ideas and they didn't lack materials.

On the other hand it was equally possible that they might pursue something more immediate and more tactical, designed to make a point and remind us of their presence and power. A single sniper could terrorize the full swath of mid-Atlantic states. One already had. Cyber attacks were an ongoing possibility. Whether they originated at the desk of an amateur or a professional made no difference; the cultural and financial chaos that resulted would be the same. That was probably not their style, however. They preferred the spilling of blood and dismembering of bodies. If they set off a few pulse bombs to destroy circuitry or released a computer virus to infect cyberspace it would likely be linked with some other initiative, something involving significant pain and noticeable loss of life.

I was working my way through various map and munition sites when my cell phone twitched. I had forgotten that I had switched it from *ring* to *vibrate* the last time I talked to Hallensby and at first I thought its movement was a spasm in my shoulder. I looked at the screen; it was Salva.

"Yes, sir?" I said.

"We've just found an Escalade," he said. "A farmer reported it. Rural Loudoun county. *Very* rural. The vehicle went off the road and down the side of a hill into some heavy woods. The farmer's dog started barking; otherwise it might have been some time before it was discovered."

"Anybody inside?"

"Yes. One person. White male. Tall, thin, size 11 1/2 jungle boots. Quite dead. Best estimate of time of death is an hour or two after they hit you and Agent Ingle."

"Suspicious circumstances?"

"Very. The steering appears to have blown out. The firewall shredded and took most of the driver's left leg with it."

"It could have been rigged to do that and a signaling device installed, so that the vehicle could be tracked."

"Right. As soon as it got to the perfect location the button would be pushed. If the driver didn't die at once or on impact, he could be expected to promptly go into shock and then quickly bleed out. That far out in the boondocks it would usually be days or even weeks before the body was discovered."

"I wonder what happened to his partner."

"Good question."

"Obviously they had a second vehicle."

"Right. Just because we didn't notice any evidence of one doesn't mean it wasn't there. There wasn't enough space for the Escalade *and* a second car under the tree where we found the SUV tracks…"

"Could have been parked on a side road or nearby driveway. Hallensby's team wouldn't have noticed anything out of the ordinary, unless there was an oil spot or some foreign material left behind. A gravel road would have plenty of tire tracks—no reason to believe that someone had actually parked there."

"Right."

"And since each driver rearranges the gravel there's little chance of finding intact tire impressions."

"Right, unfortunately."

"Maybe the partner left," I said, "and then broke contact. The Escalade driver got suspicious, figured that someone had taken his partner out. Figured he was next."

"Maybe he thought you and Richard were coming for him," Salva said. "That's why he shot first before punching the accelerator. We've never been comfortable with the random-shot-at-civilians theory. Maybe this is our explanation."

"Then everything now points in the same direction," I said.

EIGHTY

"Yes?"

"It's somebody at the Protective Vehicle Division. It has to be."

"I'm not denying that possibility," he said. "All I'm saying is that the possible suspects look pure as freshly-fallen snow. Solid careers... unblemished records...no suspicious connections.... These are family people, Gwen...lots of small kids...pictures from their trips to *Disney World* on their desks...mortgages...Toyota vans...*Chuck E. Cheese* receipts in their pockets...flag poles in their front yards..."

"I understand, sir," I said, "but somebody has been able to crack our security systems and somebody knows his way around explosives and automobiles. If they're one and the same person, the most likely place to look would be some place involving both security *and* automobiles."

"I'll get with Beehler," he said. "Meanwhile, if you'd like to visit Agent Ingle I've obtained clearance from Homeland Security. I can't guarantee that he'll be very lucid and I *can* guarantee that they'll want you out of there after about five minutes, but you can go."

"Where is he?"

"Fairfax Hospital ICU."

"Thanks, Skip, I appreciate this."

I've always had some apprehension about a hospital located on Gallows Road, but Fairfax is the place you want to be when your body's in need of significant care. The ICU was noticeably quiet when I entered and the shades had been drawn to mute the bright sunlight. The atmosphere was comforting, even in the presence of catheter tubes, large needles and beeping monitors. Richard's eyes were closed when I entered his room. Both his head and chest were heavily bandaged and his left arm and left leg were in casts.

When I put my hand on his and kissed his cheek he opened his eyes. They were glazed with sedation but his lips parted in a thin smile. He said, "Hi," but it came out as a whisper. Then he said something else that I had trouble hearing. I got closer and he said, "Kiss me again." I did, and he smiled again.

After exchanging more personal words I told him about the death of the person who most likely shot us and I recounted my theories about the Protective Vehicle Division as the most likely source of a principal suspect. He nodded in agreement, though it seemed to cause him pain to do so. He told me to be very careful.

"I don't want you ending up in bed with me," he said.

"That's not very flattering," I said.

"I mean under these circumstances," he said.

"I know," I said. "I'll be careful." I was about to say something else when the head nurse appeared at the door, pointing at her watch. I turned around and stared at her until she backed off, exchanged more words with Richard, kissed him, and reluctantly left.

I had turned off my cell phone and when I checked it in the hallway there was a missed call—from the AD. I called him as soon as I reached the parking lot. He told me that Beehler had an update that he wanted to share ASAP and told me to meet them at the *Key Bridge Marriott*.

It took me thirty minutes to get there. We met in the room that Beehler's men were using as an observation post. There were two of them on duty, one working the hallways and public areas, the other sitting at a terminal that tapped into Donovan's phone and laptop lines and afforded views of both his rental car and the door to his room.

Beehler and Salva were drinking coffee. When I entered they offered me some, along with the remains of a box of sweet rolls. I passed on the two still-intact dried rolls and assorted crumbs and opted for the coffee, which was hot and fresh. I waited for them to speak.

"First I had to dance around with them," Beehler said, "because I couldn't tip them off about our suspicions, but they're smart enough to know that I wasn't there taking a random survey, so we did a little of this and a little of that and finally got to the issues in question.

"It seems that there *is* another person. The government lists him separately because he's technically retired but hired back as a consultant, so his name doesn't come up on their current T O & E chart. They call him 'Old Fred.' Because of the Mac voice."

"I don't follow," Salva said.

"On the Mac computer…you can choose voices to read cue messages. The voice 'Fred' sounds like some old world-weary duffer who just woke up and very much wants to go back to sleep."

I had heard it, but I didn't say anything.

"His name's actually Frederick. Frederick Hoffman. Started out as the head mechanic at a Mercedes dealership in Cincinnati. He then took a job at O, H & E. He worked there for five years, then joined the Secret Service. He worked for them for eight years and then, technically, retired. Whenever anybody's on vacation or under the weather he comes in to help. He's there probably a hundred days a year or so."

"And if he needs to be there more often all he'd have to do is slip a little something into one of the other men's coffee," Salva said.

"Right," Beehler answered. "Anyway, he's been on for the last week and he was at Wolf Trap last night."

"So he's been around for nearly fifteen years," Salva said. "How about before that?"

"Germany," Beehler said. "In the service there and then working for an American company."

"Automotive?" Salva asked.

"Yes."

"How about his MOS?"

"Mechanic. Armor."

"Honorable discharge?"

"Yes. And a couple of ArComs for exceptional service. Apparently he can use a wrench the way Merlin could wield a wand."

"Lots of cells in Germany," Salva said. "Lots of time there for somebody to find him and recruit him. What else have you got on him?"

"Age 63, 6'1", 190 pounds. Here's his driver's license photo…"

His hair was dark, but with gray flecks. He had a smoker's face, with creased cheeks and thin, dark lines above and below his lips. He looked as if he could use a bath and a good shampoo, maybe with lye soap and some steel wool pads. I imagined there was sour breath to accompany his dour expression.

"He doesn't look like Secret Service material," Salva said, turning to me for a response.

"I'd say he looks like a barfly, one with a lot of anger and a lot of opinions."

"The Secret Service guys say he doesn't talk much," Beehler said. "Sticks to himself. Does his thing and then goes home."

"Doesn't look much like a terrorist either," Salva said. "More like the guy you'd see behind the desk of a cheap motel, watching a small-screen TV and doing his best not to be bothered."

"The kind of guy you'd turn your head away from," I said. "Maybe he uses that to his advantage."

"Maybe," Beehler said.

"Address?" Salva asked.

"Military Road, North Arlington."

"Pretty nice neighborhood," I said. "Not within reach of most mechanics' pocketbooks."

"Subsidiary income?" Salva asked. "I suggest we pay him a visit."

EIGHTY-ONE

"I want a full team," Salva said. "S.W.A.T., the bomb squad, the full deal. This guy could have his place booby-trapped. He could also be operating a dormitory for terrorists. At the least he could be a person who likes to blow things and people up. If he's the brains behind this operation he's been planning it for years. He would have anticipated that someone might get suspicious and make a run at his house, so he's likely to be prepared for it."

"I'll make some calls," Beehler said, pulling out his cell phone and walking toward a quiet corner.

"Gwen, I want you in reserve on this," Salva said.

"What do you mean, sir?" I asked.

"I mean I want you around but I don't want you rushing in with your gun out. You've already been banged up on this operation and the next phase is a job for the people who are specifically armed and trained for it. I want your thoughts and advice, but I don't want you to end up in the Fairfax ICU with your friend."

"I'd like to be there when you go in, sir," I said.

"No problem. You can stay in the armored van until we've cleared the area and the bomb squad gives us an all clear."

"Do you expect him to be there?"

"Not really," Salva said. "Too few possible suspects. He's got to know that he could be on our list. After years of working against us he'd also have a finely-tuned case of paranoia. A guy like this who has to look over his shoulder constantly…after awhile he would expect to see somebody there and he'd be surprised if he didn't."

"I'm wondering about his relationship with Malawi," I said. "Any way you slice it, Malawi would want to keep him at arm's length. The cells aren't permitted to overlap—too many security problems. If he's an independent contractor rather than a member of a local cell Malawi would have even more reason to keep him isolated and circumscribed. There's a higher risk that he could be government bait and now that the operation's gone belly up Malawi's suspicions that Hoffman could be working both sides of the street would intensify."

"Hard to know about personal relationships and loyalties. It's not like the old cold war days," Salva said. "Then the cells would attract bright young idealists, anxious to help everyone build the road to the workers' paradise. The longer they hung around, however, the more they saw that the workers' paradise was really a scam designed for the benefit of the elites and the apparatchiks. The more they got to know *them* the more they realized the degree to which the so-called leaders were motivated by their own self-interest. As soon as that realization set in we were able to turn them. This is very, very different. People hook up with the jihadists and figure they're interesting but maybe a little nutty. The longer they hang around with them, however, the more they realize that these people are true believers, ready to do anything. Their respect for them grows rather than diminishes and they develop the kind of extreme faith that you see in converts. That's why it's so hard to penetrate their organizations and turn their members.

"Don't get me wrong," he continued. "The boys in charge know how to send other people out with bombs strapped around their waists and they *do* keep telling them about that room full of virgins waiting for them, but it's still different than during the cold war."

I nodded in agreement.

"What about the payoff?" I asked. "If Hoffman's doing this for hire I doubt very much that he was paid in full in advance. He's not likely to just walk away now, even if things didn't turn out quite like he planned. Besides, he's incurred expenses, and, more important, he's got a reputation to protect. If he walks away without getting paid he falls to the bottom of the food chain and he can kiss any future operations good bye. At the same time, if Malawi pays him when he's failed *he* loses face, along with a significant amount of money. The fact that the functionaries at the Mountain are both probably dead could work to Hoffman's advantage. It's his way of letting Malawi tell his people that the incompetents were liquidated. Hoffman stays in the shadows and everything's copacetic. At the same time, there's still the bill to pay. I figure that Malawi should be trying to take out Hoffman and Hoffman should be trying to collect his check and then take out Malawi rather than having him hanging around as a loose end."

"Malawi's not going to get his own hands dirty," Salva said. "Besides, taking Hoffman out would be beyond his technical expertise. He's a brains and money guy, not a field agent. Also, if we can find Hoffman's home and workplace, so can Malawi. He could have already issued the order to some of his people to head for Military Road."

"And Hoffman could already be on his way to Los Angeles."

"Right," Salva said. "We'll get a larger team around Malawi and let them know about this possibility. Who knows—we could get lucky and take down both of them together. We'll also alert our guys here to the possibility that they might not be the only group intent on giving Fred Hoffman a little housewarming party."

Beehler put down his cell phone, approached us, and told the AD that the teams were ready.

"Give me ten minutes to brief the powers that be," Salva said, "and then we'll head up the Parkway and see what we can see."

EIGHTY-TWO

All of Arlington is divided into two parts and so labeled—north Arlington and south. Forty blocks in either direction, bisected by Arlington Boulevard and bounded by the river—a huge half-circle. The north is generally nicer, though there are pockets of great wealth and pockets of decay and flaking paint throughout. It was developed earlier than the suburbs and exurbs of Fairfax, Prince William, and Loudoun Counties, so the neighborhoods are established, the commutes are short and new construction—generally only after the tearing down of existing property—is rare.

Many houses date from the 50's or earlier and their modest dimensions stand in stark contrast to their elevated price tags. The streets are wide, the lawns broad and green, and in the spring the white blooms and shiny leaves of Magnolias contrast with stands of multicolored dogwoods and rows of ever-spreading azaleas. Behind the doors of the comfortable but not grandiose homes of north Arlington lived people like the late William Rehnquist and, for a time, the spy Aldrich Ames.

The tourists' Arlington is the Lee Mansion, the Cemetery, and the Iwo Jima Memorial—all engraven on the public consciousness by thousands of photographs at sunrise and sunset, sometimes with a backdrop of fireworks and sometimes without, and memories of the gravestones of Audie Murphy, John F. Kennedy, and thousands of local and personal heroes. Just beyond are the endless redbrick apartments of students and working-class commuters, the Asian restaurants and cineplexes of Courthouse Square, the Millenial apartments and shoppes of Ballston and the interspersed relics of the past—old *Sears* stores now jostling with earth-friendly groceries and fifties' service stations, diners, and palm readers' establishments cheek by jowl with Mercedes dealerships, banks, commuter law schools, and the everpresent *Starbucks*.

A short drive up the George Washington Parkway takes you to Spout Run, a heavily-wooded creek-divided road with a set of tributaries that clog at rush hour. Lorcom Lane is the first; it leads to Nelly Custis, which runs into Military Road, which then snakes its way across the neighborhood and leads to Glebe, the connector to the Chain Bridge.

In between the edge of McLean and the edge of north Arlington is North 41st Street, a sloping lane-and-a-half road with four houses. Troops encamped there during both the Revolutionary and Civil Wars—either protecting the Potomac or attempting to choke it off. Buffs come through the area with metal detectors, though the great oaks once used for target practice were removed for a major water project years before. Raspberries now grow in their place and wild strawberries spring up in the sandy soil above the street.

At the confluence of Glebe and Chain Bridge Roads, the end point for commuters from McLean and Great Falls, you are in the belly of the real estate beast, with astronomic property values and household-name neighbors. Chuck and Linda Robb live there and Teddy Kennedy once did—next door to the Sultan of Brunei. Nancy Dickerson and Jackie Kennedy grew up in the area. Townhouse 'villas' which look down upon the Potomac and across to the Palisades, go for $6 million and change.

Military Road is cheaper, but not cheap, particularly now that they're replacing tear-downs with McMansions on pipestems and postage-stamp lots. The original home lots are larger, though the buildings often require significant updating and remodeling. The land is hilly and some construction shows its considerable age, with detached, single-car garages built into the side of the hill at street level, well below the principal property—a significant trade off for those in possession of luxury SUV's and long, lowslung Lincoln and Cadillac sedans. The upside is that every house is different and every structure looks like the perfect place to eat Thanksgiving dinner, with mature trees and shrubs, Cape Cod windows, multi-gabled cedar shake and slate roofs, one-of-a-kind natural-wood doors with massive brass knockers and the overall feel of a trip over the river and through the woods to grandmother's house combined with the realization that you are no more than five or ten minutes from what the locals regularly refer to as the world's most powerful city.

It was the worst possible place in which to stage a full-court-press military assault. The lines of sight from Hoffman's house to the street were all clear and the slope was steep. The windows of the house were small and draped—no vast expanses of glass exposing the individual(s) within. The backyard was fenced and no points of access were visible from the street.

We were too far from the parkway to gain any muffling traffic noise and we would have to deal with the natural alarm system of bored neighborhood dogs, at the alert and ready to signal their concerns regarding strangers and interlopers. If we waited until dark we would cede crucial minutes and hours that we could not spare and if we sent in a single plainclothes officer we would risk tipping Hoffman to our larger purposes. He could greet the individual, welcome him inside, kill him, and trash all of his files and records while we waited, helpless, a block away.

The AD had to act quickly, since the locals would be tiring of his role in what they would inevitably begin to characterize as a local affair. Despite his juice with agency heads and the Homeland Security braintrust, the bureaucracies would soon begin to assert their normal prerogatives and retake their established turf. The chain of evidence and intuition led to Military Road, but this was likely to be his last hurrah as well as mine and any way you sliced it my role would necessarily be reduced by the injury to my shoulder and the ongoing suspicions of any group of heavily-armed men concerning a woman who was also perceived to be little more than a rookie.

We went in in two armored vans with a trailing sedan. The S.W.A.T. team went in first, one unit scaling the backyard fence to close off any escape routes and the first team going through the front door, uninvited and unannounced. The bomb squad followed directly, ready to go to work once the perimeter was secured and the house searched. I was given the task of watching the garage door. The fact that it did not appear to have been opened in years and was situated at street level, at least fifty yards below the main house, indicated that I was there, basically, to hold the snipe bag while everyone else went off on the hunt.

I did a very good job of observing the door, noting the dust and cobwebs at its windows, the now-warped slats that had been used in its construction, the collection of undisturbed leaves and soil directly in front of it, and the absence of any tread marks, footprints, or tracks of any kind between it and the sidewalk.

The other houses of that vintage generally included newly-built modern garages beside or behind the principal residence, but Hoffman's did not. The fact that his driveway was empty suggested that he was either out or sufficiently suspicious to park his vehicle somewhere else within the neighborhood so that he might gain the advantage of surprise in the case of an enemy incursion.

Ten minutes later Salva returned to the van and told me that the house was empty. "The bomb squad is going over the place inch by inch," he said, "but I doubt that they'll find anything. The place appears to be clean. If he *is* our guy and if he *was* involved in creating explosive devices, he was doing it elsewhere. The dogs aren't picking up anything at all and the building appears free of any suspicious nooks or crannies. It's been gutted and totally remodeled. Everything is very minimalist. All open spaces and simple, functional furniture. No junk, no locked cabinets, no sliding doors. We played back the messages on his answering machine. Nothing interesting, but there were three days' worth. He's either not our guy, he's at his secret workshop, or he's on his way to California."

"I could call Beehler," I said, "ask him to search databases at all the phone companies and in public record offices in the surrounding counties. I agree that he's not going to set up shop in a congested residential neighborhood. He's somewhere in the countryside."

"Thanks," Salva said, "but I already did. We already picked up a reference to him in a Leesburg paper. Some auto show event. He could be out there even as we speak."

"Easy access to Dulles from there," I said.

"Right. He could have been using it for his base for the last several days. I'm keeping the teams together. Hopefully we'll have another door to knock on soon."

"What do you want me to do?" I asked.

As he paused to answer I realized that I had suddenly become an afterthought.

EIGHTY-THREE

"How about if I stay here," I asked, "just in case he returns. In the meantime I can look around, see if I can find anything that might prove helpful."

"That sounds good," he said.

I could hear the sense of relief in his voice and could see that he was anxious to head toward Leesburg. He was listening to the clock tick in the back of his head and was anxious to seize what could be his last opportunity to be a part of the collar.

No matter what we had been able to accomplish there were still questions in the public mind about the Bureau. The brass always seemed to be defensive, trying to rehabilitate us, trying to counter the conventional wisdom that we were far too stuck in our ways, far too resistant to change. Our computer systems were still not where we wanted them to be and the interfaces with the security agencies, the Secret Service and Homeland Security units still too shaky. We still weren't over the stories about Edgar's ball gown and cocktail frock wardrobe. Maybe we never would be. There were too many powerful images fixed in a public mind that fed voraciously on such things.

That was why the Bureau worked so hard to change its public face, adding minorities to the mix…adding women…planting stories of their new-found diversity. The with-it, hip Bureau, facing down the modern world, positioned for change, countering all of the former stereotypes.

I was part of the 'new face' of the Bureau, except that my face was a little whiter than some would have liked, my features a little too

Anglo, my accent more eastern seaboard than northern plains. In their hearts they wanted somebody with 'little feather' in her name. In some ways they had forgotten one of Edgar's cardinal principles; the Bureau was designed to be a long gray line of armed lawyers and accountants, capable of fading into the wallpaper and woodwork, nearly invisible, drawing no personal attention to their face, hair, or dress; standing in the shadows, watching, waiting, recording; combing files and databases, the technicians of crime fighting; large in number but singular in purpose; spread out across the continent in dozens of field offices, but with an airtight chain of command and every path, alley, road, and highway crossing at the Director's desk, his command and control absolute, his authority unimpeachable.

It wasn't quite the same imagining him there, with his hand on the phone and his tommy gun at the ready, dressed in a late afternoon sleeveless, basic-black sheath, Clyde Tolson at his side, playing footsie and smiling adoringly. No one was ready for that much diversity.

That's probably why I preferred the long gray line. Not only did it draw less negative attention; it was ultimately more effective. Where was Eliot Ness when we needed him? A far better face for the Bureau, with an antagonist to match.

It wasn't anything that I could solve, but it was something with which I had to deal. Whether the Bureau was ready for me or not I was ready to do more than pose for a recruiting poster or sit in the back seat of an empty car and wait for somebody to put me in the game.

"Here are the keys to the sedan," Salva said. "It's parked just up the street. Be very careful. I don't want him to return and surprise you. Be sure to call me every thirty minutes."

There was little urgency in his voice. I thanked him for his concern, slipped the keys in my purse, promised to call, and walked up the driveway toward the house. Before I was halfway there I could hear the vans pulling away.

The S.W.A.T. team had done minimal damage to the front door and I did what I could to make it appear intact. If Hoffman *did* return while I was there I didn't want him to take one look at the door and disappear into the ether. As I walked from room to room I saw that everything that Salva had said was true; the place looked like an Ikea showroom after a closeout sale. There was a sprinkling of furniture, but fewer pieces than any normal person would consider necessary. The walls were blank; even the kind of perfunctory, assembly-line 'art' that one finds in hotel chains was absent. The handful of end tables contained no photographs. Neither did the chest of drawers in the master bedroom. It was a house without a past and with very little present.

There was nothing in the house that could ever be imagined as having been *collected* and nothing that spoke to a sense of style or preference beyond the purely instrumental. It looked like a piece of rental property a few days before it was actually ready to show. The refrigerator was empty except for some cans of off-brand cola, an open box of baking soda and two trays of ice cubes that had developed the onion-like smell that comes with age.

The bed had a single pillow, yellowed sheets, and an olive drab blanket. The medicine chest was bare. The only thing it contained was a rust stain on one of the white, metal shelves. The second bedroom consisted of a simple couch, a single table, and a relic of a television set— an old Sylvania with rabbit ears and a collection of dust on the screen. The third bedroom was empty. The half bath in the hallway appeared to have gone unused for months. Most of the water in the toilet bowl had evaporated and the bracket for the toilet paper roll was empty. The dining room consisted of an oblong table of oak laminate, with a single, oak chair. He didn't entertain much, at least not here.

The kitchen contained the barest collection of pots and pans and four place settings of cheap, stainless steel utensils, all of which sat on a paper towel on the sinkboard. The house reminded me of a discount hotel suite. I decided to take a closer look, beginning in the bathroom.

I started with the sink and tub drains, looking for hair and soap curd. There was nothing. I looked for a plumber's helper to see if anything had been recently flushed that was still caught in the toilet trap. There was none anywhere, including in the bare linen closet in the hallway. Either Hoffman preferred to live dangerously or he wasn't living here at all.

I did a closer inspection of the bedroom. I didn't have any luminol but I did a visual check for fluid stains. Nothing. I looked for stray hairs; there were none. No cigarette burns. No reading materials of any kind. And no telephone.

Then I had a thought. It just appeared, like an anonymous gift. I went back outside, to the front of the house, and looked into the living room through the break in the drapes. The view afforded me was very narrow and circumscribed, but it included just enough of the living room and dining room furniture and the kitchen space beyond to create the illusion that there was more. I walked around to the side of the house and looked into the dining room window. Again, the view was extremely restricted and the image conveyed a sense of plenitude in inverse proportion to the actual reality. The function of Hoffman's furniture was not to serve modest domestic purposes; it was to convey the sense (with the most minimal investment) that the house was actually inhabited.

But why?

EIGHTY-FOUR

I continued to ask myself a related question. If Hoffman's primary residence was a workshop in the woods, why go to the trouble of obtaining and paying for a place in this price range, particularly when the price tag could draw a lot of unwanted attention. Why not just get a maildrop apartment in Rosslyn or Ballston?

I walked through the house, staring at near-empty rooms and the objects therein, turning possibilities over in my mind. Then, suddenly, it hit me like a steel pipe across the bridge of my nose. It had been there all along but I had blocked it out or left it in a forgotten mental drawer. I was frustrated with myself. Why hadn't I thought of it at once? Probably because at first glance it was a simple, routine thing that only took on significance in this later context.

I hurried out to the front of the house and saw it just below the gable on the southern side of the structure: a tiny satellite dish. It looked new, not like some relic of the past that had conveyed with the property at the time Hoffman purchased it. Then the obvious question: who needs a satellite dish when the only television in the house is a museum-level clunker with no cables to carry the signal and everything about the place said that it contained absolutely nothing that could be considered superfluous? Answer: I hadn't yet found the rest of the house.

Salva had said that there were no secret passageways or sliding panels. That was certainly true in terms of the basic floorplan, which was spare and straightforward. There were no wings or additions visible from the outside that were unaccounted for after my series of walkthroughs. The likeliest candidate—the old garage—*was* sealed like a tomb and there was no evidence, *none,* at street level, of any ingress or egress within recent memory.

I hurried down to the basement. At first glance it was nothing more than a blank expanse. The gas furnace was an aging Lennox, probably thirty years old or more. In this area the newer trend is toward heat pumps, but little else had been upgraded in the house, so I didn't expect the furnace to be. The hot water heater was a Ruud, eighty gallons rather than the usual forty. That was a surprise; the larger version had probably been purchased by an earlier owner with a family that included teenagers. The pilot lights were on in each. Neither carried one of those repairman's labels that record the dates of a service contract or solicit your future business. The central floor drain was dry, as were the walls and window wells. I looked at the foundation. Cement, not cinder block, but again, no sliding panels or pivoting bookcases, just a universal blank. While essentially clean, there was enough dust along the floor and enough cobwebs around the windows and in the rafters and corners to indicate that this was not a heavily-trafficked area.

The corner steps leading to the old cellar door were clear. Nothing interesting had been tracked in, not even in the remote past, and the light coating of dust on the horizontal surfaces and curtain of webs in the vertical spaces remained undisturbed.

I went back outside and checked the garage a second time. It was as tight as I remembered it and the door was nearly flush with the side of the hill. There was no space that would have permitted a secondary entrance. I went back up to the principal residence and explored the exterior. Nothing. Then I went back in the house, walked through the kitchen, and entered the fenced backyard. It was interesting that there was no door in the fence. The only way in and out was through the house or over the top. Not a big deal. Anyone who's had a dog escape through an open gate or door would consider such a fence; they were also common with houses with pools—both in-ground and above (especially when the latter violated neighborhood association rules)—and cheaper for someone whose overriding priority was privacy.

I was running out of options as I surveyed the few hundred square feet of space within the walls of the fence. There was a newish, plastic shed in the corner, containing a lawn mower, gas can, two rakes, and a shovel. The bare necessities. The lawn had been mowed recently, but there were no garden areas and no decking, just a simple wooden porch off of the kitchen. I looked all around the plastic shed and was able to see open space between its floor and the ground below. It was approximately 6' x 6' and both simple and functional. There was a slight incline on the front which enabled the mower to roll down onto the lawn. There were some tiny tire marks on it.

I wondered how the rest of the lot was mowed—almost surely by some lawn service or neighborhood freelancer, since no one would want to roll a gas mower with debris in the tires and blade well through the house. That thought led to another: anyone who could afford Military Road could afford a gate. There was no pool and there were no pets in evidence. Perhaps the gateless fence was designed for maximum privacy, even though there was nothing in the yard that suggested the need for privacy. I couldn't imagine Hoffman as a nude sunbather, and even if he was he could have purchased a windowless gate with an interior lock.

The only remaining object in the yard was the cellar door—uncommon today, but common when this neighborhood was initially developed. I closed the door on the shed and walked toward it, knowing that by now I had run out of any other alternatives.

EIGHTY-FIVE

The lock on the cellar door was new and it was a deadbolt, not a padlock. That was a first, particularly given the fact that there was nothing in the basement and nothing in the house worth stealing. I took my nail file from my purse, but quickly realized I would be unable to pick the lock with it. I slipped it into my hair, above my ear, figuring I might be forced to try it again, but for now I hurried into the house and went down the basement stairs, hoping I might get lucky and be able to open the lock from the inside. The only tools I had available otherwise were a shovel, the tines of a rake, and my Bureau automatic.

No such luck. There was a keylock on the deadbolt both inside and out. The good news was that Hoffman was hiding something and I was getting closer to finding it. Time was of the essence. I took out my automatic and blew out the bolt. There would be noticeable damage, no matter where I shot, but the basement would at least muffle most of the sound. I heard some dogs bark immediately afterwards, but I had heard them earlier whenever I walked around the property—no more than white noise to the local residents.

The cellar door was heavy and I had to use my good shoulder to raise the left half of it. Climbing up into the open air I saw what Hoffman had been hiding. The opening in the basement was smaller than the span of the double cellar door. Looking down from above, the additional space on the left was earth and gravel. On the right there was a narrow, second stairway leading to previously-unexplored space.

I took out my cell and called Salva. He told me to call him the moment I found something of interest. He also warned me to be careful. "*Very* careful," he added.

There was a glow of light at the bottom of the stairs, but I left the cellar door open and started to descend. No dust and no cobwebs. The steps had been in recent use. There were eight steps in all and they led to a hallway with indirect light running along the edge of a low—probably 7'—ceiling. The floor was cement but with a runner of oriental carpet. The space was very dry. I passed a room with a large dehumidifier positioned above a floor drain. I had both of my hands on my automatic and my back near the edge of the wall as I made my way down the hallway. The next room—on my right this time—was a bedroom. It wasn't large by above-ground standards, but it was huge in this subterranean space, probably 12'x16'. A queen-size bed sat on wall-to-wall beige carpeting. A flat-screen TV hung from the wall at its foot. A small table, floor lamp, and leather armchair were in the corner; a walk-in closet and bath completed the suite. Again, there was a glow from recessed lighting, this time positioned inside the extensive crown moulding which ran along the room's ceiling.

The next room—on the left—was dark, but the light from the hallway was sufficient to enable me to see the work benches, tool boxes, supply cabinet, and boxes of parts for electronic devices of various kinds. The floor was bare, but clear and, as far as I could see, clean. Hoffman's workshop.

I took another eight or nine steps and came to the end of the hall, which abutted the entrance to a large, dark room. The light from the hallway illuminated the first few square feet of open floor space, but I could not see the area beyond. I thought twice before flipping the light switch, fearing that it could be linked to a signaling system of some sort, but then I reasoned that the entire subterranean space (and, for that matter, the cellar door itself) could have contained any number of sensors that had already registered my presence. I decided to go ahead.

The switch was actually a rheostat button. I clicked it and the room was bathed in bright light. And suddenly it was all there...everything that I had anticipated, and more.

EIGHTY-SIX

Communication Central. Two tables forming a 90 degree angle on adjoining walls, each with a bank of recording equipment across the back and ample workspace along the front. There was a multi-buttoned land-line handset, a charging station for cell phones, and a computer set-up that looked like something out of a futuristic technothriller. In effect, Hoffman had two long desks at which to work and a high-back, leather office chair on casters to pilot between them. The floor was carpeted and the chair sat on an oversized plastic mat to facilitate its movement. The ceiling was acoustic tile. I closed the door and could hear the movement of air as I did so. The space was as tight as a top-record-label recording studio's, where the budget was deep and the margin for error narrow.

On the far wall was a kitchenette, with a mini- refrigerator, a single sink, and two-urn coffee maker. The refrigerator was stocked with Evian water and Paulaner beer. The urns were empty, but clean. There was a gold filter, a bag of Seattle's Best beans and an electric grinder. No artificial creamer and no artificial sweetener. He obviously liked his coffee fresh and black and he didn't share it with guests.

Above the appliances was a set of built-in cabinets. The first contained cups, spoons, forks, knives, napkins, and both small and large bone china plates; the second was his liquor cabinet and nothing inside it was second-class. From Johnnie Walker blue label scotch to thirty year-old Armagnac, his tastes were carefully indulged. The glasses were heavy, cut crystal. Judging from the upstairs kitchen I figured that most of his meals consisted of upscale carryout. My guess was that he ate like a K Street lawyer, working late but billing his clients for every bite. To the side of the kitchenette was a black, plastic garbage receptacle with a pivoting lid. The liner was fresh and empty.

There was no whirr of tape in any of the recording devices, but the power was on and the indicator lights were glowing. The screen saver on the computer was a set of interlocking triangles, organizing and then reorganizing themselves in multiple, changing patterns.

On the fourth wall was a rack of audio cassettes with a list of names and dates. The names were abbreviations such as S-1 and S-2, F-1 and F-2. Secret Service no. 1? FBI no. 2? Next to the storage rack was an oblong steel cabinet with an industrial-strength lock.

From all appearances his operation was beautiful in its simplicity and ease of execution. At each White House or Homeland Security event—an interagency meeting or field operation, for example—the sedans, vans, and SUV's of the various security organizations would assemble and Hoffman would have the opportunity to install or replace electronic devices. As a trusted, senior engineer as well as an agent with the highest security clearance he would have access to every vehicle. In some cases he would have formal responsibility for them and even if he could not directly transmit the conversations within the fleet of presidential vehicles he could record them for later use and directly transmit the conversations within the agency sedans.

The potential value of the intelligence he could collect was inestimable. I wondered if he was a Malawi mole or an independent contractor. I suspected the latter, since his name had not surfaced in any current files within the Bureau's databases. He could have established his terrorist bona fides back in Germany and then come to the United States, kept his nose clean and polished for years and then, when the time was right, gone into business for himself.

He could act on the intelligence he collected or sell it, perhaps even auction it in some cases. Once he had consistently demonstrated the accuracy and dependability of his information its price would skyrocket.

Very tidy. And he didn't need to run out to the countryside to do his work. He could maintain his north Arlington address and easy commute, keep snoops at bay with his upstairs movie-set house while enjoying his upscale living space and high tech facility below stairs.

He was strictly old-school, with racks of hard copy recordings, immediately visible and accessible. They also appeared to be more 'real', particularly if they were to be put up for auction.

The one point in common between the space upstairs and that below was the complete absence of anything personal. There were no pictures, no books, no artwork. No images of a life, either real or imagined. The parallels that sprung to mind were those of an operating room or an execution chamber. For all of his involvement in pain and death, in rage and in hatred, there was a personal detachment, a sense of distance and anonymity. He may have been *behind* it all, but he was also determined to be *beyond* it or *above* it all. An experimental scientist at Auschwitz, wrapped in a white lab coat, perhaps, or the faceless calibrator of precision instruments of torture.

There was a certain irony in the fact that he had turned the instruments of our own technological success against us. I thought about the endless analyses of the end of the cold war and how communication-age advances had forced once-closed societies to either open or wither economically. Hoffman's twisted genius was in utilizing what some would consider passé technology in tandem with more contemporary instrumentation. A theorist of tactics and strategy might use him and his system for a case study, but for me there was a second way of seeing him and his activities, one more immediate and more personal. Either directly or indirectly this man had attempted to kill someone I cared about deeply and he had come close to succeeding.

I didn't have the time to nurse the anger that was churning inside me. I took out my cell phone and hit the first button on my speed dial. Salva was on a fool's errand. There *was* no workshop in the woods.

Moment by moment the backup that I needed was driving farther and farther away from me.

"Put that away," a voice said. Within the small space the words were piercingly loud. Then I heard the sound of a round being chambered in a handgun.

EIGHTY-SEVEN

I turned around and looked into the barrel of an automatic pistol. The angle wasn't very good, but it appeared to be a Sig Sauer P220. Again, old-school; a product from 1975. Not that it made a lot of difference. At that distance any weapon would do. Hoffman had lost weight since our file photo was taken. The furrows in his face had deepened and the circles under his eyes had darkened. His hair had thinned, but it still appeared to be in need of a good washing.

"Open your jacket," he said.

When I revealed my sidearm he ordered me to remove it from its holster and place it on the adjoining table, then step back. He took my gun, checked it and slipped it inside his belt.

"Who are you and what are you doing here?"

I thought about it for a second and then decided to roll the dice.

"I represent Karras al-Malawi," I said. "He's asked me to speak with you directly."

"Do you now?" he asked, his voice heavy with skepticism.

"He recognizes the difficulty of your position and he's asked me to inform you of his decision."

"Really? Go on."

"Your operation failed, Mr. Hoffman. There were some casualties on the beltway bridges and a great deal of inconvenience resulting from the gridlocking of the capital area, but nothing like the level of effect he had been led to expect. The New York operation failed utterly. You know that and he knows that."

"Go on," he said. "This is extremely entertaining."

"You have received a preliminary payment. You realize, of course, that he cannot pay you for an operation that has failed and he realizes that you know that and will seek to silence him in an effort to salvage your own reputation."

"So you believe that he would announce his association with a failed operation to third parties?"

"There are only a few such parties who matter, Mr. Hoffman, and you are not in a position to know which of them are privy to Mr. Malawi's thoughts and intentions. As you know, his dealings are carefully compartmentalized."

"So, does he have an alternative to propose?"

"Yes. He is prepared to pay one-half of your remaining fee in return for an agreement of mutual non-aggression."

He paused for at least twenty seconds, then continued. "I have to say this, you are either uncommonly resourceful, foolhardy, or a complete imbecile."

"What *I* am hardly matters, Mr. Hoffman. Mr. Malawi asked me to convey this information and I have done so. I have no other business with you."

"Agent Harrison," he said, "it is not beyond the realm of possibility that a person of Mr. Malawi's stature would be able to place an operative in a significant position of trust and then call on them, as needed, some time later. It is quite clear that *you* are not such a person. Kneel down and put your hands on your head. I want you to hear something."

I tried to give as little indication as possible of the pain in my shoulder but was unable to kneel without favoring my opposite arm. He was watching me carefully but I couldn't tell how much he had been able to observe. Once I was in place he walked over to the rack, ran his finger along the back of what appeared to be the most recent set of audio cassettes, selected one, and inserted it in a machine at the end of the table which contained his computer. After a second or two of rushing noise a voice came on. It was Salva's. Hoffman turned up the volume.

"Yes, sir, she's quite good, particularly for a rookie, but she was injured and I don't think it's fair to expect her to do full-bore fieldwork under the circumstances…yes, sir…yes…her shoulder actually…"

Hoffman stopped the tape. "He's talking to the FBI Director. He always calls him 'sir'; he refers to the Homeland Security head as 'Mr. Secretary.' When he talks to people in the Secret Service he tries his best to avoid titles of respect. Inter-service rivalry, I suppose."

I realized then that I should have disguised my voice. Hoffman had obviously heard it before and the moment I attempted to present myself in the role of a Malawi agent he had identified me.

"You really did quite well, all things considered," he said. "And you were lucky. You should not have survived the attack at Naked Mountain."

"You overheard our conversation and ordered the attack."

He smiled. "How is your little friend, by the way?"

"I should think you would already know, Mr. Hoffman," I said. "Did you neglect to put a transmitting device in his hospital room?"

"I chose not to," he said, smiling again. "The information gained would not have been worth the risk. Pity you won't have the opportunity to join him at Fairfax Hospital. I know you would have enjoyed seeing him again. Unfortunately that will not be possible."

My mind raced to various possibilities, but it fast became clear that Hoffman had anticipated them. "By the way, Agent Harrison," he said, "when your cell phone rings I want you to answer it. I want you to tell Assistant Director Salva that you have nothing new to report and that you will check back with him regularly. If I see any indication whatsoever that you are attempting to signal him I will kill you in a way that you will find extremely unattractive. Understood?"

"Understood," I said.

"Good," he said. "Now we must go."

EIGHTY-EIGHT

While the place he intended to take me was relatively unimportant (any place remote enough in which to hide my body would work) I was interested in the fact that he seemed to be in a hurry. Perhaps he had some reason to believe that Malawi was coming for him. Perhaps he was thinking about Salva and our standard operating procedure that we stay in contact in thirty-minute intervals. So long as the AD remained unsuspicious our conversations would be brief and perfunctory. The moment he thought something was wrong he would key in on my location by satellite and send a response team. That was something that Hoffman would definitely want to avoid. Of course, he could simply turn off my cell phone and drive me quickly to his killzone, but he had ordered me to talk to Salva when he called, so he must have been interested in keeping him on the sidelines as long as possible.

The answer was clear (or at least I thought it was)—he still had work to do on Military Road. The most likely possibility was that he wanted to kill me quickly, then return to clear his files and bag up his tapes and hard drives. There were also the contents of the locked, steel cabinet. They might have been heavy as well as extensive. His materials were no doubt extremely valuable—at least in his eyes—and he would not want to abandon them and all of the money and sweat he had invested producing them. At the same time, he would not want to deal with me, them, and potentially other agents at the same time and he couldn't just kill me or crack me on the head, because he'd have to carry me all the way to the street and risk drawing the attention of the neighbors and any potential passers-by. Most important, if he was able to assemble all of his essential materials and transport them to a location that was safe and secure he might escape prosecution, since all we had, at bottom, was a case based on circumstance and inference. The presence of my body would change that, so if he killed me now he would have to remove the evidence of the action and he was smart enough to know about the persistence of blood under the scrutiny of modern technology. The various records that he had built with his surveillance systems were a second clincher; they would have to be removed. My best guess was that he would drive me to his killzone, force me to contact Salva and tell him that I'd have to go offline for awhile—perhaps to recharge my phone—then take me out and hurry back to Military Road.

Moreover, if I suddenly disappeared I could be temporarily skapegoated for some of his actions. Who was I, after all? Some kid, new to the Bureau, who had been jumped from case to case a little too quickly...somebody they may have recruited in the heat of the moment—hungry for diversity headlines, anxious to make a point. Oh, so politically-correct, but this time it came back to bite them. And they should have anticipated it, what with all the things they had done to the Indians over the years. It was me who had put the transmitting devices on the vehicles at Wolf Trap. I couldn't have put recording devices in the presidential vehicles, but there was no way of being sure that Hoffman knew that we even suspected him of doing that. As best I could remember, our principal discussion of that possibility had occurred in a coffee shop, not in a Bureau vehicle.

Maybe I was fantasizing or obsessing, but I had to find some explanation that fit the general situation. Whatever was happening appeared to be happening quickly and if I was going to prevent it I'd have to stay a step ahead. Since he had both of our guns I was very short on options. The cell phone wouldn't do me much good. Even if I could somehow signal Salva with it, all Hoffman had to do was get me to his car and kill me before any reinforcements would have a reasonable chance of arriving.

"Where are we going?" I asked.

"Someplace nice," he said. "You'll like it."

"Somehow I doubt that," I answered.

"You're probably right," he said, smiling.

As he ordered me down the hall toward the cellar door exit I kept my hands on the top of my head. With the inside of my wrist I could feel the edge of my nail file. I coughed, trying to create enough of a distraction to enable me to palm it. Then I coughed again.

"How do you live in this cave?" I asked.

"Shut up," he said. "The socializing's over."

As we approached the bottom of the steps I stopped walking, stood still, bent over and coughed uncontrollably.

"God *damn* it," he said. "I'll kill you right here if you don't move," and came forward to shove me with his left hand. I moved quickly to the right and as he fell forward I jabbed the point of the file into the side of his throat. His eyes popped, his pistol discharged, and I felt as if a white-hot steel poker had been thrust into my body.

I shoved him and he fell backward. I rushed up the steps, my shoulder screaming in pain, and I threw down the cellar door behind me. If he had any sense he'd know that I could be waiting for him behind it, holding one of his rakes and hoping for the opportunity to bury its tines in his face. Instead, I hurried through the house, figuring I could buy a few extra moments of time while he floundered.

I might not have much of it left, now that my already-weakened shoulder was sodden with blood, but I hurried into his front yard, moving from tree to tree, slaloming down his lawn to the Bureau sedan, waiting to see if he would follow. There were several cars parked on the street and in the driveways near his house and I had no way of knowing which was his.

A few seconds later he came hobbling down his driveway, his gun in hand and his eyes flashing wildly. I was wedged in the driver's seat of the Bureau sedan as low as I could get and still see him. Apparently he couldn't see me, since he looked in both directions briefly and then put his key in the door of a black Audi sedan. I turned on the ignition, put the car in gear, and accelerated toward him, hoping to either kill him or disable his car and prevent his escape. As he pulled away from the curb I sideswiped him hard. He hadn't yet buckled his seatbelt and was disoriented enough to be forced to stop and gather his thoughts. As he did I backed up quickly and hit him a second time, hoping to at least make his car undrivable, while I called Salva and anybody else who could possibly come to my aid.

As I backed up he suddenly turned toward me. His hand came up as his window came down and I drove off to the sound of 9 mm rounds shattering the glass and piercing the frame of the sedan.

EIGHTY-NINE

I drove about a quarter of a mile, slowing down to see if he was going to give chase. When he didn't appear in the next several moments I turned abruptly and drove toward him. I could see him in the distance, heading in the opposite direction, toward Glebe Road. I accelerated and got close enough to see that his car had sustained significant damage. There was smoke coming from the engine compartment and when I got closer still and rolled down the window I could hear a grating sound. The car seemed to be listing to the left as if the frame had been bent and I could see something dragging beneath the undercarriage.

I accelerated again and rearended his car at approximately thirty miles an hour. His body jerked but this time he had had the foresight to strap himself in, so his face didn't go into the windshield. He quickly turned to his right and fired directly toward me, shattering his rear window. I ducked as the rounds broke my windshield and headlights and hit the car's grillwork and—I feared—the radiator behind it.

He accelerated and I followed. He turned right onto Glebe, heading toward Chain Bridge. At that point on Glebe the traffic is generally slow, with cars easing down the steep road, through the woods, past North 41st Street, and onto the bridge. At rush hour it can back up for a half-mile or more.

My fear was that he might choose instead to turn left on Chain Bridge Road, just before the bridge, and head up into McLean, assuming that his car could function that long and assuming that he was still able to breathe properly and drive. Once into a residential neighborhood it would be far more difficult to locate and then track him, particularly if he had a few minutes' lead time.

When I turned onto Glebe there were other cars besides Hoffman's in front of me. He couldn't be too far ahead because the traffic was too dense, but the road curved sharply to the left and then sharply to the right and for the moment he was out of my line of sight. I inched along and eventually passed the blind curve, but as the road straightened I was still unable to see his vehicle. At the bottom of the hill I could see Chain Bridge Road, but the traffic heading up the hill was coming out of the District, from across the bridge. There was no car in the left lane, waiting to follow them. Either he was ahead of the Chain Bridge Road traffic or he was on the bridge itself, but as yet I still couldn't see him.

Suddenly I caught a break. In the corner of my left eye I could see smoke coming from a vehicle on North 41st Street. There were two other cars—parked more closely to the bridge, under the overpass for the GW Parkway—but I figured that the third car might be Hoffman's. I turned left and I was correct, but I didn't see anyone behind the wheel. I parked, approached cautiously, and looked inside. Hoffman was gone; his car had been abandoned. There was no sign of him heading up North 41st and the woods there were sufficiently clear to afford me a view of the areas on either side of the roadway. There was no sign of him there either.

I turned around and looked across the bridge and could see a figure moving on the left side, along the pedestrian walkway. He was holding on to the rail and his stride was labored. My shoulder was now soaked with blood and the adrenalin rush was yielding to a heavy throb of pain, lightheadedness and slightly-blurred vision. I may have been in better shape than Hoffman, but not by much. I hurried down to the intersection and made my way through the traffic turning off the bridge and onto Chain Bridge Road. Two of the cars honked at me as they were forced to slow down and I didn't see any facial expressions that suggested the possibility of the sudden appearance of a Good Samaritan. If anything I was lucky that they hadn't run over me.

As I moved across the bridge I saw Hoffman turn and then disappear. He was taking the stairs at the side of the bridge that led down to the old C. and O. Canal below that paralleled the river and gave its name to Canal Road on the District side of the Potomac. It was a favorite of walkers and joggers. To the southeast was Fletcher's Boat House, but I didn't expect him to be going there. He knew I still had my cell phone and could call in reinforcements to every flash point in the area.

It was a long walk to the boat house, probably a mile and a half in length, and a straight shot along the canal. I could follow along the road above and—assuming I wasn't crushed against the wall by incoming traffic—follow his movement easily. If he tried to shoot I could simply drop down behind the stone wall separating the road from the canal. It was thick and, except for a few places in which steel dividers had replaced stone, the complete wall was still largely intact. That's not where he was heading. I knew his destination and I knew that I had to hurry or risk losing him forever.

NINETY

His best chance was to make his way to Arizona Avenue—the first available exit from Canal Road, work his way through the intervening woods and go into the Palisades, the residential area along MacArthur Boulevard. His logical destination might then be Sibley Hospital, just northwest of Arizona and MacArthur. Sibley was the country club hospital in the District, the destination point for the wealthy in Northwest D.C. who were going in for elective surgery or other routine care.

It wouldn't be easy though, since there was no entry point to the canal itself from the intersection of Canal Road and Arizona. The closest was at the Reservoir Road exit, next to the boat house, another mile or so to the southeast. To get to Arizona Avenue he'd have to ford the canal, then make it up and over the wall, or scale the support structure of the abandoned railroad bridge which formed an ersatz pedestrian overpass above the intersection.

Hoffman was smart enough, however, to remember that I still had my cell phone and would quickly call Salva so that Sibley could be staked out and everyone put on notice that they were soon going to receive a visit from a terrorist-for-hire with a bleeding neck wound. I then figured he'd turn right rather than left and head for one of the doctor's offices along MacArthur Boulevard. There was at least six blocks' worth of small businesses between the intersection of Arizona and MacArthur and the Georgetown Reservoir—physicians, veterinarians, and even some private schools that would include nurse's offices. He might even go into a dentist's office—anywhere that would contain what he needed: a person capable of doing some elementary suturing and in possession of a ready supply of painkillers. The only other requirement was that the person would be responsive when he brandished a 9 mm automatic (his or mine) and threatened to kill them if they did not stitch him up forthwith.

On the latter point, the degree to which he was armed was an open question. As far as I knew he had my weapon and one full magazine of ammunition. He had his own weapon, from which he had fired the equivalent of a full magazine, but he could have pockets filled with additional magazines. There was no way that I *could* know, except by drawing his fire and waiting to hear a click rather than the discharge of a live round. The fact that he was probably becoming groggy and disoriented was a point in my favor, but this was also no time for foolhardiness. If he was able to shoot me and get away he might be able to escape forever. I wish I had had a sword or Bowie knife to jab in his throat rather than a nail file.

My first decision point came at the stairway linking the bridge with the canal. I was unarmed and he could be waiting below. Rather than tempt fate I made my way through traffic to the other side of the bridge, where I could get a better view of the towpath along the canal. The traffic in was gridlocked, but the traffic out was moving briskly. I had to be careful in moving across the bridge and again my actions prompted honking from various cars.

Standing on the southeast side of the bridge, looking down the towpath, I could see movement in the distance. It was Hoffman and he was approximately 50 yards ahead of me. I re-crossed the bridge, dodging impatient drivers, and went down the stairs to the canal. I was grateful for the handrail, since my vision was blurring again and my shoulder was pulsing with increasing pain.

I stood within the grillwork of the stairwell and saw Hoffman in the distance. He was turning around nervously, looking to see if he was being followed. As soon as he looked to the front I hurried after him, positioning myself behind the available foliage along the side of the towpath. At points it was dense. When the river flooded it rose above the towpath and even at average depths the stands of scrub between the Potomac and canal could be subjected to standing water. The result was a combination of woods, marsh, or flood zone, depending on the vagaries of the weather.

I buttoned my jacket and turned up the collar, the green of the fabric and darkening blood stains creating a large patch of camouflage. As I walked beside the path I looked for blood droplets in the ground clay and gravel, but as yet had seen none. I thought I had seen a line of blood beneath Hoffman's neck, but if it actually was blood there was not much of it. The puncture wound had startled him momentarily and it was no doubt annoying and frustrating him, but he was still able to navigate the terrain. I thought I saw a partial handprint on the bark of a sycamore that appeared to be streaked with blood—perhaps the result of his clutching at his shirt to relieve pressure on his throat—but I didn't have time to linger and check it.

As he got closer to the point below the intersection of Canal and Arizona he began to hurry. I wondered why; perhaps he had caught a second wind. Suddenly he turned and caught a glimpse of me before I could reach a point which would afford some cover or concealment. Without hesitating he began firing at me. I leaped off of the edge of the path as splinters of wood flew above my head. When the shooting stopped I crawled toward the path and saw him hurrying past Arizona Avenue. He was either heading toward the boat house and the Reservoir Road intersection with Canal or planning to go on toward Georgetown.

I followed him, trying to close the gap between us without getting so close to him that I presented an easier target. At one point he stopped and raised his left hand to his neck. His body was slightly hunched forward, but only for a few seconds. Then he began to move again. I gained ten or fifteen yards in the process.

When he got to the Reservoir Road intersection he left the towpath and headed up toward the Palisades. The roadway was far less steep than Arizona Avenue and residential properties began just above Canal Road. It was easier for him to navigate and an easier area in which to hide, even if it had required him to walk much farther than he had probably liked. It also forced me to make choices. Following him along the towpath was easy. Following him between homes and behind townhouses was far more difficult and I would have to choose both the likeliest route for him and the safest one for me. It was the perfect location for an ambush.

NINETY-ONE

I knew that I would be the most vulnerable when I first emerged on Reservoir Road, so I backtracked to the northwest, coming down Canal Road and going into the woods a few hundred feet before Reservoir. I couldn't see Hoffman waiting anywhere, but I moved forward very slowly for the last few dozen yards. I tried to catch some hint of a scent, which was nearly impossible with the exhaust fumes along Canal Road. The acrid smells of catalytic converters were everywhere, along with the strong presence of diesel fuel and even a hint of alcohol. I was hoping for the copper-like scent of blood but would have happily settled for sweat and body odor.

At the edge of Reservoir Road—there a narrow strip of blacktop with crumbled shoulders—I looked for droplets of blood. I hadn't seen them before when I was following Hoffman's direct path but at a time when I had nothing else to go on I was still living on hope.

Suddenly I got something better—a set of muddy footprints. They were fresh and largely undisturbed by the heavy traffic which came down from MacArthur Boulevard. I pulled out my cell phone and called the AD.

"Salva," he answered.

"Skip, it's Gwen."

"I was just going to call you," he said.

"I'm following Hoffman on foot. He's just left the C. and O. Canal and is heading up to MacArthur Boulevard via Reservoir Road."

"How close are you?"

"I'm not sure. I'm not more than a couple minutes behind him. He's armed and I'm not, so I'm trying not to walk into the open and present him with a target."

"Where do you think he's headed?"

"I think he's looking for a place where he could get some quick medical attention. I was able to stab him with my nail file."

"In the heart, I hope."

"Actually in the throat."

"Close enough for government work," he said. "Well done."

"Unfortunately he's still ambulatory."

"I bet it's still getting his attention though."

"I think so."

"He's a long way from Sibley and probably not much closer to Georgetown Hospital."

"Right. I figure he's looking for a private practitioner's office along MacArthur."

"Safe bet. How are you?"

"Shot in the shoulder but also ambulatory. A little woozie."

"Don't put yourself at any unnecessary risk. I'll cover the area with agents and cops. I'll send an ambulance also."

"Thanks," I said, and clicked off. There was no reason to hold him on the phone when he needed to make calls. For the next five minutes I worked my way between the local residences on either side of the road. There was no sign of Hoffman. Two minutes later I was at the edge of MacArthur Boulevard and I finally saw him.

I was wrong about his plans. He wasn't looking for any local medical help. That may have been his earlier intention; he probably had hoped to drive to Sibley. Going into the Palisades on foot was his second choice; he wouldn't want to go up Chain Bridge Road to McLean on foot because the homes there are often gated and high security is a neighborhood constant. There are also guns in Virginia...lots of them.

Now that he knew that I was behind him and that I had a cell phone he had to get out of the area immediately. The easiest way to do that was by car and the easiest way to get a car was to commandeer one at the Exxon station at the corner of Reservoir and MacArthur.

He was standing at the front, driver's-side window of a Buick sedan, pounding on the roof and window with the butt of his pistol. The driver had not turned off his ignition and he suddenly accelerated forward onto the boulevard. Hoffman was angry and rattled and fired two rounds at the car, which continued up to and through the red light opposite the reservoir. Better traffic court than the morgue.

One of my questions was answered; he was not yet out of ammunition. I saw him turn and enter the middle of the three repair bays. I came around toward the front of the station. There were three cars in the parallel bays, one parked on the ground, the two others up on their respective lifts. Hoffman was yelling.

Just then a car pulled into the station for gas. I waved to the driver, indicating that he should get out of there. He must have seen the blood on my shoulder because he didn't hesitate. He hit the boulevard so hard, so fast, and at such an odd angle that the rear bumper of his car smashed into the curb.

I hurried into the station office, looking for some field expedient that would serve as a weapon. I was hoping for a pry bar or large screw driver. Time was short. Hoffman was now screaming and cursing at the attendant, demanding the keys to a functioning vehicle and threatening him with death if he didn't comply immediately. I looked around. The only items on the service counter were the keys to the men's and ladies' rooms and a tire pressure gauge. The keys were attached to small tin plates. The tire pressure gauge was one of the larger ones, the kind used to check truck tires, with a circular clock-like gauge at one end, the chuck at the other, and 10"-12" of flexible cord in between. I stepped behind the counter. On the shelf was a large rubber hammer.

The sounds of my footsteps were muffled by the noise from the workbench radio. Hoffman's back was to me, but I looked first to see if there were any reflecting surfaces in which he might be able to see me. The attendant saw me, but didn't signal the fact to Hoffman, who was now jamming his pistol into the man's throat.

The most lethal shot would be to the temple, but only if it connected perfectly. I decided instead to go for shock and awe. I came in on Hoffman's right, tightened my grip on the hammer's wooden handle, and swung with all of my strength. The face of the hammer struck Hoffman on the bridge of his nose. Even with the radio blaring I could hear the crunch as the bone snapped like a dried branch. Before he could fully realize what had happened I bent the pistol backwards, breaking his index finger in the process, and securing his full attention.

As he fell backward I pounced on top of him, pushing the pistol out of his reach. The attendant came back to life now that Hoffman no longer had a gun at his throat, put his workboot on Hoffman's good hand and began to make some threats of his own, most of them involving various forms of damage to Hoffman's groin area. I pushed my left thumb into the wound in Hoffman's throat and pinched his now bloody and rubbery nostrils shut with the thumb and index finger of my right. "Now," I said, as he gulped and churned and the sounds of the police sirens grew louder and louder, "can we all please just get along?"

TWO MONTHS LATER

Richard is still splinted and bandaged and sore, but he has decided that we have earned a week of leave, which we are spending in Honolulu. We are at the *Hilton Hawaiian Village*, a collection of hotel towers, shops, restaurants, and pools. There are parrots everywhere and even a small penguin rookery. He is wearing silk shirts with palm trees and sunsets on them and I am wearing bathing suits, my self-consciousness over my red, yellow, black and blue shoulder finally beginning to fade. We cool down with tropical drinks and watch teenagers taking surfing lessons and Japanese honeymooners taking pictures of everything. I thought I saw Charo this morning.

The Bureau is as happy as the Bureau gets. Hoffman's files are opening new doors and leading to new indictments. After a week strapped to Charlie Dolan's polygraph the outlines of his story are becoming much clearer. The New York operation was a subcontracted afterthought. The Wolf Trap event was the pivot point from the beginning. Two things saved us in New York—the medical technology and savvy that enabled us to determine that Charles Pierson's death was a homicide and the sheer luck in seeing their operatives escaping from a sewer on Third Avenue. The AD has been working overtime to convince me that we *do* sometimes get lucky, but he's acknowledged that my skepticism is a healthy counter to those with absolute faith in the system and those with absolute faith in the power of prayer.

We expect to begin making arrests in New York within the week. Hoffman's files disclosed the fact that he served as the go-between in delivering the explosives to Malawi's cell. We have the names of the receivers and one is now actively cooperating. The wealth of information in Hoffman's audio files has sent a collective chill across official Washington, where it's always a short step from captured information that jeopardizes our national security to delicious gossip that wrecks careers, exposes the nudity of emperors and energizes the sippers of white wine at Georgetown cocktail parties. As best we can determine, the notion of a U.S./U.K. reunion at Wolf Trap was initiated by the President months ago, in a call to the embassy in Wandsworth from one of the presidential limos. There *were* voice-activated recorders in the limos, but the Secret Service does not yet agree on their location or locations. The body of the second man at Naked Mountain was found in rural Fauquier County, also shredded by a blast from behind his vehicle's firewall. Hoffman is the prime suspect for that murder, as well as for the murder of the driver of the Escalade, Bigfoot.

Malawi has left the country but the Israelis are getting closer to him day by day. The Secret Service is taking major heat for hiring Hoffman and the Bureau is breathing a deep sigh of inter-governmental relief. Salva is the man of the hour because of his and his rookie's work and the New York field office is thinking about some new paint, new carpet, and a whole lot of slack at appropriation time. The mainstream media are having a p.c. orgy over my success and their counterparts at the other end of the political spectrum are talking about my having "gone on the warpath big time." I've been praised in a series of multicultural circumlocutions and awarded a succession of stereotypical nom-de-guerre nicknames. I didn't want any of it and when Richard offered me the chance to put four or five thousand miles between them and us I started packing before he could complete his next sentence.

For a person who still looks vaguely like the Mummy he smiles a lot. He kissed me last night and said sweet things, things he had never said before. He's sleeping now, stretched out on a canvas chaise longue, beside the Ali'i Tower pool—the top-of-the-line venue in the Village. I've been sipping a flavored daiquiri—peach, I think. I've let it melt while I've been concentrating on the people around the pool. It's still sweet and vaguely fruity, but becoming watery in the afternoon sun.

On the other side of the pool are two lawyers. They're standing in waist-deep water. Each has a heavy gold bracelet and one is smoking a cigar. Their hair is meticulously groomed and their voices are a little too loud. Their wives are behind them, in deck chairs, flipping through magazines.

I've heard a woman telling her life story to a stranger on the near side of the pool. She's a part-time professor at Pepperdine and wants to go full-time, but can't because she's not a member of the university's church. She said something about it to one of the lawyers but he didn't seem interested in her case. He *did* seem interested in a sunbather wearing a flesh-colored thong bikini and an iPod. Her eyes were closed and she was chewing gum.

Into this mix of humanity came a man in a three-piece wool suit. It was one of those light plaids with delicate lines, the sort that Prince Charles wears. The shirt, tie, and pocket square were a perfect match and the shoes—more English than Italian—looked like they cost as much as a decent secondhand car. He walked through the assortment of chairs, umbrellas, and chaise longues. He was clearly looking for someone but he was unable to find her there. He didn't speak to anyone and he didn't take out a cell phone.

Who was he? Why was he dressed that way? Where was he going? Why did he expect to find someone at the pool? And where was she? Did she know what she was passing up or did she know only too well what she was consciously avoiding?

No one dresses like that in Honolulu. Thank God I had brought some light tennis shoes and a slip-on jumpsuit. I leaned over and kissed Richard, who smiled in his sleep. "I'll be back in a little while," I said.

"You rest," I added and followed the man at a safe distance as he walked toward the courtesy phone in the hotel lobby.

ACKNOWLEDGMENTS

Very special thanks to my friend Charlie McCaffrey, retired Secret Service agent, who kept me on the factual straight and narrow and supplied the crucial information on SCIFs. This story actually began years ago, over drinks with Charlie and his wife Katie in the stern of the *McThruster*, on the Potomac and on the Chesapeake. Thanks also to my friend Freddie Campo for his insider's perspective on the Army logistics command's Pentagon offices and the events of 9/11 and to Colonel Leon Hoffsette for information on Air Force fighters and their likely responses to terrorism.

The terrorist attacks affected everyone I know in some direct, personal way. Each of us has lost friends or friends of friends as a result of that day's actions. My friend and Georgetown colleague Leslie Whittington died in the Pentagon crash, with her husband and her daughters and, in an odd twist of fate, the family remains were identified by our distinguished Missouri alumnus and friend, Dr. Tom Holland. Most of all I am haunted by accounts of the cries for help which came from a friend's assistant at Cantor-Fitzgerald when her office was enveloped in smoke and flames. I had visited there shortly before the towers were struck and she had been kind and helpful, as always.

Bernie Cantor was one of America's great businessmen. He was also one of the greatest salesmen of war bonds during World War II and the most important private collector of Rodin in the world. For many years there were parts of his collection in Cantor-Fitzgerald's headquarters. The Guinness Book of Records recognized this facility with the unique designation of the *highest* museum in the world, a place of art and beauty as well as commerce. Rodin's masterful *Burghers of Calais* commemorates six citizens who volunteered themselves as hostages to Edward III in exchange for his lifting the siege of their city during the Hundred Years War. Ground Zero is (among many things) a monument to those who were willing to sacrifice themselves in the hope and belief that others might be safe.

Finally, my most profound thanks and love go to my most conscientious reader, closest friend and life companion, my wife Judith. I have a soft spot for Special Agent Harrison, but Judith remains my favorite heroine.

ॐॐॐ

www.ingramcontent.com/pod-product-compliance
Lightning Source LLC
Chambersburg PA
CBHW032048020426
42335CB00011B/240